THE AFRICAN AMERICAN NEWSPAPER

Medill School of Journalism
VISIONS *of the* AMERICAN PRESS

GENERAL EDITOR
David Abrahamson

Other titles in this series

HERBERT J. GANS
Deciding What's News: A Study of CBS Evening News, NBC Nightly
News, Newsweek, *and* Time

MAURINE H. BEASLEY
First Ladies and the Press: The Unfinished Partnership of the Media Age

PATRICIA BRADLEY
Women and the Press: The Struggle for Equality

DAVID A. COPELAND
The Idea of a Free Press: The Enlightenment and Its Unruly Legacy

MICHAEL SWEENEY
The Military and the Press: An Uneasy Truce

DAVID R. SPENCER
The Yellow Journalism: The Press and America's Emergence as a World Power

THE AFRICAN AMERICAN NEWSPAPER

VOICE OF FREEDOM

Patrick S. Washburn

Foreword by Clarence Page

MEDILL SCHOOL OF JOURNALISM

Northwestern University Press
Evanston, Illinois

Northwestern University Press
www.nupress.northwestern.edu

Printed in the United States of America

10   9   8   7   6   5   4   3   2   1

ISBN 978-0-8101-2290-1

Library of Congress Cataloging-in-Publication Data

Washburn, Patrick Scott.
  The African American newspaper : voice of freedom /
Patrick S. Washburn ; foreword by Clarence Page.
    p. cm. — (Visions of the American press)
  Includes bibliographical references and index.
  ISBN 978-0-8101-2290-1 (pbk. : alk. paper)
  1. African American newspapers—History—20th century. 2.
African American newspapers—History—19th century.   I.
Title. II. Series.
  PN4882.5.W37 2006
  071.3089'96073—dc22

                                        2006020577

For my wife, Glenda,
who has always been there for me.

CONTENTS

FOREWORD

Clarence Page

I have never worked for any of the black newspapers whose history Patrick Washburn so admirably explores in this volume. But, like many other black journalists of my generation, I often have relied on them.

Even as a child in the 1950s, I enjoyed the adventure that was offered up to my eyes and my imagination by the vast landscape of pictures and stories that our family "papers" offered, spread out on the floor of our living room in our southern Ohio factory town. But I took special delight in the pages of the "colored" newspapers like the *Pittsburgh Courier,* the *Michigan Chronicle,* the *Chicago Defender,* and the *Cleveland Call & Post.* Their vast landscape offered something that the big "white" newspapers left out: pictures and stories about black doctors, lawyers, politicians, business folk, society ladies, church leaders, and other "Negroes of quality," as my elders called the classy people of color who were more economically fortunate than we were. The comments and cartoons in the "colored newspapers" had a mission to bluntly and reliably ridicule anyone perceived as standing in the way of black progress. In the rapidly, feverishly growing television age, the Negro press gave African Americans something no other media were ready or willing to offer: visibility and a voice.

When I decided as a high school student that I wanted to be a journalist, the black press offered me something else: a possible career safety net. It was the winter after President John F. Kennedy's assassination, Martin Luther's King Jr.'s "I Have a Dream" march on Washington, and the Ku Klux Klan bombing deaths of four little girls in a black Alabama church. History was happening before my eyes, thanks to the media, and I wanted to get out there and be an eyewitness to it. Trouble was, despite their widely held liberal image today, the mainstream media were only beginning to slowly and reluctantly open their newsroom doors to journalists of color. Unlike my young white friends, I had to prepare myself for the possibility that the same white newspapermen who were eager to have me sell and deliver newspapers in my hometown would not, because of my complexion, hire me to report for those same newspapers. No matter, I assured my worried parents; if the white newspapers wouldn't let me compete, maybe the "colored newspapers" would give me a chance—as they had Langston Hughes, Louis Lomax, Ida B. Wells, W. E. B. Du Bois, and my other black journalistic role models. I held high hopes.

It was the summer of 1965. I had just graduated from high school, and Ohio University's journalism school awaited me. Like other major journalism schools at the time, it had almost no black journalism majors, a sign of how unwelcoming the industry had been to aspiring nonwhites. "Just prepare yourself," my optimistic grandmother calmly advised. "Someday soon the doors of opportunity will open up and, when they do, you must be ready to step inside." Little could Mother Page or anyone else have known how widely or how soon those doors would open up, thanks to an unexpected and perverse form of affirmative action: urban riots.

Beginning that summer in the Watts section of Los Angeles, more than four hundred civil disturbances would rock the streets of urban America in the late 1960s. White newsrooms, in print and broadcast, pressing suddenly to find reporters and photographers who could be dispatched to America's inner cities without looking too conspicuous, snatched up the few black students who, like me, had decided to take the gamble of pursuing a journalism career. They also raided the vast talent pool they long had ignored in the newsrooms of black newspapers and magazines. By the early 1970s, black reporters and photographers were winning Pulitzers and other major awards for the *Chicago Tribune* (where I still work) and other major newspapers that had passed over their talents for generations.

Yet the black press, though damaged by the talent drain, did not disappear. Like any other industry faced suddenly with radically changed times, the giants of black journalism had to reconsider their mission. They took a new look at their communities and at the value of their brands. Even as black Americans integrated as never before into America's melting-pot mainstream, many of us continued to look to these sources. Their ability to fill the enormous gap in news, features, commentary, and target advertising left behind by the newly sensitized mainstream media kept the black press alive, and it continues to live today.

To figure out where black media or any other media are going in today's rapidly changing Internet and cable TV world, it is helpful to know where they have been. Black America's unique circumstance as America's only involuntary immigrant group produced, from its very beginnings, a black press with attitude. The publication of America's first black-owned newspaper, *Freedom's Journal,* in 1827 gave African Americans a voice of their own to "plead our own cause," in the words of editors John Russwurm and Samuel Cornish. From then to now, black newspapers offered passionate advocacy for black rights, opportunities, and visibility against the community's common enemies. "Objectivity," it is important to note, was not a popular notion in America's press until the early twentieth century and, even then, never caught on as well with black audiences as it did for the mainstream press.

After all, despite their vaunted "objectivity," the big white newspapers almost never covered black community news unless it involved crime or, in later years, sports.

The black press not only covered black history as it happened, but also made it happen. The *North Star,* edited by Frederick Douglass, an escaped slave who became the premier black journalist, diplomat, and leader of his times, added a strong black voice to a mostly white-led abolitionist chorus. Harvard graduate William Monroe Trotter launched the *Guardian* in 1901, boldly dedicated to opposing "discrimination based on color and denial of citizenship rights because of color." Ida B. Wells's *Memphis Free Speech* crusaded against lynching until white mobs forced her to flee to the North. There she continued her writing and joined Trotter, W. E. B. Du Bois, and others to found the National Association for the Advancement of Colored People (NAACP), America's oldest and largest civil rights organization. Robert Sengstacke Abbott's *Chicago Defender,* founded in 1905 and eagerly sold across the deep South by Pullman porters, spurred the "Great Migration," perhaps this planet's largest and fastest peacetime movement of any ethnic group from one place to another. As *Defender* editorials demanded antilynching laws, its "help wanted" ads from northern industrialists and domestic employers beckoned black workers, and its advice features helped the new migrants maneuver their new big-city lives after they arrived.

As we wonder where America's media are headed, we can gain important insights from Patrick Washburn's thoughtful examination of where we have been. The challenges posed by the Internet and the cable TV era offer new opportunities to today's generation of black editors and publishers and to those who aspire to join them. The new media are tailor-made for the niche markets in which black-oriented media always have operated. Today almost anyone with Web access has the ability to be a publisher, with all the joys and headaches that come with that lofty position. It is important for them and for the rest of us to know the obstacles faced by those who came before us, as well as how those obstacles were turned into opportunities.

PREFACE

This book is the culmination of a personal, lifelong voyage of racial discovery. I grew up in a white society—not by design but by happenstance. I went to public schools in Texas, Missouri, Kansas, and Oklahoma all the way up through high school, but in all that time I had only two black classmates, and for only one year. I did not know either of these students personally, and my only interaction with other blacks was when I competed against them athletically. I did not care about the color of other athletes' skin, and there was never any racial animosity or trash talking—all of us simply played hard and tried to win. Nothing in this regard changed when I went to Baylor University, which was segregated, or in my first four years out of college, which I spent as a newspaper sportswriter in Texas, Virginia, and Georgia. None of my coworkers were black, and only occasionally did I interview any blacks. That phase of my career was followed by four years in the college sports information field at Harvard University and the University of Louisville, where I did know some of the black athletes, but again, everyone I worked with was white.

I do, however, have strong memories of comments about blacks made by white people in the South. My landlady in Charlottesville, Virginia, who belonged to an all-white country club, told me, for example, that while a black caddie was okay, she would never play on a course if a black was playing at the same time. When I asked her what difference it made, she had no explanation; that was just the way it was. Then, there was the time at the newspaper when I ran a wire-service photograph of three black college basketball players celebrating in the locker room after a big win, and the publisher complained. He said he did not mind running pictures of black athletes, but he did not want any more nonaction photos that had only blacks in them. That was followed in 1969 by Bernard "Peck" Hickman, the athletic director at Louisville and a former highly successful coach of the Cardinals, talking about how more and more blacks were playing college basketball. Then, he made a remarkable observation, "But you can't play more than two blacks at a time or you'll have trouble." Huh? I still wonder what he thought a little more than a decade later when Louisville won the coveted NCAA championship in 1980 with a team that was predominantly black.

After earning a master's degree at Indiana University, where I actually knew some of my black classmates and sometimes ate with them, and spending six and a half years as a reporter in Rochester, New York, where Gannett made an effort to hire a few blacks in the newsroom, I returned to Indiana for a doctorate. My life changed forevermore in the fall of 1980 in a history class about the presidents and the press. I was required to write a paper on the *Pittsburgh Courier*'s Double V campaign in World War II, and for the first time, I read a black newspaper. I remember being stunned by what I found. Growing up as I had, I unconsciously had come to believe that there were no equals to the white press, and therefore I was mesmerized when I discovered a power and a passion in the *Courier* that I had never seen in any white paper. And particularly intriguing to me was the style of writing. There was a noticeable lack of objectivity. This was an advocacy press, which sometimes mixed objective statements with editorialized comments from paragraph to paragraph, and it was a potent, interesting mix that was highly entertaining and effective.

But my racial education might have stopped there if fate had not intervened. As a result of my paper on the *Courier*, I discovered a book by Walter White, executive secretary of the National Association for the Advancement of Colored People, who claimed that the government had illegally cut back on newsprint supplies to some black newspapers in World War II in order to try to force them to tone down their criticism. He said he told President Franklin D. Roosevelt, who ended the illegal cutbacks. I wrote the Roosevelt Library in Hyde Park, New York, to see what documents it had about this and was disappointed to find there was nothing. However, an archivist said there was a lengthy wartime report by the FBI on blacks that had been at the library for three years but had been totally ignored by researchers. Twenty-five pages dealt with black papers, and he wondered if I wanted to see them. I purchased copies for twenty-five cents a page, and it was the best money that I ever spent. It started me on a fascinating four-year odyssey through the federal government's investigation of the black press in World War II, which no other historian had examined, and I quickly became a heavy user of the Freedom of Information Act in going after documents from the Justice Department and the FBI. In the end, I did a dissertation, which then became an acclaimed book published by Oxford University Press in 1986.

Over the past twenty years, I have continued to research the black press in World War II and have spoken about it at numerous places, including twice at the Smithsonian Institution and also at the National D-Day Museum. And everywhere I have gone, I have been struck by the same thing: Although both blacks and whites have been intensely interested in the stories that I have told, virtually none of them ever before realized that black newspapers provided the foundation for the civil rights era, which then pushed onward for even greater rights for blacks. In fact, it became obvious that most audiences knew little about black history in the period before the civil rights era beyond something about slavery, the fact that Booker T. Washington and maybe Frederick Douglass existed, and, of course, that there were early black sports stars, such as Jesse Owens, Joe Louis, and Jackie Robinson. Essentially, I found they believed that blacks made few gains until the civil rights era erupted in the 1950s. Thus, the tales that I told them were compelling, opening up a new vista of American history for them.

Over the past quarter of a century, I have thought a lot about these glaring gaps in the public's knowledge of black history, and I gradually decided that I wanted to write a book that would address them in terms of the black newspapers. Therefore, I was pleased when David Abrahamson of Northwestern University asked me to author such a book. Finally, I had my "canvas," and I think the reader will find, just as I did, that the story that follows is remarkable.

Some readers may find that there are more quotations than they are accustomed to coming across in a book of this nature, but that was done purposely. I believe it is important to hear exactly what was said or written, rather than paraphrases by others, when looking at blacks and the black press. This is a story steeped in controversy, as well as racial hatred and superiority at times, and to appreciate the strong emotions that were aroused in both blacks and whites, it is necessary to let the words ring out, no matter how jarring or disquieting to our sensibilities. Then, and only then, can one truly appreciate what occurred and understand it. The striking words simply put things into context. Some readers also may be disappointed that some newspapers are not mentioned or that some events are not given a wider display. But this book does not pretend to be an encyclopedia. It paints a broad picture over a period of more than 160 years and cannot mention everything. Instead, it is focused, like a laser, on one subject: how and why the black newspapers rose and fell in influence. Readers will find the explanations here.

Finally, I hope this history will encourage readers to think deeply about the evils of racism in this country. It was not written with that as a goal—the story is told with the rigor of a hard-core historian who is determined to avoid bias and let the evidence speak and lead us wherever it goes. Nevertheless, I think it is difficult to read what happened to blacks from the 1820s to the 1990s and not feel ashamed if you are inclined to not treat someone equally because of the color of their skin, whatever it is. If this book makes readers think about that, that alone will make it a worthwhile book to have written.

PATRICK S. WASHBURN

ONE

INTRODUCTION

The Negro reporter is a fighting partisan.
—Percival Prattis, *Pittsburgh Courier*

The *Pittsburgh Courier,* self-proclaimed at the top of its front page as "America's Best Weekly," did not indicate to readers that its October 22, 1966, issue was special. The newspaper simply contained the same things in its sixteen pages that it had been running for fifty-six years: items about, or of interest to, blacks. One article noted that New York congressman Adam Clayton Powell Jr. had recently denounced controversial black radical Stokeley Carmichael, both in his weekly sermon at the Abyssinian Baptist Church in New York and then afterward at a press conference. He accused him of being one of those who "run through the streets drunk with the 'wine of violence,' shouting 'black power' in a purposeless scorched-earth orgy." Another story discussed "the Pill" and its value for women over forty who worried about becoming pregnant. It quoted an endocrinologist, who had said, "I see no reason why any woman in the autumn of her life should not experience an Indian summer instead of a 'winter of discontent.'" And there was the weekly advice column by Lady Fortune. A man in Fort Lauderdale, Florida, wrote to her saying that he suspected his wife of having an affair with his brother, and he asked how he could find out. She replied: "Now don't do nothing rash. Follow the steps I'm going to give you and you will know for sure what's happening when you're away from home. Make up your bed before you leave home in the morning. Take an egg and stick it between the mattress and the bedsprings. If the egg is broken when you get home that night, then brother, you should have no doubts that there's a 'new mule kicking around in your stable.'"

There also were editorials, editorial cartoons, letters to the editor, church news items, entertainment stories, society briefs, wedding announcements, recipes, a book review, a comic strip, and sports news. It was what readers in Pittsburgh, as well as in other cities across the country where the newspaper was sold, had come to expect over the years.

But the biggest story on that Saturday was missing in the *Courier.* Without any advance notice to readers, the newspaper had been purchased by its longtime rival, the *Chicago Defender.* When it was next published two weeks later, it was not the same. It was now the *New Pittsburgh Courier,* and it had a slightly different look. A one-column story that started at the bottom right-hand corner of page one and jumped inside discussed the sale almost in a matter of fact way, as if it were talking about the wake of a paper located somewhere else that *Courier* readers did not know or care about. The article did note that under former publisher Robert L. Vann, the *Courier*'s distribution had included southern towns "where Negro newspapers were forbidden to be read," and that he had "developed a platform to help free his people from segregation and oppression which is still being carried out in the pages of the *Courier* today." But no other significance was attributed to the paper. Nothing on that day, or in successive issues of the *Courier,* indicated it had ever had much, if any, national prominence. No more news stories. No news analyses. No feature stories. No editorials. No letters to the editor. Nothing.

The absence of further comments of any kind was striking. But then the mainstream press virtually ignored the end of the original *Courier.* The *New York Times,* the only national newspaper of record, failed to write about it, and so did the *Wall Street Journal,* the country's main paper devoted to business news. The *Chicago Tribune* ran a three-paragraph United Press International story about the sale on page seven of its second section on October 22, and the mainstream *Pittsburgh Press* ran an equally brief story on page thirteen on the same day. Neither attributed any importance to the *Courier.* Three days later, the *Defender* ran the same article that would appear in another week and a half in the *Courier.* There were no accompanying articles or editorials in the paper on that day, or afterward, discussing the sale.

On the face of it, it would seem that there would have been little reason for the press to pay attention to the takeover of a black weekly newspaper with only about 25,000 circulation. After all, it was not one of the last existing black newspapers—they are still around today. But judging the newsworthiness of the sale of the *Courier* merely by its size, and by the fact that it was not a mainstream paper, demonstrated a marked ignorance of mass communication history.

Near the end of the 1940s, the *Courier* had more than 350,000 circulation, which made it larger than any other black newspaper before or since. But far more important than its circulation was its power and its influence. In 1948, famed novelist James Baldwin appraised black newspapers in the United States and called the *Courier* "a high class paper" and "the best of the lot." It was the only black newspaper for which he had nothing but praise. At that time, it was still enjoying the prestige of being the nation's top black newspaper, a reputation that it had solidified in World War II, when it leaped upward in only four years by 160,000 circulation, a spectacular 84 percent increase. Within two months of the country entering the war in December 1941, following the savage and devastating attack by the Japanese at Pearl Harbor, the *Courier* began a famous "Double V campaign," which stood for victory over totalitarian forces overseas as well as over similar forces in the United States that were denying equality to blacks.

Within six months, the campaign attracted 200,000 card-carrying members, and the Double V became a nationwide battle cry for blacks throughout the war as they pushed for and won innumerable rights that they had never had before. These included staggering job-related gains, particularly for black women, who not only streamed into government jobs as secretaries and stenographers but also as assembly-line workers with white women at war plants, where they helped to inspire the image of "Rosie the Riveter"; far less discrimination in the hiring of blacks and higher pay for them; admission into all branches of the armed forces at an unprecedented level and with far less discrimination; large amounts of advertising in the black press for the first time by white-owned companies; the first black White House correspondent (Harry McAlpin); and the first meeting in history of an American president with a group of American blacks (the Negro Newspaper Publishers Association). As Joseph D. Bibb, a columnist on the *Courier,* had predicted on October 10, 1942: "When the war ends the colored American will be better off financially, spiritually and economically. War may be hell for some, but it bids fair to open up the portals of heaven for us."

And so it did, and the *Courier* basked in the warm adulation that came from its readers. The paper, it could be argued, brilliantly led those readers in their push upward rather than merely reacting to what they wanted. But fame is sometimes fleeting, and by the early 1950s the *Courier* and other black newspapers were starting to spiral downward in influence and circulation in what became a stunning free fall. This decline did not stop with the *Defender*'s purchase of the Pittsburgh paper in the fall of 1966, but in a way, the death of the original *Courier* marked the end of a significant era. The black newspapers' influence and power were gone, taken over by white newspapers, and to a lesser degree television, and have never returned. This book will examine that sudden decline and explain why it occurred. It is an interesting, absorbing tale that is considerably more complicated than it appears at first glance. It also is a sad story. Some would call that progress, but what occurred in black newspapers at that time was a wrenching process and clearly not deserved by a medium that had served blacks boldly, courageously, and successfully for more than a century.

But this book is more than just a history of the dramatic decline in black newspapers in both circulation and influence in the 1950s, 1960s, and beyond. To appropriately understand what occurred following World War II, and to truly appreciate the tragedy that it was, it is necessary to begin the story in 1827, when the country's first black newspaper was published, and to examine what occurred over the next century and a half. Operating against a background of continual inequalities for blacks and a white America that routinely, and sometimes fiercely and even illogically, fought the granting of any new rights, black newspapers came to be in the vanguard of the struggle. Because white newspapers virtually refused to cover blacks unless they were athletic stars, entertainers, or criminals, blacks were forced to read their own papers to learn about everyday black life in communities across the country. Not surprisingly in this atmosphere, both black preachers and black newspapers had more influence among blacks in the twentieth century than anyone else, but the latter had the most power because a single paper could speak to a far larger audience every week than a preacher could, particularly since readership was much higher than circulation. Each issue was passed around avidly from reader to reader.

Their coverage, however, sometimes went far beyond mundane meetings and crimes and weddings and athletic events and church news. Ida B. Wells, for example, began a lengthy fight in the late nineteenth century on black papers in Memphis, New York, and Chicago against the lynching and murder of blacks. "She has become famous as one of the few of our women who can handle a goose-quill, with diamond point, as easily as any man in the newspaper work," said T. Thomas Fortune, publisher of the black *New York Age*. ". . . She has plenty of nerve, and is as sharp as a steel trap." Then there was Robert Abbott, the founder and first publisher of the *Chicago Defender*. Searching desperately in 1910 for more circulation because he had little advertising revenue, he dramatically changed his paper by modeling it after the sensational "Yellow Journalism" of William Randolph Hearst and Joseph Pulitzer in New York. When his circulation skyrocketed, other black publishers across the country eagerly followed his lead, changing black newspapers forevermore as they became outspoken and blunt advocates for blacks—and, as a result, the objects of intense and largely secret federal investigations from 1917 onward.

Abbott's chief competitor, Vann, turned the *Pittsburgh Courier* from a small, inconsequential weekly in World War I into the country's largest black newspaper by World War II. Besides its memorable Double V campaign, the paper was one of the leaders in important fights, such as the drive to allow more blacks into the

Army and the tireless campaign to break the color line in professional baseball. The latter paid off in 1947 when Jackie Robinson joined the Brooklyn Dodgers as the first black player in the modern major leagues. During the war, John Sengstacke, who had taken over the *Defender* when Abbott died, faced off against U.S. Attorney General Francis Biddle, who threatened in a 1942 meeting at the Justice Department to try some of the black newspaper publishers for sedition because their criticism of the government was supposedly hurting the war effort. Refusing to apologize for the black press attacking obvious inequalities, Sengstacke wrung a significant promise out of Biddle: None of the publishers would be taken to court during the war if they did not publish anything more critical than what they already were writing. And there was McAlpin, who became the first black White House correspondent in 1944. Finally, only a little more than sixty years ago, blacks had the opportunity to directly question the president.

These were extraordinary journalists who lived in extraordinary times, and telling their stories and the stories of their newspapers is important because it is a tale that is largely unknown by both blacks and whites. By examining this history, and how it fit into what was occurring in America, one begins to get a better perspective of the country's past than can be gained by studying only the usual lily-white picture. Over the past thirty years or so, scholars increasingly have begun to remedy the general lack of knowledge of the black press by producing books that have examined various parts of its history—from newspapers before the Civil War to their interactions with the federal government in two world wars in the last century to biographies of leading journalists and papers. But the overall history of the rise and fall of black newspapers has largely been ignored, with two prominent exceptions: a somewhat encyclopedic book by Armistead S. Pride and Clint C. Wilson II in 1997 and an eighty-six-minute PBS documentary, *The Black Press: Soldiers without Swords,* in 1999. The latter was produced over five years by an independent filmmaker in Harlem and won the highest honor given in broadcasting, a duPont/Columbia Award. Thus, this book examines a period that has not been mined heavily by other historians, and it will do so with the intent of providing new insights and provoking discussion.

It particularly strives to make an important historical point: The civil rights movement that began in the 1950s and then increased in momentum in the 1960s and the 1970s, sometimes leading to violence by both blacks and whites, owed a heavy debt to black newspapers. This is not to suggest that the black press caused the civil rights era. But its continual push for more black rights from 1910 to 1950, using a powerful and compelling form of advocacy journalism rather than the standard objective style found in most white-owned newspapers, allowed those who began pushing nationally for equality in the 1950s to start at a far higher level than if the black press had not existed. This point has largely been missed by Americans, who seem to believe that the civil rights era suddenly erupted from a dead standstill like a dormant geyser. In other words, they think there was no prologue. But that is not the way history occurs. Quite to the contrary, for four decades the black press had stoked the flames of black discontent, using whatever it had at hand. This varied from the Brotherhood of Sleeping Car Porters, who secretly delivered black newspapers on their trains to the South before World War I, to black newsboys, who dared to deliver black newspapers onto Army posts in World War II despite the possibility of being beaten and having their papers burned, to black editors, who nervously faced subtle censorship from one of the most frightening of the governmental agencies, the Federal Bureau of Investigation. Their courageous actions, as well as numerous others, led to enormous gains by blacks and set the stage for the civil rights movement, and the black press deserves everlasting praise for what it accomplished. It is time to set the record straight and give credit where it is due.

Finally, as the reader moves through this story, it should be remembered how Percival Prattis, the executive editor of the *Pittsburgh Courier* during World War II, described the role of the black press: "The Negro reporter is a fighting partisan. He has an enemy. That enemy is the enemy of his people. The people who read his newspaper . . . expect him to put up a good fight for them. They don't like him tame. They want him to have an arsenal well-stocked with atomic adjectives and nouns. They expect him to invent similes and metaphors that lay open the foe's weaknesses and to employ cutting irony, sarcasm and ridicule to confound and embarrass our opponents. The Negro reader is often a spectator at a fight. The reporter is attacking the reader's enemy and the reader has a vicarious relish for a fight well fought." That type of writing, which was highly charged with emotion and showed up again and again, was at the heart and soul of the history of the black press.

TWO

===========================◇===========================

THE EARLY BLACK PRESS

We wish to plead our own cause.
   —John B. Russwurm and Samuel Cornish,
     Freedom's Journal

On March 16, 1827, a new weekly newspaper appeared in New York City. *Freedom's Journal* had four columns of type on each of its four 10-inch by 15-inch pages, and at the top of the front page was the motto, "Righteousness Exalteth a Nation," which set its tone. The country's first black newspaper had finally arrived.

It had been a long time coming. Although the English established their first permanent settlement in the New World at Jamestown in 1607, which was followed by the Pilgrims landing at Plymouth in 1620, a printing press did not arrive in the colonies until 1638 in Cambridge near Boston. The government and the clergy tightly controlled what was printed, and as a result the first newspaper in the colonies, *Publick Occurrences Both Forreign and Domestick,* was not published until September 5, 1690, in Boston. The British immediately shut it down after only one issue because Benjamin Harris did not have the required government license; thus, he had not "Published by Authority." Although *Publick Occurrences* was not published regularly, a requirement for a newspaper that distinguishes it from a poster, a pamphlet, or a handout, historians still consider it the first paper in the colonies because it reported news like English papers of the time and it looked like a paper. It would be another fourteen years before a second newspaper, the *Boston News-Letter,* was published in America, and the publisher, who obviously recognized the importance of staying in business, was careful to always show the British what he was going to publish before the newspaper was printed. Consequently, even with the prior censorship, it was published regularly because it did not alienate the government—in fact, it has been called "savorless journalism" that was "libel-proof, censor-proof, and well-nigh reader-proof"—and newspapers in America have existed ever since. In fact, by 1828, when a black newspaper finally existed, there were almost 900 papers in the country.

By the time the first newspapers were published in the colonies, blacks had become commonplace. In 1619, the first group arrived when a Dutch privateer unexpectedly brought twenty of them, at least three of whom were women, to Jamestown. While they were not slaves, they were not free either. They were sold by the colonial government as indentured servants and were thus required to work for a certain period of time to pay for their trip to the colonies before they were set free. By 1700, however, slavery had become the more common situation for blacks because it offered an enormous advantage to their owners—slaves were bound to their masters for life, while indentured servants eventually earned their freedom, at which point they had to be given their "freedom dues," which might be clothing, money, or land. But slaves were not entitled to own any of these, and they replaced themselves and increased their numbers by having children: Their offspring belonged to whoever owned them. They were simply cheaper than indentured servants, even though the slave owner did have to furnish clothing and food and a place to live.

The mention of servants, many of whom were black, showed up quickly in white-owned American newspapers. In the first issue of the *Boston News-Letter* in 1704, publisher John Campbell ran an advertisement looking for revenue: "[A]ll Persons who have any Houses, Lands, Farmes, Ships, Vessels, Goods, Wares or Merchandizes, &c., to be Sold or Lett; or Servants Runaway; or Goods Stoll or Lost, may have the same Inserted at a Reasonable Rate; from Twelve Pence to Five Shillings." Such ads for runaways became common in colonial newspapers, as did ads offering blacks for sale.

As the number of white-owned newspapers slowly increased in the colonies—from five in 1725 to twelve in 1750 to forty-eight in 1775—news stories about blacks, particularly about slave rebellions or crimes committed by slaves, showed up frequently. As one historian noted, "Innuendo about slave activity was sometimes all that was needed to produce a news story that created panic among the white population. Often the activities of blacks were referred to in newspapers as 'The Proceedings of the Rebellious Negroes.'" While the stories were usually short, they seldom suggested equal treatment for blacks. An early example of an article about blacks appeared in the *Boston News-Letter* in April 1712 and referred to slaves setting fires to homes and businesses in New York City and conspiring to murder whites: "We have about 70 Negro's in Custody, and 'tis fear'd that most of the Negro's here (who are very numerous) knew of the Late Conspiracy to Murder the Christians; six of them have been their own Executioners by Shooting and cutting their own Throats; Three have been Executed according to Law; one burnt, a second broke upon the wheel, and a third hung up alive, and nine more of the murdering Negro's are to be Executed to morrow [sic]."

Another typical crime story, this time about blacks poisoning their master, appeared in the *Boston Evening-Post* on July 7, 1755: "Last Tuesday died at Charlestown, after a few Days illness, capt. John Cedman of that Town, strongly suspected to have been poisoned by a Negro Fellow of his own. After taking the poisonous Potion, he was seized with most exquisite Pain in his Bowels, and when dead, all his lower Parts turned as black as a Coal, and being opened, some of the deadly Drug was found undissolved in his Body, which . . . we hear, was found in the Negro's Chest. He is committed to Goal [sic] and 'tis hoped will meet with his just Desert. . . . " A follow-up story on August 25 read: "Last Tuesday in the Afternoon, at the Assizes held at Cambridge, in the County of Middlesex, Phillis, a Negro Woman, and Mark, a Negro Man, Servants to the late Capt. Cedman of Charlestown, deceased, who were found Guilty of poisoning their Master, received Sentence of Death:—The said Phillis to be drawn to the Place of Execution, and there burnt to Death; and the said Mark, to be drawn to the Place of Execution, and there to be hanged by the Neck 'till he be dead."

But blacks were not always guilty, and the newspapers noted that, too. In February 1735, Boston's *New England Weekly Journal* wrote: "On Wednesday and Thursday last at the Superiour Court holden here two Negros were Tried, one for Burglary, and the other for setting on Fire his Master House &c. but the Evidences on the part of the King not being strong enough to convict them in the apprehension of the Jury, they were both acquitted." And Philadelphia's *Pennsylvania Journal* noted in January 1755 that an autopsy of a black servant showed he had died because of the "Cruelty of his Master a few Days before in chastising him for some Misdemeanour." As a result, his owner was charged with murder and put in jail.

Then, in the 1770s in New England, newspaper coverage of blacks entered a new phase as the abolition of slavery became an important and highly charged topic that would last until the Civil War in the 1860s. In May 1772, in one of the early examples of this type of journalism, Connecticut's *New-London Gazette* criticized Christian slave owners for not setting their slaves free. "It is esteemed very laudable to us to contend for Liberty, and to 'value our freedom more than our Lives,'" it wrote, "but should one of these poor Blacks assert that he was naturally free, and that it was unjust (as in truth it is) to enslave him, what might he expect from his Christian Master but to be severely punished?"

Although a black newspaper did not exist until 1827, the groundwork for it and those that followed, as well as for the protest themes that would appear in their pages, was laid long before in various forms of black self-expression. Beginning in the first half of the 1600s, for example, slaves sang folk songs and spirituals, and although many were not written down, these were what one historian, Carter R. Bryan, has called the slaves' "first literary expressions." As another historian, Benjamin Quarles, noted, the spirituals were not necessarily what they appeared to be, simply because the slaves could not afford to be openly critical of their white masters:

> On the face of it, the words of the spirituals suggest resignation to one's lot, but many of the black singers read into the songs a double meaning. It may be straining to say that whenever the world "hell" appeared in a spiritual, the singer consciously equated it with slavery as he knew it, and that every time the word "heaven" appeared, the singer equated it with freedom up

North. But it is undoubtedly true that the slave found a way of saying in his . . . songs some things he dared not say in any other way. Even the most sluggishly minded slave could hardly miss the dual meaning of these lines:

> I got a right—we all got a right,
> I got a right to the tree of life.

What slave would not instantly identify his master with Pharaoh in two of the best known spirituals, "Go Down, Moses" and "Pharaoh's Army":

> Go down Moses,
> Way down in Egypt's Land,
> Tell old Pharaoh
> To let my people go.

> Mary, don't you weep, don't you mourn,
> Pharaoh's army got drownded,
> O Mary, don't you weep.

Also important in contributing to the startup of black newspapers was oratory, which ranged from powerful sermons against slavery by black preachers to the simple eloquence of a black mother as she was being auctioned off as a slave. And there was prose and poetry. Briton Hammon's autobiographical Narrative, which was published in Boston in 1760, was the first book by an American black, and in the following year, the first piece of black poetry, "An Evening Thought: Salvation by Christ," by slave Jupiter Hammon (it is unknown whether the Hammons were related), came out as a broadside. The latter also was the author of a far more important antislavery publication in 1787, "An Address to the Negroes of the State of New York." Partly because of it, New York passed legislation in 1797 that banned slavery by 1827. In addition, autobiographical accounts of escaped slaves, which were usually published as pamphlets, increased by 1800. "These works . . . were influential in creating and arousing anti-slavery sentiments; but they were important also as antecedents to the start of Negro newspapers," noted Bryan. But this is not to suggest that white-owned newspapers carried much written by blacks. If they carried anything by them, and many papers refused, they only did so occasionally.

But while black self-expression was important in setting the stage for black newspapers, the final impetus was provided unquestionably by Mordecai M. Noah, a Jewish editor of the white *New York Enquirer,* which he founded in July 1826. One of the leaders of a strident campaign against blacks in the city that had begun in the early 1820s, he attacked black men daily in his newspaper for their lack of integrity and courage, questioned the chastity of black women, supported slavery, and railed against setting slaves free. He also referred to black men around Broadway as "an abominable nuisance" and complained that free blacks in the city "swell our list of paupers, they are indolent and uncivil." These continual attacks were so vicious that one black historian labeled him "the most vile protagonist" in the city, and another called his paper a "perpetrator of evil."

As a result, a group of free blacks met in New York and decided that starting a weekly newspaper was the best way to counteract Noah's antiblack campaign because other avenues of communication were largely closed to them. Thus, *Freedom's Journal* was born, and two of the men at the organizational meeting, John B. Russwurm and Samuel Cornish, were persuaded to publish the paper. The former was in charge of editorial duties while the latter looked after business matters. Their appointments were particularly striking since neither had any journalistic experience. Cornish, who was born about 1795 in Delaware, attended the Free Africa School and Princeton, became an ordained minister, and helped found the First Colored Presbyterian Church in Manhattan in 1821. Russwurm was born in 1799 in Jamaica to a white man and a black woman and then schooled in Canada. He graduated in 1826 from Bowdoin, where, by less than two weeks, he was the second black college graduate in the country.

In the paper's first issue in 1827, Russwurm and Cornish set forth their goals, which included being basically an abolitionist newspaper, under the heading "To Our Patrons":

> In presenting our first number to our Patrons, we feel all the diffidence of persons entering upon a new and untried line of business. But a moment's reflection upon the noble objects, which we have in view by the publication of this Journal; the appearance at this time, when so many schemes are in action concerning our people—encourage us to come boldly before an enlightened publick. For we believe that a paper devoted to the dissemination of useful knowledge among our brethren, and to their moral and religious improvement, must meet with the cordial approbation of every friend to humanity.
>
> The peculiarities of this Journal, renders it important that we should advertise to the world our motives by which we are actuated, and the objects which we contemplate. We wish to plead our own cause. Too long have others spoken for us. Too long has the publick been deceived by misrepresentations, in things which concern us dearly, though in the estimation of some mere trifles; for though there are many in society who exercise towards us benevolent feelings; still (with sorrow we confess it) there are others who make it their business to enlarge upon the least trifle, which tends to discredit any person of colour; and pronounce

anathemas and denounce our whole body for the misconduct of this guilty one.

The civil rights of a people being of the greatest value, it shall ever be our duty to vindicate our brethren, when oppressed; and to lay the case before the publick.

Freedom's Journal did not have a particularly long life. Cornish opposed sending free blacks to other countries as colonists, which became the paper's position, while Russwurm took the opposite view. After six months of disagreement, Cornish quit in September 1827 to return to his ministry, and Russwurm took over as editor. Within several months he came out in favor of Liberian colonization. Unhappy over racial conditions in the United States and lamenting that there was "no probability" that blacks would make the effort to rise from "ignorance and degradation," Russwurm either resigned or was fired in March 1829 and went to Liberia. In his final editorial, he called the editor's job "thankless" and noted that he had "been slandered by the villainous" and that his name was a "byword among the more ignorant." He concluded: "Prepared, we entered the lists; and unvanquished we retire, with the hope that the talent committed to our care, may yet be exerted under more favorable auspices, and upon minds more likely to appreciate its value." Cornish returned to editing the paper, changing its name to *Rights of All* in May 1829, but it was closed down in October because it did not have the money and support to continue publishing.

In its two and a half years of existence, *Freedom's Journal* (and *Rights of All*) was a continual, formidable foe of slavery, which an early black historian described dramatically as "a volcano of sin and oppression . . . riveted about us with a most tenacious grip." Sometimes the paper treated the subject with sarcasm and irony.

On April 6, 1827, for example, it wrote: "Blessings of Slavery! Mr. John Hamilton of Lanesborough County, Va., was murdered on the 9th ult. by his slaves. Seventeen of them have been committed to the county jail to await their trial." Then, a month later, it attacked an editor at another newspaper in an editorial, "Slavery in the West Indies": "The venerable Editor of the *New-York Evening Post,* (Mr. Coleman) has assumed the responsibility of palliating the crime of slavery. For this absurd attempt, we can make but one apology; that is, old age. The many years he has been permitted to enjoy the goodness of Providence, perhaps, have impaired his mind, and left it . . . without sufficient vigour to guide his decisions. This is the most charitable view we can take of such an effort."

But common sense dictated that *Freedom's Journal* had to temper its antislavery diatribes to some degree. Before the Civil War, a black editor who was too outspoken, like some white abolitionists, might be attacked and killed and his press destroyed.

Nevertheless, *Freedom's Journal* and *Rights of All* set the stage for the black newspapers that were to follow by covering a much broader range of subjects than just slavery in editorials and articles, sometimes "stealing" material verbatim from other papers. The importance of education for blacks, for example, showed up in the first issue of the newspaper in 1827. "Education being an object of the highest importance to the welfare of society, we shall endeavor to present just and adequate views of it," said the paper, "and to urge upon our brethren the necessity and expediency of training their children, while young, to habits of industry, and thus forming them for becoming useful members of society." Then, two weeks later, the paper criticized blacks for spending too much money on "balls, theatrical and numerous other trivial amusements," instead of using it for education, which was necessary for them to advance in their jobs.

The paper also offered advice to blacks on manners, on how they should dress, and on how they should comport themselves. One example was on January 16, 1829, when it addressed mistakes that blacks should avoid when walking down the street:

> It don't look well to see a gentleman going through the streets eating apples, nuts; nor does it look any better to see them breaking open letters and sauntering along with their faces buried in them, leaving other people to turn out for them.
>
> It don't look well after passing ladies and gentlemen in the street to wheel around, stop, and gaze at their persons and dress. I am ashamed to walk the streets with a person so indiscreet yet there are very fashionable folks that do it.
>
> It don't look well for you to stop exactly in the center of the sidewalk and gabble with friends without regard to others' convenience and rights.

Black women readers were not forgotten, either. Not only did *Freedom's Journal* cover their organizations, such as the Dorcas Society in New York, which helped poor children, but it urged them to improve themselves just like the men, offered advice, and sometimes printed letters from them. On October 3, 1828, a twenty-two-year-old black woman, who described herself as "elegant," wrote the paper that she was beginning to become frustrated because she had been engaged for more than two years and yet her husband-to-be had not set a wedding date. She added that she had been scrutinized by him so much that it had become an "ordeal," and she was "bored" with his company when they had tea. However, she said she still believed they would get married, and thus she did not want to end the engagement. A historian noted that it was striking for a woman at that time to write to a newspaper about such matters and that she probably had written to *Freedom's Journal* because no white publication would print her letter, since she was black.

Other topics covered in the paper included religion, science, politics, children, fashions, crime, U.S. and foreign news, speeches, and ship sailings. It also addressed temperance, ridiculing those who drank too much. On May 16, 1828, it ran the following verse about the "advantages" of being drunk:

> If you wish to be always thirsty, be a drunkard; for the oftener and the more you drink, the oftener and more thirsty you will be.
>
> If you seek to prevent your friends raising ahead of you in the world, be a drunkard, for they will defeat all your efforts.
>
> If you wish to starve your family, be a drunkard; for that will make the task easy.
>
> If you would become a fool, be a drunkard; and you will soon lose your understanding.
>
> If you would get rid of your money, without knowing how, be a drunkard; and it will vanish insensibly.
>
> Finally, if you are determined to be utterly destroyed in estate, body and soul, be a drunkard and you will soon know that it is impossible to adopt a more effectual means to accomplish your end.

On first glance, the broad array of topics covered in *Freedom's Journal* and *Rights of All* would seem to have been designed largely for blacks, but historians have differed on this point. Roland E. Wolseley believed that the low literacy rate of blacks in the United States meant the paper was written mainly to influence whites, who not only had the money needed to help the publication, which most blacks did not, but "were in a position to help free the black man." Jane and William Pease agreed, feeling that "much" of the pre–Civil War black press's coverage "sought to mold white attitudes." Quarles took the middle road. He said that although black newspapers before the Civil War were written for blacks, the writers and publishers also "hoped to attract white readers, thus furnishing an evidence of Negro abilities as well as an exposure to his viewpoints." Clint C. Wilson II, however, believed the articles in *Freedom's Journal* were primarily aimed at blacks, citing as evidence that the paper had been founded by a group of leading blacks in New York City. Furthermore, he noted that "[t]he evidence at least suggests that a level of financial commitment was made by that group prior to launching the enterprise," and that Cornish also had the support of his church congregation, which may have put money into the paper. Martin E. Dann agreed with Wilson. Since black editors probably knew that slavery conditions in the South were something on which they could have "little direct influence," he said, they aimed their publication at ex-slaves and free blacks, who were mostly in the North and "were becoming upwardly mobile."

Whatever the case, *Freedom's Journal* established a template for the early black newspapers that followed until the end of the Civil War in 1865. There is disagreement among historians about how many black newspapers were started in this time period, or even how long some of them lasted, principally because copies of some of them do not exist in archives and libraries. But one of the best lists appears to be the one compiled by Bryan in 1969. Counting *Freedom's Journal* and *Rights of All* as two papers, even though they were really the same with only a name change, he listed thirty-eight black papers that were established in six states and one territory of the United States before the end of the war. The state with the most papers was New York, with twenty-one, followed by Pennsylvania with six, Ohio with four, Louisiana with three, California with two, and Massachusetts and Kansas (a territory) with one apiece. City-wise, New York City had the most black papers, with twelve; Philadelphia was second, with four; and New Orleans and Albany, New York, had three apiece. The papers in New Orleans were the only ones in the South, and west of the Mississippi River, two were started in San Francisco and one in Lawrence, Kansas Territory. The longest-running paper on his list was the *Christian Recorder* in Philadelphia, which published from 1852 to 1864, and the shortest was the *Weekly Advocate,* which only lasted for two months in New York City in 1837.

Like the titles *Freedom's Journal* and *Rights of All,* a number of the names of the newspapers alluded to equality, some more obviously than others. These included: the *Colored American,* the *Genius of Freedom,* and the *Mirror of Liberty* (New York City); the *African Sentinel and Journal of Liberty,* the *Northern Star and Freeman's Advocate,* and the *Elevator* (Albany); the *National Reformer* and the *Colored American* (Philadelphia); the *Alienated American* and *Herald of Freedom* (Cleveland, Ohio); the *Palladium of Liberty* (Columbus, Ohio); the *Liberty Party Paper* (Syracuse, New York); the *Emancipator and Free American* (Boston); and the *Kansas Herald of Freedom* (Lawrence). Similar themes showed up in the mottoes of some of the papers. The *Mirror of the Times,* which began in San Francisco in 1855, predicted, "Truth, Crushed to Earth, will rise again," while the *Anglo-African,* which started four years later in New York City, had as its motto, "Man must be free; if not through law, then above the law."

More black newspapers were not started by 1865 because the odds were against their survival. Bryan noted that none of them made money, which was not surprising, since "none was founded and published purely from motives of economic self-interest." The financial problems of the papers were compounded because until the end of the Civil War most blacks were slaves without any education—state laws in the South, where 90 percent of them lived, banned the formal education of blacks—and few had any money. Thus, there was a high illiteracy rate, particularly in the South, and many of the blacks who could read could not afford a newspaper. Even in the northern states, all of which by 1804 had established deadlines for the elimination of slavery, only a third of the blacks could read, and they were the victims of prejudice, job discrimination, and limited political rights. While they legally could express their opinions about these and other inequalities as well as advocate an end to slavery, few of the literate northern blacks had the skills necessary to write or edit a newspaper, and even fewer had the necessary money. But those who managed to do so were held in high esteem. The *Herald of Freedom,* a white abolitionist paper in Concord, New Hampshire, praised the black editors: "They have got their pens drawn, and tried their voices, and they are seen to be the pens and voices of human genius; and they will neither lay down the one, nor will they hush the other, till their brethren are free."

As if publishing for a black audience was not enough of a financial handicap, black newspapers also had problems obtaining advertisements. White-owned newspapers began in the 1830s to become more and more dependent upon advertising to make a profit, but most of the early black newspapers contained no commercial advertising. Certainly little, if any, came from white companies; instead, what small amount of advertising they did have consisted mainly of personal ads from middle-class blacks playing up values espoused by newspapers, such as "intelligence, sobriety, moderation, and industriousness," according to historian Frankie Hutton. She noted, for example, that in 1840 a woman placed the following advertisement in New York's *Colored American:*

WANTED

The subscriber is desirous of meeting with a female companion, middle-aged or elderly, of good common education, true religious principles, good character, temper, etc., who would be happy in a very economical way of living. Such a Christian might in all probability find a pleasant home for life, with the lady advertising. Address, for further particulars to M.N.O., Nelsonville, in Athens, Co., Ohio.

Then there was the "colored gentleman," a thirty-eight-year-old widower with a fifteen-year-old daughter who advertised in New York's *Anglo-African* in 1859 looking for a wife. He lived in the country, where there were few blacks, and wanted to meet "a lady of intelligence." He wrote that he would supply references as to his character and sobriety.

Other advertisements were by free blacks seeking employment or promoting businesses. Music, dance, and voice instructors offered their services, providing what Hutton called "perfect opportunities for young blacks to meet others of gentility and talent." There also were ads from hotels and boardinghouses, which were looking for "genteel" black men and women. "Only those polite people of manners and means were welcome as boarders," she wrote. Not surprisingly, funeral directors and undertakers joined in, with their number of ads showing a small, steady increase as the period wore on. "Heaven became the 'perfect extension of life' and, more and more in black communities, burial procedures took place in specialized houses for the dead, that is funeral parlors or homes," explained Hutton.

Low circulations contributed to the black papers' financial woes. While it is impossible to verify circulation figures, it is estimated that the papers sold only between 1,500 and 3,000 copies weekly. Readership probably was considerably higher, however, because those who subscribed or purchased papers unquestionably shared them with others eagerly. In an attempt to get more subscriptions, some of the black papers hired agents. One of them for the *Colored American* of New York City passed out the paper's prospectus to 500 persons, which netted twenty subscriptions, and another walked through the rain and snow for twenty-six miles to get five new subscribers. But getting subscribers did not always mean getting more money. Quarles noted that delinquency in paying for papers was common: "'Pay Us What You Owe Us,' ran the title of an editorial in a colored weekly. 'Will friend Glouces-ter (J. H.) please to transmit us some money," begged another publisher: "We hope our Philadelphia patrons will be punctual in paying.' The editor of the *Impartial Citizen* [Syracuse, New York] observed that many Negroes took the paper on credit for two or three years and then stopped it 'without paying up arrearages.' Doubtless some of these delinquent subscribers were well-intentioned optimists who simply never were able to get enough money." In addition, subscription money was sometimes stolen. The *Colored American* warned its Ohio and Michigan readers in 1838 to be on the lookout for a man named Skipworth, who claimed to be soliciting subscriptions for the paper even though he had no connection to it.

In the midst of these problems, one editor towered above the others, attaining national influence, in the early period of the black press. Frederick Douglass did not seem a likely candidate for fame, at least based on his early life. Born Frederick Augustus Washington Bailey in 1817 to a white man and a black slave in Maryland, he ran away from his master in 1838, and he and his wife ended up in New Bedford, Massachusetts, where he worked for an average of one dollar a day at various jobs, including loading oil on a ship, being a chimney sweep, sawing wood, driving a coach, and waiting on tables.

Meanwhile, less than six months after escaping from Maryland, he began subscribing to the *Liberator,* a famous abolitionist publication put out by William Lloyd Garrison. He read it avidly every week and said it became "in my heart second only to the Bible." In August 1841, while attending an abolitionist meeting in Nantucket, he was asked to speak, and despite his halting style, he impressed an agent for the Massachusetts Anti-Slavery Society, who invited him to become a lecturer for the group. As John A. Collins later wrote Garrison, he felt the public was "itching" to "hear a colored man speak, particularly a slave." Douglass immediately became a major attraction at the society's lectures, particularly because of his ability to express himself memorably. "I appear before the immense assembly this evening as a thief and a robber," he began at a meeting in January 1842. "I stole this head, these limbs, this body from my master, and ran off with them." But his effectiveness was not solely because of what he said—his voice and his physical presence also commanded attention. Quarles noted: "His voice struck the ear pleasantly, and as he gained experience he capitalized on it to the fullest. Melodious and strong, it varied in speed and pitch according to its use, whether to convey wit, sarcasm, argument, or invective. A first-rate speaking voice was not Douglass's only asset—he caught the eye, a man people would come to see. Six feet tall, broad-shouldered, his hair long (as was the custom) and neatly parted on the side, his eyes deep-set and steady, nose well formed, lips full, and skin bronze-colored, he looked like someone destined for the platform or pulpit."

In 1845, fearful that his newly found fame might attract slave catchers, who would return him to his master, Douglass went to England, Ireland, and Scotland for twenty months, lecturing extensively to large, enthusiastic crowds on slavery and on what it was like to be a slave. According to Garrison, at these events he was "the lion of the occasion." Some of his British friends at this time purchased his freedom from his master for $700 and gave him the bill of sale. The transaction brought unexpected criticism from American abolitionists, who said this was recognition of "the right to traffic in human beings." The *Liberator* covered the controversy extensively for three months, with one letter writer saying, "I am not surprised that the English should purchase Douglass. They are accustomed to buying slaves."

Douglass claimed that his time in England changed him from "a beast of burden to a man of words," and this was quickly evident when he returned to the United States in 1847. He nominally became editor of the *Ram's Horn,* which had been started in New York City that year to protest the treatment of blacks, but he rarely wrote in the paper and contributed little to it. Instead, he was there mainly because of his famous name, which guaranteed the paper importance—and readers. He also bought a press and type with $2,174 donated by English friends, and on November 2, an announcement appeared in the paper: "PROSPECTUS for an antislavery paper; to be entitled *North Star.* Frederick Douglass proposes to publish in Rochester [New York] a weekly Antislavery paper, with the above title. The object of the *North Star* will be to Attack Slavery in all its forms and aspects: Advocate Universal Emancipation; exalt the standard of Public Morality; promote the Moral and Intellectual improvement of the COLORED PEOPLE; and hasten the day of FREEDOM to the Three Millions of our Enslaved Fellow Countrymen." Quarles speculated that one reason for the paper's name may have been Douglass's familiarity with a song sung by runaway slaves. Two lines said: "I kept my eye on the bright north star, / And thought of liberty."

The *North Star* began publishing on December 3, 1847, as the first paper printed in the United States on a press owned by a black. Its masthead proclaimed an antislavery mission: "Right is of no Sex—Truth is of no Color—God is the Father of us all, and we are all Brethren." Warning it would be a "terror to evil doers," the paper said it would be "freely opened to the candid and decorous discussion of all measures and topics of a moral and humane character, which may serve to enlighten, improve and elevate mankind." Thus began the *North Star,* which merged in 1851 with the *Liberty Party Paper* and was renamed *Frederick Douglass' Paper,* lasting until 1860.

As historian Waldo E. Martin Jr. wrote, the *North Star* was the result of Douglass's "deep desire to express more fully his burgeoning intellectual independence." Quite simply, he wanted to prove that a black could put out a newspaper that was both intellectually and journalistically as good or better than those published by whites. He said he felt this would raise the status of the black man, "by disproving his inferiority and demonstrating his capacity for a more exalted civilization than slavery and prejudice had assigned him. In my judgment, a tolerably well-conducted press in the hands of persons of the despised race would, by calling out and making them acquainted with their own latent powers, by enkindling their hope of a future and developing their moral force, prove a most powerful means of removing prejudice and awakening interest in them." As a sign of his high journalistic standards, and wanting to prove what a black could do, he made sure that his paper rarely had a typographical error and that it never had awkward grammatical phrases.

Douglass had to be pleased by the immediate praise that the *North Star* received from Rochester's white papers, which was not totally surprising because they served a community that had an antislavery sentiment even though there still was segregation and racism. After the first issue of his paper appeared, the *Rochester Daily American* observed that it "bears marks of much ability. . . . The fact that so creditable a journal is published and conducted by a colored man, is to us full of interest." The *Rochester Daily Democrat* said it was "well printed and gives promise of ability"; the *Rochester Daily Advertiser* noted "its mechanical appearance is exceedingly neat, and its leading article indicates a high order of talent"; and the *Rochester Evening Gazette* called it "a beautiful sheet." However, the latter paper also advised Douglass that it was necessary to be discreet in what he wrote in order to further the cause of abolition. "[E]xhibitions of violence, either in language or otherwise, only tend to retard its advance, whilst calmness and dignity win respect for our arguments and ourselves," it said. A further sign that Douglass and his paper were held in high regard locally came in January 1848 at an annual press dinner, where he was honored with two toasts. He wrote in the *North Star* that "the vulgar and senseless prejudice against colored persons, so prevalent in our land, was utterly repudiated by the gentlemen of the press in this city. . . . Prejudice against color cannot long exist." Interestingly, in praising the reception that he received from the Rochester papers, Douglass did not tell readers for six months that he and another black man on his paper were initially denied entrance to the dinner because they were black.

As would be expected, particularly because Rochester was the last stop on the Underground Railroad before blacks escaped to Canada, and Douglass, by his own admission, was heavily involved in this, both of his papers continually wrote about slavery. For example, in the first issue of the *North Star,* he noted: "There has just left our office, an amiable, kind, and intelligent looking young woman, about eighteen years of age, on her way from slavery. A rehearsal of her sad story thrilled us with emotions which we lack words to express. On her right arm between her wrist and elbow, the initials of the name of her infernal master, is cut in large capitals. Oh! the wretch!"

Five months later, on May 12, 1848, Douglass told his readers what happened to a black boy in Mississippi when he picked up a stick to defend himself after a white man tried to "chastise" him: "The overseer told the boy to lay the stick down or he would shoot him; he refused, and the overseer then fired his pistol, and shot the boy in the face, killing him instantly. The jury of inquest found the verdict, 'that the said Wm. A. Andrews committed the killing in self-defense.'" As a result of such incidents, and the continual threat to blacks from slave hunters, Douglass urged his readers to fight back. In *Frederick Douglass' Paper* in June 1854, he wrote: "Every colored man in the country should sleep with his revolver under his head, loaded and ready for use. Fugitives should, on their arrival in any Northern city, be immediately provided with arms, and taught at once that it is no harm to shoot any man who would rob them of this liberty."

With his circulation quickly reaching about 3,000, Douglass ranged widely for news. He had correspondents not only in Europe and the West Indies but also throughout the United States. One historian noted that the *North Star* was the first black newspaper to have a large circulation among whites, and another said it operated "on a much higher plane than any of its predecessors." Famed writer Henry Ward Beecher had an article in the *North Star* on "Abolition of Slavery in New England," and there also were stories on abolitionist speeches by renowned women's rights advocate Lucretia Mott as well as by Douglass.

Editorials were one of the strengths of his newspapers. In 1848, for example, Douglass criticized a South Carolina senator in the *North Star* for proposing that the federal government support slavery: "Poor mistaken Senator! even this will not do anything to save your darling institution. It is 'doomed.' It is a 'great lie,' which all your buttresses of legislation cannot support. The 'spirit of fanaticism,' as you are pleased to call it, which in other words, means the 'spirit of truth,' is stronger than the spirit of slavery, and all your 'measures to avert the evil' will be vain and unavailing."

Besides attacking slavery, Douglass in his editorials continuously addressed problems faced by the black masses, who had to deal with enormous prejudice even as freemen in the North. In a May 1853 issue of *Frederick Douglass' Paper*, he wrote that blacks had to "learn trades or starve" because whites were taking over jobs formerly done by blacks, such as loading and unloading ships, making bricks, and working as porters on trains. In fact, he recommended going to work rather than getting an education, because blacks could always learn on the job, but education would not give them a trade. "The American Colonization Society tells you to go to Liberia," he wrote. "Mr. [Henry] Bibb [an escaped slave] tells you to go to Canada. Others tell you to go to school. We tell you to go to work."

As might be expected, not everyone liked Douglass's newspapers. While some in Rochester felt it was a disgrace to have an abolitionist paper edited by a black in the community but accepted it with resignation, others took action against it. Douglass's house was set on fire, twelve bound volumes of his paper were destroyed, and the *New York Herald* wrote, "The editor should be exiled to Canada and his presses thrown into the lake." But those were not his only problems. Douglass received more financial support for his newspapers than any other publisher in the black press's early period. The Colored Ladies of Philadelphia held bazaars to raise money for him, delegates at black conventions voted to support him, and people at public meetings from coast to coast took up collections. Nevertheless, in May 1848, he was forced to make his first of a number of appeals for more subscribers. "We have exerted ourselves to obtain subscribers, and have succeeded to an encouraging extent," he wrote in the *North Star,* "but it is impossible in our circumstances, commencing as we did with but a small number of subscribers, to obtain a sufficient number to float unencumbered from week to week." Finally, he got help from a friend, Julia Griffiths Crofts, who became the paper's business manager, and he was able to pay off his debts as well as a mortgage on his house.

After the *North Star* was renamed *Frederick Douglass' Paper* in 1851, the only real change was that Douglass's articles no longer contained "F. D." at the end of them. As for problems, they continued in several forms. Following John Brown's brief capture of the federal arsenal at Harper's Ferry on October 16, 1859, Douglass was forced to temporarily relinquish his editorship of the paper and flee secretly and hurriedly at night by boat to Canada. There was proof that he had provided prior assistance to Brown, though he had refused to join the famous raid. Later in the year, he went to England, and it was not safe for him to return to the United States and resume his editing until April 1860. As for the financial condition of the paper, it was no better off than the *North Star,* and mounting debts made it necessary in 1859 for him to reduce its size in order to spend less on newsprint. But after continuing to lose $25 to $30 a week in the first six months of 1860, he was forced to cease publishing. Douglass, who spent more than $12,000 of his money on the paper over eight years, told a friend that he was "very sorry to give up the struggle," but he was not through with journalism. For the next three years, he published an abolitionist magazine, *Douglass' Monthly,* which helped the cause of the North in the Civil War, though aimed at a British audience, and in 1870 he became the contributing editor of the *New Era,* which was designed to help the now-freed blacks, and then the editor of the renamed *New National Era.* After a $10,000 loss, it closed in 1875.

Quarles summed up Douglass's career as the country's first great black newspaper editor:

> With the launching of the *North Star,* Douglass became a Negro leader in the totality of his interests and outlooks. His attention reached out to the question of Negro exclusion from "white" churches, to the practice of racial segregation in the public schools, and to an analysis of the whole principle underlying separate accommodations for white and colored. While anti-slavery rather than Negro protest, Douglass' weekly mirrored his concern with all problems growing out of the color line. . . .
>
> [Furthermore] Douglass' periodicals contributed to the development of Negroes other than their editor. Race-conscious Negroes could experience a vicarious pride at the sight of a well-edited Negro sheet. Colored poets, essayists and letter-writers could gratify the American love of seeing one's name in print. College-trained Negroes could give public expression to literary

urges which otherwise might have totally escaped posterity. Colored leaders used the columns of the weekly to express their views and denounce detractors of the race. . . .

A final influence exerted by Douglass' weekly was its effect on white readers. . . . Here was a paper that stood comparison with the best-edited weeklies of the ante-bellum period. Here was a paper free from . . . rhapsodies in bad grammar. Here—and this was the most telling point of all—here was the work of a Negro who had spent twenty years in the prison-house of slavery.

Several things stand out about the content of black newspapers up through the end of the Civil War in 1865. Instead of continually and militantly challenging white leaders on significant issues to blacks, which might anger them and could lead to violence, they frequently ran uplifting and positive messages and played up the best things blacks did. They believed this would impress whites and hoped it would help to end the racism and stigma of inferiority under which they were forced to live. All of this also was a sign and encouragement to the country's most downtrodden blacks that even they could rise despite their lowly stations in life.

In addition, they continually wrote about middle-class blacks. "In a nutshell, these newspapers cajoled, charmed, and attempted to sell their readers on the idea that at least some people of color— the middle class and those aspiring to it—were working together successfully in spiritual unison with America's democratic ideals," said Hutton. "This was true even as the democratic ideals they held dear had precious little applicability to people of color." So, they doggedly played up "social responsibility, education, morality, temperance, and upright living" as well as a "spirit of patriotism" during the war, hoping it would uplift blacks and lead to their acceptance by whites.

For the remainder of the century, some things about the black press would remain unchanged. Black journalists would continue to write about many of the same themes, and although slavery was gone, lynching would replace it as a new evil that drew the ire of the black press. As for the number of black newspapers, they escalated sharply, but their life expectancy remained short in many cases for lack of circulation, advertising, and money. According to Hutton, however, the black press "miraculously" survived up through the Civil War and for the remainder of the 1800s.

THREE

STRUGGLING BUT SURVIVING

We are aliens in our native land.
　—T. Thomas Fortune, *New York Globe*

May 18, 1896, was a pivotal day in the history of blacks and black newspapers. On that date, the U.S. Supreme Court announced its decision in *Plessy v. Ferguson,* sending a tremor through black communities as it firmly established racism as the law of the land for almost the next sixty years.

At the heart of the case was Homer Adolph Plessy, a New Orleans black man in his late twenties who made custom leather boots and shoes. He was recruited by a local Creole committee that wanted to test the constitutionality of an 1890 Louisiana law that segregated railroad cars by race, thus creating a separate but equal atmosphere. Playing a part in his selection was the fact that he looked white and was an "octoroon," that is, he had both black and white grandparents—in his case, his lineage consisted of seven white grandparents and one black one.

On the afternoon of June 7, 1892, Plessy purchased a first-class seat for a two-hour trip to Covington on the Mississippi border and boarded an East Louisiana Railroad train at the Press Street depot in New Orleans. Wearing a suit and a hat, which was normal attire for gentlemen in first class, he looked no different than the whites on the car. But when the conductor came to punch his ticket, Plessy uttered a sentence that he had carefully rehearsed, "I have to tell you that, according to Louisiana law, I am a colored man." This was a reference to the state defining blacks as anyone with black ancestors, no matter how few, and thus black blood. The conductor, who was surprised, since Plessy looked no more like a black man than anyone else in the car, informed him that he would have to move from his comfortable cushioned seat to the wooden benches of a "colored" car, which was usually directly behind the locomotive and had a dirty and unhealthy mixture of smoke and soot in the air. When Plessy refused to move, pointing out that he had purchased a first-class ticket in the car in which he was sitting and thus was entitled to ride in it, and with the other passengers becoming restless because the train was being held up from leaving the station, the conductor called the police. They took Plessy to jail, where he spent the night until a bail bondsman came for him.

The case slowly moved up through the courts, and the Supreme Court ruled on it almost four years later. As legal historian Harvey Fireside noted, the narrow question posed by the case was whether a southern state could force blacks to ride in a separate train car. But he pointed out that the issue led to a broader question before the court: "[C]ould southern states replace the caste system of slavery with a set of legal racial barriers to keep African Americans in a status inferior to whites, despite the constitutional changes after the Civil War that had extended federal protection of basic rights to all citizens?"

Seven of the eight justices on the Supreme Court upheld the

constitutionality of the Louisiana statute. After stating in their majority opinion that the Constitution could not "abolish distinctions based upon color," or force the two races to mix, which was different from guaranteeing political equality, they continued:

> [We] consider the underlying fallacy of the plaintiff's argument to consist in the assumption that the enforced separation of the two races stamps the colored race with a badge of inferiority. If this be so, it is not by reason of anything found in the [Louisiana] act, but solely because the colored race chooses to put that construction upon it. [The] argument also assumes that social prejudices may be overcome by legislation, and that equal rights cannot be secured to the negro [sic] except by an enforced commingling of the two races. We cannot accept this proposition. If the two races are to meet upon terms of social equality, it must be the result of natural affinities, a mutual appreciation of each other's merits, and a voluntary consent of individuals. [Legislation] is powerless to eradicate racial instincts or to abolish distinctions based upon physical differences, and the attempt to do so can only result in accentuating the difficulties of the present situation. If the civil and political rights of both races be equal one cannot be inferior to the other civilly or politically. If one race be inferior to the other socially, the [Constitution] cannot put them upon the same plane.

In a sharp, ringing dissent, Justice John Harlan noted that the Constitution was "color-blind, and neither knows nor tolerates classes among citizens," which meant there was no "superior, dominant, ruling class of citizens" in the United States or any caste system. However, he predicted that statutes such as the one in Louisiana, which clearly made blacks inferior and degraded them because they could not ride on train cars with whites, would arouse race hatred and distrust. Labeling the law's end result virtual servitude, he concluded, "The thin disguise of 'equal' accommodations for passengers in railroad coaches will not mislead any one, nor atone for the wrong this day done."

Fireside, whose extensive examination of the case resulted in a 2004 book that clearly expressed its tenor in its title, *Separate and Unequal,* labeled *Plessy v. Ferguson* one of the Supreme Court's two most "shameful" decisions. He noted that its effect quickly went far beyond whites and blacks riding separately on trains:

> [T]he . . . ruling was applied during the next decades to justify racial barriers in all aspects of life, literally from cradle to grave: colored hospitals for babies, segregated schools for children, job discrimination for adults, fenced-off parks, partitioned public accommodations and churches for families, and, finally, segregated cemeteries. The "Jim Crow" caste system was rooted in the South, but its tendrils extended into the border states and even into much of the North. Despite the legal formula—"separate but equal"—everyone knew that there was no real equality for Negroes; nonetheless, the highest court in the land had established the constitutionality of separateness. Who would dare to challenge it?

However, that is looking at the *Plessy* case with hindsight, which is always a dangerous thing to do in studying history. At the time, the outcome resulted in no national protests and was scarcely mentioned by many white newspapers. On the day after the decision, the *New York Times* put it on the third page of the second section next to railroad news. Nevertheless, Fireside noted, the northern papers that wrote about it generally were critical of the result. The well-regarded *Springfield (Massachusetts) Republican* pointed out that the case's outcome was expected in the South, "where white supremacy is thought to be in peril," and it predicted that such laws would "spread like the measles" in that part of the country. Then, it asked sarcastically, "Did the southerners ever pause to indict the Almighty for allowing negroes [*sic*] to be born on the same earth with white men?" The *New York Daily Tribune* called the decision "unfortunate" and said separate train cars for whites and blacks were no more necessary than they were for Catholics and Protestants.

As might be expected, the reaction was considerably different from southern white newspapers. The *New Orleans Daily Picayune* applauded the outcome, noting that all of the states touching Louisiana had similar laws segregating the races on trains, as did most other southern states. It said such laws were necessary because without them "all would belong to everybody who might choose to use it. This would be absolute socialism, in which the individual would be extinguished in the vast mass of human beings, a condition repugnant to every principle of enlightened democracy." The *Richmond Dispatch,* meanwhile, predicted that other southern states would pass laws like the one in Louisiana because of how "disagreeable" some blacks were on trains.

Black papers, however, were not only critical of the *Plessy* decision but also frequently outraged. While a *Cleveland Gazette* editorial merely labeled the decision "ridiculous," the *Richmond Planet,* a far more militant black paper, was grimly blunt: "We can be discriminated against, we can be robbed of our political rights, we can be persecuted and murdered and yet we cannot secure a legal redress in the courts of the United States. Truly has [*sic*] evil days come upon us. But a reckoning day will come and all classes of citizens, sooner or later realize that a government which will not protect cannot demand for itself protection."

The *Washington Bee,* known for being as outspoken as the

Planet, directly addressed the reference to "a reckoning day." It predicted ominously that if a constitutional amendment ensuring blacks equality was not passed, and then upheld by the Supreme Court, whites would "suffer the consequences and the dangers that confront and threaten this Nation. We shall no longer play fool nor shall any more shackles bind the limbs of the once oppressed." Another major black newspaper, the *Baltimore Afro-American,* did not specifically mention the *Plessy v. Ferguson* case, but it agreed with the *Bee* that a nonpeaceful clash between blacks and whites might be unavoidable. Noting that history taught that no "people" had ever achieved full rights unless they were willing to fight for them, it said, "Justice sometimes waits on slaughter, and liberty on victory." It expressed sadness if force became necessary for blacks to achieve equality, but it said reality dictated that unless a black "manifests a willingness to fight, he never can become free."

But not all of the black papers were so outspoken. Instead, some were just discouraged. An editorial in the *Indianapolis Freeman* was indicative of the mood that permeated black America, even among militant newspapers, after the *Plessy* decision: "The decision will have a demoralizing effect. It will do much towards destroying the faith that Negroes may have in any institutions that white men control. At the reception of this news the Negroes of this country will ponder well his situation. It may not be the setting sun of his hopes, but such decisions are drastic upon his reasoning powers. . . . No matter what direction the Negro turns opposition stands like a stone wall."

Such statements from black papers, while noteworthy, were not unusual. After all, they had been writing about equality, sometimes militantly, since *Freedom's Journal* began publishing in 1827. But what made this point in black newspaper history particularly important was that it forced the publishers and editors to make a difficult choice: Would they be accommodating, basically accepting whatever rights white America wanted to give them, or would they aggressively continue to push for more rights, despite the fact that this probably would anger whites and might lead to drastic repercussions? To understand how this dilemma evolved, and why it was the most significant thing to happen to black newspapers in the last third of the nineteenth century, it is necessary to return to 1865.

With the end of the Civil War, blacks and black newspapers had reason to be optimistic about the future. Not only had the North won, vanquishing the South and its well-established system of slavery, but the Thirteenth, Fourteenth, and Fifteenth Amendments to the Constitution were ratified between 1865 and 1870. Respectively, these ended slavery; granted citizenship to former slaves; and said no one could be deprived "of life, liberty, or property, without due process of law," or be denied the right to vote or have that right curtailed because of race or color or the fact of having formerly been a slave. In addition, Congress passed civil rights acts in 1866, 1870, 1871, and 1875. At the same time, the federal reconstruction of the Confederacy, which was designed to bring the southern states back into the union, attempted to ensure that blacks did not lose their new rights.

It quickly became apparent, however, that not even with the end of slavery, and with all of the overwhelming force brought to bear by a victorious federal government, could white supremacy be vanquished or easily tamed in the South. The most famous proponent of it was the Ku Klux Klan. The KKK began innocently enough in December 1865 in Pulaski, Tennessee, when six young men, all of whom had been in the Confederate Army, were sitting around a fireplace discussing ways to amuse themselves and relax.

They decided to form a secret club, took their name loosely from the Greek vocabulary, and named their meeting place the Den. Wanting to avoid military or political titles, and liking weird and impressive ones, they named their leader the grand cyclops; other officers included the grand magi, the grand turk, and the grand scribe. Those not holding an office were referred to as "ghouls."

Then, it was time to announce themselves flamboyantly to the town, as historian Stanley Horn noted in his history of the beginning years of the KKK: "Bubbling over with the excitement of their new-found plaything, the young members of the new Ku Klux Klan decided to make a public manifestation of themselves; so, borrowing the familiar idea of the easy Hollowe'en disguise, they wrapped themselves in sheets, mounted their horses and galloped through the streets of the little town, greatly enjoying the sensation they created—particularly the alarm and dismay of the negroes [sic], to whose superstitious minds the sight of white-sheeted figures suggested nothing but spirits risen from the grave, and who accordingly fled to their homes in panic-stricken terror." Satisfied with the effect that they had had, the club members adopted as their official costume a white robe, a white mask, and a white headdress. The latter was shaped from cardboard, and its pointed top added impressively to a wearer's height and fearsome nature.

While the original members of the KKK were only having what they considered harmless fun, it soon was noticed that blacks were frightened by the ghostlike horsemen whom they sometimes would encounter at night, and this made them reluctant to go out of their homes after dark. "[T]his gave birth to the idea that perhaps the Klan might be used as a means of subduing the undue bumptiousness and the nocturnal prowlings of some of those who seemed incapable of using their new-found freedom discreetly," said Horn. Consequently, the Klan began making unannounced nighttime visits to blacks who were considered out of line. Sometimes no words were spoken, and they relied on a black's superstitions and fears to accomplish the desired goal. But other times they made frightening verbal threats, such as: "We boil niggers' heads and make soup," "We'll skin you alive," "We'll take you for a trip over the moon," and "We live off fried nigger meat."

While there was no intention of violence at first, it quickly slipped into that by the end of the 1860s, with whippings, beatings, and even murders occurring as the organization spread rapidly across the South. The Klan moved almost inevitably into these illegal activities because whites were alarmed with what they considered to be irresponsible and disorderly free blacks, and they saw no way to control them through the courts. They also adopted twisted logic to justify what they did. Horn noted that in congressional hearings on the KKK, witnesses frequently said such things as, "It is a desperate remedy, but there is no denying that it has done a lot of good"; "It was the only manner of punishing criminals in this country, and they think they did exactly right"; and "It is a terrible thing for such a thing as this to occur, but ultimate good will follow from it."

But the South resorted to far more than extralegal actions to reestablish white supremacy. During Reconstruction, which officially began with the end of the Civil War in 1865 although President Abraham Lincoln had made moves in that direction in the preceding year, states such as Mississippi and South Carolina immediately passed legislation placing restraints on blacks. Some of it was hauntingly reminiscent of the former fugitive slave laws because of provisions legalizing the capture of runaway apprentices and contract laborers. Such legislation alarmed many northerners, who were convinced that a new form of slavery was emerging in the South, and they believed black suffrage was required if their rights were going to be upheld. Consequently, the radical majority in Congress was adamant that federal troops should remain in the South, and it passed a bill in 1866 continuing the Freedman's Bureau, which had been formed to protect refugees and freedmen from the former Confederate states. Meanwhile, as the three new amendments to the Constitution were ratified along with the new civil rights acts, all of which specifically protected blacks, the southern states slowly adopted new constitutions under guidelines established by Congress. But black suffrage, although a goal, was never achieved. Georgia, North Carolina, Tennessee, Texas, and Virginia quickly ended up controlled by whites, followed by Florida, Louisiana, and South Carolina, and Alabama and Arkansas reestablished white supremacy in new constitutions in 1874. Two years later, Reconstruction ended when federal troops were withdrawn from the South, and the disenfranchisement of blacks in those states began in earnest and would not be overcome until after World War II.

As white supremacy rose again in the South with a renewed vengeance and strength, black newspapers continued in many ways as before the Civil War. Black publishers still found it difficult, if not impossible, to make a living solely from putting out a paper, and consequently they had other jobs, too. That is why they were commonly called "sundown editors": They worked on their papers at night after they finished their more lucrative daytime jobs. Financially, their problem partly was literacy based. In 1865, only 5 percent of the country's blacks could read and write, and while this figure rose to 55.5 percent by 1900, it still greatly limited the number of possible subscriptions. Equally important were advertising constraints. Unlike white papers, which increasingly were moving toward advertising as their main source of income—

ads would account for 44 percent of their income in 1880 and 55 percent by 1900—black newspapers had few ads beyond what they could obtain infrequently from small, local black businesses. This brought in little income, and consequently they were forced to continue to exist largely on circulation. As a result, black papers appeared and disappeared in increasing numbers, some lasting only a few months.

The exact number of black newspapers during this period will probably never be known. In 1891, historian I. Garland Penn noted there were only 10 black papers in the country in 1870, 31 in 1880, and 154 in 1890. Other historians came up with figures for other years. George W. Williams wrote in 1885, for example, that there were 56 black papers in 1882. Adding to the confusion is that some historians have reported how many black newspapers were started rather than how many existed at a specific time. For example, Henk La Brie III wrote that more than 1,200 black newspapers were founded from 1866 to 1905, 70 percent of which were in the South. Armistead S. Pride and Clint C. Wilson II were more specific but limited themselves to certain years, noting that 58 black papers began publishing between 1866 and 1877, and that another 49 started in the next two years. Moving to the end of the century, they found that 81 new papers opened in 1898, and another 99 in 1902. Meanwhile, figures for the number of black papers that died are nonexistent. As Pride and Wilson noted, the number of papers in the last third of the nineteenth century "were to come and go by the scores, like foot soldiers storming a fortress."

Information on circulation figures for black newspapers at this time is equally uncertain. T. Thomas Fortune claimed in the 1880s in his paper, the *New York Freeman,* that it had a circulation of 5,000, which apparently made it the largest black paper in the country at that time. Meanwhile, as before the Civil War, numerous papers had circulations of fewer than 1,000. However, historian Martin Dann warned that such figures were not indicative of the readership of the black papers—or their potential influence. "Whatever the printing, it is clear that these papers reached far more people," he wrote. "Papers passed from hand to hand or, in the time-worn tradition, were posted in a local pub or other common meeting place. In this way, a single paper may have been (and probably often was) read by a hundred people." La Brie noted the same thing. Because black family income levels were so low, which meant that many could not afford a black paper even if they could read, one copy of a paper was sometimes passed throughout an entire neighborhood.

What they read in black newspapers after the Civil War was in some ways no different from what they had read before. Historian Frankie Hutton noted that some of the black editors remained idealistic for the remainder of the century as they continued to optimistically support the country's democratic goals. For example, the *Elevator,* a black paper in San Francisco, wrote in October 1868 that it was hopeful the blacks' struggle for equality would result in them seeing "the light of political glory beam forth with its full refulgence." To some extent, such optimism had been renewed by Lincoln's Emancipation Proclamation on January 1, 1863, which freed the slaves, and the apparent gains of blacks in the Reconstruction era after the war. The optimistic attitude was never more evident than in the *Elevator* on June 21, 1867, when it wrote, "All agree [that if blacks] could or would become an intellectual people that prejudice would be destroyed." Hutton pointed out that those same words could have been written by Samuel Cornish in *Freedom's Journal* in 1827.

The papers also continued to push for gains in education, employment, and politics. They particularly played up the success stories of those blacks who were articulate, who were buying property, and who were moving upward economically. As Dann noted: "Black newspapers urged their readers to work for their own progress, for recognition in their professions as black men and women, with dignity and self-respect. The accomplishments of black people as doctors or lawyers, teachers or workmen, became a major theme in these papers. In such a way, the press was able to instill a positive sense of the progress and future of black people which was imperative to resisting persistent attempts by white racists to undermine the black community."

Thus, black newspapers became increasingly indispensable to blacks, primarily because white newspapers largely refused to write about them, which meant there was essentially no other place for blacks to get news about themselves other than in conversations or in church. Black papers also became essential because their stories of black inequities put them at the swirling core of a growing push for equality and the fight against white racism. Quite simply, they promoted solidarity through racial pride, which had largely been denied blacks until the end of the Civil War, and central to this was the belief that blacks had the right, just like whites, to determine their own destinies, whether it was in education, work, politics, or anything else. All of this united blacks, particularly because it stressed their capabilities, and encouraged them to press ahead doggedly despite numerous artificial barriers erected by whites.

Meanwhile, by the late 1870s, southerners came up with new ways to legally force blacks into servitude, partly because they were threatening to gain equality and also because of the need for cheap labor on the plantations, on the railroads, and in the mines. One was the convict-lease system. Any black arrested, no matter what the offense, could be sent to a prison farm and hired out to a private company, which paid a few pennies a day toward the prisoner's fines. At that rate, it took a long time for the fine to be paid off. "It was not surprising that when the demand for labor was high," wrote Dann, "the number of arrests was correspondingly high." Then there was sharecropping. In this system, a black family was given land to farm and guaranteed a portion of what it could raise, with the rest going to the landlord, who provided food and supplies. Because sharecroppers depended on landlords for support, they started out in debt, and with landlords keeping the books, the farmers found it almost impossible to earn more than they owed. This made it difficult, if not impossible, for them to get out of what Dann has labeled "subjection." As if this was not enough, whites often ignored the Fifteenth Amendment to the Constitution and refused to allow blacks to register and vote, particularly if their votes might alter the balance of power, and if they persisted and did vote, they were sometimes murdered. As for the Ku Klux Klan, it was spreading rapidly throughout the South and gaining power. Black newspapers continually wrote about the KKK's attacks on blacks and called for government protection, but their pleas were largely unsuccessful. Nevertheless, they persisted in pointing out injustices and calling for equality, which gave blacks hope for the future and the strength to continue fighting against both the legal and extralegal methods used to hold them back.

On October 15, 1883, blacks' optimism that they were gradually achieving equality received a severe jolt when the U.S. Supreme Court ruled that Congress's 1875 Civil Rights Act was unconstitutional. The act had guaranteed "the full and equal enjoyment of the accommodations, facilities, and privileges of inns, public conveyances on land or water, theaters, and other places of public amusement; subject only to the conditions and limitations established by law, and applicable alike to citizens of every race and color, regardless of any previous condition of servitude." It had been passed to counter post–Civil War black codes enacted by southern states that limited personal contact between whites and blacks. "Attempts to give the freedmen political and economic equality threatened the old ways of life," explained historian Rayford W. Logan, referring to the reason behind the southern codes. "Social equality—the mingling of the races in schools, inns, theaters and on public carriers—would encourage black men, it was asserted, to dream of cohabitation with white women."

Historian David Domke found that the northern black press greeted the Court's decision with outrage, while the southern black papers were more reserved in their comments because of their fear of whether whites would allow them to continue to publish if they were too outspoken. The *New York Globe* editorialized angrily that the Court had ruled that blacks had no civil rights. Fortune wrote: "Then, what is the position in which the Supreme Court has left us? Simply this—we have the ballot without any law to protect us in the enjoyment of it; we are declared to be created equal, and entitled to certain rights, among them life, liberty and the pursuit of happiness, but there is no law to protect us in the enjoyment of them. We are aliens in our native land." The *Cleveland Gazette* also was outraged. It noted in an editorial that the decision would result in "hundreds" of hotels, amusement parks, and other public facilities being closed to blacks. Then, a week later, it wrote, using italics to stress its point, "Representative men of all races stigmatize [the] decision . . . as *infamous, outrageous and not in accordance with the will of the people.*"

Despite such strong statements, however, Domke found that all of the black newspapers he studied remained optimistic about the future and advised patience. Fortune, for example, told the *Globe*'s readers that they should not "be browbeaten into servile compliance by adverse decisions [because] we are free men; we are American citizens." The *Gazette* said blacks should not give up hope because "intelligent" Americans "of all races" realized how ignominious the ruling was, and the *Washington People's Advocate* said that the blacks' "march of progress" could not be stopped by one Supreme Court decision because it was "so advanced" across a large part of the country. As for the *Washington Bee,* it said it believed the Constitution would continue to protect all U.S. citizens, whatever their color and regardless of whether they had formerly been slaves.

In the South, the *Mobile Gazette* also criticized the decision, being careful, however, to attribute its criticism to specific individuals. But in an editorial, the paper's editors were more positive and stressed that southern blacks had never been pushy:

> Practically, the decision . . . will have no effect in this section of the south other than possibly to re-open the race issue which has been regarded as settled.
>
> The colored people of the south have not been obtrusive. . . .
>
> The whole community was settling down to the conviction that equal rights for all was a principle firmly established; but the colored element did not offensively demand any social rights.

The *Charleston New Era* urged readers to "be patient" and said that whites' fears about "commingling" unreservedly with blacks could be overcome by education and other methods that would make blacks "more presentable" than they were during slavery. However, it predicted that this would take time. The *Huntsville (Alabama) Gazette* ran a letter saying the 1875 act had never been very important, and in its only editorial comment, wrote, "Worse things have happened to the Negro than the Civil Rights decision and he is still here stronger than ever."

Blacks got some comfort from the fact that fifteen northern states, as a result of the 1883 Supreme Court decision, soon passed civil rights legislation, and three other states beefed up existing laws. But then came the *Plessy v. Ferguson* decision of 1896. Domke found that the black press's reaction to the case was considerably different from its reaction after the earlier Supreme Court ruling in 1883. While there was still outrage, with some papers again being more reserved in what they wrote than others, the black press was far more discouraged in 1896, and its advice to readers was split between renewing the fight for equality or accepting what they had without pressing aggressively for further rights.

To understand the Supreme Court's reasoning in the *Plessy* case, as well as the black newspapers' reaction to it, it is necessary to look at several powerful influences that were prevalent in the country at the time. One was Social Darwinism. Some sociologists and academicians took the nineteenth-century animal kingdom theories of Englishman Charles Darwin, which talked about natural selection and the survival of the fittest through biological evolution, and applied them to humans, arguing persuasively to many (particularly whites) that some races were superior to others. Thus, they reasoned that the best society would evolve naturally, rather than through government intervention in business and economic matters or in judicial decisions. As a number of historians have noted, these views quickly were used to justify the innate inferiority of blacks. For example, William G. Sumner, one of the leading advocates of Social Darwinism, said in the mid-1890s: "Nothing is more certain . . . than that inequality is a law of life. . . . No two persons were ever born equal. They differ in physical characteristics and in mental capacity. . . . In fact no man ever yet asserted that 'all men are equal,' meaning what he said. Thus if you asked Thomas Jefferson, when he was writing the first paragraph of the Declaration of Independence, whether in 'all men' he meant to include negroes [*sic*], he would have said that he was not talking about negroes [*sic*]." As a result of such beliefs, according to historians Pride and Wilson, those who accepted Social Darwinism had no difficulty feeling that whites were superior. This disadvantaged blacks enormously. "While whites were busy exercising their rugged individualism and self-determination," they wrote, "the Negro population was left to make do without any of the tools required to compete in the economic environment of a society that had adopted the posture that social mores could not be changed by legislation or judicial decree."

Another important influence at this time was Booker T. Washington, who was one of the country's most famous blacks. Born on April 5, 1856, on a Virginia plantation to a white father and a black slave, he worked after the Civil War in a salt furnace and in coal mines before entering Hampton Normal and Agricultural Institute in 1872 as a student. He also served as a janitor-on-trial at the school to pay for his room and board. Samuel Chapman Armstrong had started the school in 1868 with a specific aim, which unquestionably had an effect on Washington's future: "To train selected youth who shall go out and teach and lead their people, first by example, by getting land and homes; to give them not a dollar that they can earn for themselves; to teach respect for labor; to replace stupid drudgery with skilled hands; and to these ends to build up an industrial system for the sake of character." After graduating in 1875, Washington taught for several years in his hometown of Malden, Virginia, and then attended Wayland Seminary in Washington before returning to Hampton as an instructor in

1879. There he organized a night school and was in charge of an industrial training program for seventy-five Native Americans. In 1881, the Alabama state legislature appropriated $2,000 for faculty salaries at a new school for black teachers at Tuskegee, and Armstrong named Washington as its principal and organizer. Starting with no faculty, staff, students, or buildings, he built it into a major agricultural and industrial training center with an endowment of $2 million by the time he died in 1915.

While Washington did not invent vocational education, another term for industrial training, he became the leading proponent of it in the country, feeling blacks could earn a good wage by mastering a trade or skill. Historian Benjamin Quarles noted his influence:

> At Hampton Institute . . . and at Tuskegee, the young women became proficient at cooking, sewing, and nursing, and the young men learned how to become better farmers or were taught the trades of carpenters, blacksmiths, plumbers, and painters. "I have never seen a commencement like Tuskegee's before," wrote Mary Church Terrell. "On the stage before our very eyes students actually performed the work they had learned to do in school. They showed us how to build houses, how to paint them, how to estimate the cost of the necessary material and so on down the line."
>
> Washington was aware that many Negroes resented industrial education, connecting it with slavery. But the type of education he advocated developed character as well as mechanical skills. In 1907 Washington stated that he had made a careful investigation and had not found a single Tuskegee graduate "within the walls of any penitentiary in the United States."

In February 1895, when Frederick Douglass died, Washington

immediately became identified as the country's most prominent black leader, at least by whites. Seven months later, at the opening of the Cotton States and International Exposition in Atlanta, he reached new heights of national fame after delivering one of the opening speeches. When he was introduced by an ex-governor of Georgia, blacks in the audience cheered wildly, while there was only scattered applause from whites. But Washington, who was an eloquent and talented speaker, quickly won over the whites as well with what Logan called "one of the most effective pieces of political oratory in the history of the United States."

He began by pointing out that blacks, who made up one-third of the southern population, could not be ignored if that part of the country was going to move forward. Then, in what became one of the most controversial parts of his speech, he recommended that blacks should not migrate to other countries to better themselves and should not underestimate how important it was to build friendships with white southerners. Instead, he encouraged blacks, "'Cast down your bucket where you are'—cast it down in making friends in every manly way of the people of all races by whom we are surrounded." After urging blacks in the South to work in agriculture, mechanical fields, commerce, and domestic services as well as other similar professions, he stated, "No race can prosper till it learns that there is as much dignity in tilling a field as in writing a poem." He admitted it might mean that blacks would have to begin at the bottom of some profession instead of the top, but he said they should not allow past grievances to cause them to overlook opportunities. He also encouraged whites to "cast down their bucket" among the 8 million blacks, and he predicted that they would find them to be the "most patient, faithful, law-abiding and unresentful people that the world has seen." Then, holding his hand aloft dramatically, he uttered one sentence that was to be quoted more often than any other in his speech: "In all things that are purely social we can be as separate as the fingers, yet one as the hand in all things essential to mutual progress." The applause was thunderous.

But Washington was not through renouncing social equality. "The wisest among my race understand," he continued, "that the agitation of questions of social equality is the extremest folly and that progress in the enjoyment of all the privileges that will come to us must be the result of severe constant struggle rather than of artificial folly." And he predicted that any race that could contribute to the markets of the world would not be "ostracized." He concluded by praising the exposition for encouraging and bringing about friendship among the two races and promised that whites would get "patient, sympathetic help" from blacks as the South continued to make progress. Furthermore, he said that if "sectional differences and racial animosities and suspicions" could be put aside, and people followed the law, this, coupled with increasing prosperity, would "bring into our beloved South a new heaven and a new earth."

At the conclusion of the speech, the ex-governor rushed over to shake his hand, as did the others on the platform—a startling violation of southern etiquette as it applied to blacks and whites—and the applause from the whites in the audience was among the loudest that had ever been heard in that part of the country. By the next day, a deluge of congratulatory telegrams poured in, and several days later Washington was offered $50,000 for making a series of speeches around the country, which he declined. Meanwhile, President Grover Cleveland thanked him enthusiastically for what he said in his speech, and a year later, Harvard University became the first New England university to confer an honorary degree upon a black when it gave him a master of arts degree.

The white press around the country, particularly in the South, praised the speech highly. The *Atlanta Constitution* called it the "hit of the day" and labeled it "the most remarkable address delivered by a colored man in America." Other papers commended his "wisdom" and "common sense," and the *Charleston News and Observer* called Washington "one of the great men of the South," adding, "His skin is colored, but his head is sound and his heart is in the right place." Then there was the *Cincinnati Enquirer*. It lauded the speech as "the greatest single event" of the exposition's opening day and noted that it was so "inspiring" that Washington had to stop speaking several times because of cheering. After referring to the "baneful doctrine of social equality," it added dramatically, "If peace hath her victories no less renowned than war, then the battle of Atlanta of 1895 was as decisive a victory over race prejudice as the world has ever seen. Separate socially, but in all things else united, is the new doctrine that is bound to lead the South back to glory and supremacy once more."

Given Washington's extensive background at Hampton and Tuskegee with industrial education and the less than equitable (and worsening) conditions that existed for blacks at the time, particularly in the South, the positions that he advocated in his speech were not unexpected. But not all blacks were impressed. W. E. B. Du Bois, who would become one of the twentieth century's leading blacks, derisively called it "the Atlanta Compromise," and it led to a major split between the two men. Some historians were not any kinder. Herbert Aptheker noted in 1951 that Washington's "policy [of accommodation] amounted objectively to an acceptance by the Negro people of second-class citizenship." Three years later, Logan took the same position, saying that the speech "accepted a subordinate place for Negroes in American life." He was not surprised, however, by what Washington said: "The preeminent significance of the speech stems from the acceptance of the doctrine of compromise by a Negro with close personal contacts with powerful [white] men who had made compromise the national policy."

It may never be known whether Washington's "compromise" position had an impact on the Supreme Court's deliberations in the *Plessy* case less than a year later. Wilson, noting Washington's "conservative philosophy of submissive acceptance of a separate agrarian economic role" for blacks, wrote that it was "possible," and Logan believed the speech may have "consoled the consciences" of the justices as they "wrote into American jurisprudence one of its least defensible doctrines, the constitutionality of equal but separate accommodations." But there is no doubt that Washington's position had an impact on black newspapers when the decision was announced. They had to make the difficult decision whether to renew the fight for more equality for blacks or accept the accommodationist, self-help approach championed by Washington.

Domke, in his 1994 study of the reaction to the 1896 Supreme Court decision, found that three of the seven black newspapers he examined supported accommodation. The *Savannah (Georgia) Tribune,* for example, praised the Tuskegee educator in an editorial: "Booker T. Washington is earning fame for his race, and making [Tuskegee] one of the most famous [educational institutions] in the country. Prof. Washington does not attempt to boss the politics of his state and consequently he receives the support and applause of all classes of people." It added that Georgia needed someone like him to upgrade the education of blacks in that state just as he had done in Alabama. The *Kansas City American Citizen,*

while not mentioning the *Plessy* case or Washington, also supported his views editorially two weeks after the Court's decision
as it gently chided blacks for their behavior: "Although the advancement of the Negro race is wonderful, yet we can accomplish
much by exercising privelges [*sic*] which present themselves. We
are fond of idleness, we will dance, have socials[,] excursions and
various other enjoyments [although when] one is born we have no
means to supply them properly, and when one is out raged [*sic*] we
haven't the means or the qualifications to see that justice is carried
into effect. This is because many of our race [are] as so many giddy
children rather like some thing that they do not under stand [*sic*]."

Because blacks had been advocating a philosophy of self-
help and economic advancement long before Washington's Atlanta speech, Domke found it understandable that some of the
black newspapers he examined openly supported this in 1896. But
he was still critical of accommodation, noting that by avoiding
confrontation, this stance "was doomed because it demanded ac-
quiescence to white Americans without offering a concrete means
of effecting social change." In contrast, those black papers that
renewed the fight for more black rights "engendered pride and
self-respect among blacks, integral components for an African
American self-definition." Nevertheless, whatever their stance on
accommodation, most of the papers were outraged at the *Plessy*
decision, which made blacks realize that "social and cultural acceptance" could only come from their own race. This, in turn,
made black papers even more important because black communities depended more than ever upon them to shape and reflect their
values.

But deciding whether to adopt an accommodationist role or to
renew the fight for equality did not mean that black newspapers on

both sides of the issue did not continue to vigorously attack evils that plagued blacks. And one of the most prevalent (or at least horrific) at this time, which continued past World War II, was lynching. According to figures compiled by Tuskegee Institute, 3,426 blacks were lynched in the United States from 1882 to 1947, with this illegal activity reaching its height between 1890 and 1900, when 36 percent of the lynchings (1,217) took place. The latter period also contained the highest one-year total in U.S. history for lynchings of blacks, with 161 being murdered in this fashion in 1892. Some parts of the country were clearly more dangerous than others. About 82 percent of all lynchings (which also included whites) from 1889 to 1899 occurred in the eleven former Confederate states as well as Missouri, Kentucky, and Oklahoma Territory.

Lynchings of blacks were reported commonly in white newspapers, varying from lengthy, gruesome accounts, which spared no details, to brief stories. Even the articles that fell between the two extremes were striking for the matter-of-fact way in which they were written, for some of the prejudicial language that was used for blacks, such as referring to them as "brutes" or "monsters," and for the common mention of "Judge Lynch." For example, on May 20, 1896, the readers of the *Atlanta Constitution* found a typical story on page two under the headline "Swung from a Limb":

> New Orleans, May 19—This morning's early pedestrians who happened to pass the courthouse and jail in St. Bernard parish were horrified to see swaying in the breeze the body of a man.
>
> The news quickly spread and many hundreds viewed the grewsome specticle [*sic*].

Sheriff Nunez was informed and hastening to the scene immediately ordered the body cut down and took it in charge. This was done and it was seen that the distorted features, made hideous by Judge Lynch's swift justice, were those of Jim Dazzle, alias Jim Glemley, a negro.

The news reached the city limit last evening from St. Bernard parish that a negro had attempted to ravish a white woman Sunday morning in front of the Poydras plantation. The news of the attempted outrage spread throughout the parish and in a short while every one was on the trail of the ravisher.

The victim is a married woman named Mrs. Moleso. She formerly resided at Delacroix Island, which is almost thirty miles below the city. A short while ago she moved to the Poydras plantation along with her family. Mrs. Moleso accompanied by her younger sister and child proceeded to an adjoining plantation. While on the way they met the negro and when he got near the ladies, the brute seized Mrs. Moleso before she could realize his intentions.

The woman screamed for aid and was heard by a man in a road cart, who, suspecting the ladies were in trouble, hastened to the scene and arrived just in time to see the negro escape, and gave chase. The negro was captured and placed in the parish prison of St. Bernard, which is located in Terre-aux-Boeufs.

Dazzle was a stranger in St. Bernard. He was working on a plantation near the place of the crime.

From their inception, black newspapers covered lynchings with obvious outrage. On August 3, 1827, only four and a half months after *Freedom's Journal* began publishing in New York City as the first black paper, it wrote about an Alabama lynching of a black man and then the burning of his body until only ashes remained by a mob numbering seventy to eighty. It called the act a "horrid occurrence," "disgraceful to the character of civilized man," and "one of those outrageous transactions."

While such comments were repeated over and over, it took a remarkable woman in the last decade of the nineteenth century to spearhead the black papers' revulsion against lynchings and turn it into a national issue. Ida B. Wells was not the first woman journalist in the country. Seventeen women in the colonial period before 1800 had worked as printers, some of them even as publishers. Nor was she the first black woman journalist. The *Freeman,* a black newspaper in Indianapolis, ran a lengthy article by a woman in February 1889 that discussed ten black women journalists, and while the story was generally vague about when they began their careers, at least one started six years before Wells. The paper noted that black women journalists were doing "right well," asserting that "sex is no bar to any line of literary work, that by speaking for themselves women can give the truth about themselves and thereby inspire the confidence of the people." The article concluded: "When we remember the very difficult circumstances of the past, [and] the trials and discomforts of the present, we are indeed cheered with the prospects. In the busy hum of life it is difficult to make one's way to the front, and this is true of all races, hence, we are not at all discouraged since our sisters have had such ready access to the great journals of the land. When the edge of prejudice shall have become rusted and worn out, the Negro women shall be heard most potently in the realm of thought, till then shall we strive."

Wells definitely was one of those women who was "heard most potently." Born a slave in Holly Springs, Mississippi, on July 16, 1862, to a carpenter and a cook, her life changed dramatically at the age of sixteen when a yellow fever epidemic killed her parents as well as a brother. She took over the family, pulled her hair on top of her head in order to look older, and began teaching in a rural school. Then, in 1884, after being hired to teach in Memphis, she became an activist when she purchased a first-class train ticket and sat among white women in the ladies car until a conductor told her that she would have to move because blacks were only allowed in the smoking car. When she refused to budge, he tried to force her from her seat and she bit his hand, which resulted in three men dragging her from the car as the white passengers stood and clapped. She sued the Chesapeake & Ohio Railroad, but after she won in circuit court and received $500, the Tennessee Supreme Court reversed the decision.

At this point, while continuing to teach full time, Wells began writing articles part time for a number of black newspapers. This brought her to the attention of Fortune, now editor of the black *New York Age,* who noted that while she was "girlish looking in physique," she also was "as smart as a steel trap." He also complimented her as a journalist: "She has become famous as one of the few of our women who can handle a goose-quill, with diamond point, as easily as any man in the newspaper work." Soon after this, she began to be called the "Princess of the Black Press."

Wells became a one-third owner of the *Memphis Free Speech,* a Baptist weekly newspaper, in 1889, and two years later wrote an article criticizing the disgraceful conditions in the city's black schools, where she taught. As a result, she was fired as a teacher. Now a full-time editor whose only salary came from the paper's sales, she traveled throughout Tennessee as well as two adjoining states, Arkansas and Mississippi, seeking subscribers. Within a year, circulation climbed from 1,500 a week to 3,500, which finally made the paper profitable. Her no-nonsense articles drew attention to the paper and helped it to grow. One of her pieces referred derisively to "good niggers," who tried to impress whites by taking advantage of other blacks, and another encouraged blacks to "steal big"—since they were going to jail for stealing no more than five cents while whites were getting away with thefts of thousands of dollars.

By 1891, Wells was attacking black lynchings. One article in the *Free Speech* noted that blacks in Georgetown, Kentucky, had burned down every white-owned building in town after a local black had been lynched. After complimenting the "manhood" of the town's blacks, she minced no words as she continued: "So long as we permit ourselves to be trampled upon, so long we will have to endure it. Not until the Negro rises in his might and takes a hand in resenting such cold blooded murders, if he has to burn up whole towns, will a halt be called in wholesale lynchings."

But nothing was as pivotal in her life as 1892. In the spring, when three of her friends, who ran a grocery store in a black section of Memphis, were killed by a black mob, Wells encouraged blacks to leave the city because it was not a safe place for them to live and because they were not treated fairly in the courts. When about 2,000 blacks heeded her call, it hurt the local economy badly, and white businesses asked her to stop writing such editorials. She not only refused but became even more outspoken as she began examining lynchings. Carrying a loaded pistol in her purse for protection, she visited the sites where lynchings had occurred and discovered, according to historian Rodger Streitmatter, that every case involved a white woman who had consented to sex with a black man and then accused him of rape when what had occurred became known and she wanted to protect her reputation. This outraged Wells and led to one of the most famous editorial statements of her career: "There are many white women in the South who would marry colored men if such an act would not place them beyond the pale of society. White men lynch the of-fending Afro-American, not because he is a despoiler of virtue, but because he succumbs to the smiles of white women."

Events quickly came to a head in late May when Wells wrote yet another inflammatory editorial in the *Free Speech* about the same subject, saying no one in the South believed black men raped white women. She predicted that if southern white men contin-ued to make that spurious claim, it would result in an adverse pub-lic reaction that would lead to a conclusion "which will be very damaging to the moral reputation of their women." Memphis's white papers were not about to ignore such outspokenness from a black, particularly one who was challenging deeply ingrained be-liefs that were at the core of what whites thought about blacks. The *Commercial* responded angrily four days later: "The fact that a black scoundrel is allowed to live and utter such loathsome and re-pulsive calumnies is a volume of evidence as to the wonderful pa-tience of Southern whites. But we have had enough of it. There are some things that the Southern white man will not tolerate, and the obscene intimations of the foregoing have brought the writer to the very outermost limit of public patience." On the same day, however, the *Evening Scimitar,* not realizing that the writer of the editorial was a woman, was not inclined to show any patience as it issued a not-so-veiled threat of not only branding but castration: "Patience under such circumstances is not a virtue. If the negroes themselves do not apply the remedy without delay it will be the duty of those whom he [the writer of the editorial] has attacked to tie the wretch who utters these calumnies to a stake at the inter-section of Main and Madison Sts., brand him in the forehead with a hot iron and perform upon him a surgical operation with a pair of tailor's shears." Threats of lynching for those who worked at the *Free Speech* followed as a mob formed that evening. The paper's business manager, who owned half of the paper, fled the city to escape the mob and was warned not to return. Meanwhile, Wells, who was in New York on vacation, also received threatening letters and telegrams, and the paper and its press were destroyed.

Unable to return to Memphis, Wells accepted a one-fourth interest in the *New York Age* in exchange for giving Fortune her subscription list for the *Free Speech*. Immediately, she launched a national antilynching campaign that lasted until she died in 1931. "Wells turned the *Age*'s front page into the closest thing America had to an official record of the chilling acts of racial abuse, filling the paper with the details surrounding dozens of lynchings she had investigated first hand," noted Streitmatter. The first story, on June 25, 1892, headlined "Exiled," took up the entire front page and sold 10,000 copies, which was a single-day record at that time for black newspapers. Fortune described it as being "full of the pathos of awful truth." It included three proposals by Wells on how to end violence against blacks. The first was economic reprisals of the type she had encouraged successfully in Memphis, and the second was a demand that the country's newspapers condemn lynchings. The third was the most controversial: Blacks, she said, should defend themselves against violence. Mirroring words that had appeared in *Frederick Douglass' Paper* in June 1854, she wrote: "A Winchester rifle should have a place of honor in every black home. . . . When the white man knows he runs a risk of biting the dust every time his Afro-American victim does, he will have greater respect for Afro-American life. The more the Afro-American yields and cringes and begs, the more he is insulted, outraged and lynched."

Wells then branched out in her campaign, publishing booklets and pamphlets such as "Southern Horrors: Lynch Law in All Its Phases," which included a letter of praise from Douglass. "Brave woman!" he wrote. "[Y]ou have done your people and mine a service which can neither be weighed nor measured." That was followed over almost the next forty years by speeches, an overseas tour, the organization of local and state antilynching societies, and political lobbying for a national antilynching law. The latter effort failed, but all of this earned her the title of the "Black Joan of Arc." After she died from a kidney disease, Du Bois said in a fitting eulogy that she "began the awakening of the conscience of the nation."

While Wells's crusade was the first real campaign in black newspapers, it would not be the last. Others with national significance followed before World War I and during World War II. There were other firsts, as well, in the last third of the nineteenth century, and while not of the magnitude of what Wells did, they nevertheless were signs of the continuing maturation of the black press. For example, *La Tribune de la Nouvelle-Orleans* (the *New Orleans Tribune*) became the country's first black daily newspaper in late 1864, and it continued to publish each day until 1869, when it became a weekly. Then, in 1875, thirteen editors from around the country met in Cincinnati at the first Convention of Colored Newspapermen. P. B. S. Pinchback, a black who was formerly the acting governor of Louisiana, told the group that their first goal should be to make black papers profitable, even though no one expected that would occur. He continued bluntly, charting a course that he felt was necessary if the black papers were going to survive: "Our people, as a class, are not largely a reading class, but it is on them that we must rely for patronage. Of the four millions who were recently in slavery we cannot expect any large portion of them to be readers; but we must look to their children as they grow up. We can not expect, for sometime, to derive much income from advertising, not until our people become active and enterprising in business matters." Soon after this, Henry J. Lewis apparently became the first black political cartoonist in 1879 when his work appeared in *Harper's Weekly;* ten years later, his work appeared on a regular basis in the black *Indianapolis Freeman*. And only the year before, the latter paper had become the first black illustrated paper.

But more, much more, would occur in the first twenty years of the twentieth century as the black press became a power to be reckoned with and truly flexed its muscles for the first time.

FOUR

A NEW TYPE OF NEWSPAPER

Anywhere in God's country is better than the Southland.
—Robert Abbott, *Chicago Defender*

T. Thomas Fortune, the outspoken but well-regarded editor of the *New York Age,* which was the country's leading black newspaper at the turn of the century, was at his fiery best in 1900 during a meeting in Brooklyn to honor the 100th anniversary of the birth of abolitionist John Brown. In one of the notable early salvos against an accommodationist position, he urged blacks to stage a "revolution" to halt disenfranchisement. "It took tons of blood to put the fifteenth amendment [which guaranteed blacks the right to vote] into the constitution and it will take tons to put it out," he said. "You want to organize and keep your powder dry, and be ready to demand an eye for eye and a tooth for a tooth, for there is coming a great crisis for the negro in this country." While there was ample evidence supporting his claim that "a great crisis" was approaching, his words drew national condemnation from the white daily press. He also was criticized by some prominent blacks, including Booker T. Washington, who met later that year to form a black party and draw up a slate of candidates for the upcoming presidential election.

Fortune's criticism of Washington's accommodationist approach was interesting because he had been one of the educator's major supporters for years; moreover, his newspaper had been Washington's favorite outlet for disseminating his conservative views nationally. As such, the *Age,* as well as some other papers published by blacks adhering to Washington's views, was subsidized financially by what was known as the "Tuskegee Machine." It was part of Washington's extensive propaganda program, as historian Edgar A. Toppin noted: "Washington's 'Tuskegee Machine' influenced black newspapers and magazines. The Tuskegee news bureau . . . sent out a flood of news releases and canned editorials. By placing or withholding ads, the well-endowed Tuskegee clique persuaded many black editors, most of whose publications were in financial straits, to carry these materials favorable to Washington's views. Moreover, the Tuskegee cabal secretly purchased several black periodicals, controlling them unbeknownst to the public."

The struggle over Washington's conservative position as he articulated it in his Atlanta speech of 1895—"Cast down your bucket where you are," which meant accepting what historian Clint Wilson II called "a separate agrarian economic role" for blacks—would continue to escalate, remaining one of the most heated points of contention in black America until Washington's death in November 1915. But like a wide, deep river, other important, powerful, and to some extent dangerous currents not only existed but competed for attention from blacks in the first two decades of the twentieth century. Out of their confluence came the modern black newspaper and a heightened push for more civil rights that was national in scope and escalated a massive migration of blacks out of the South. All of this, in turn, attracted the attention of the federal government like never before and led to serious threats against the black press.

Three years after Fortune's call for a "revolution," attacks on Washington's philosophy escalated into a major division among blacks. At the forefront of the charge was one of the country's best-known black intellectuals, W. E. B. Du Bois, who had joined the faculty at Atlanta University in 1897, teaching economics and history. Born into a family whose ancestry was a mixture of black, French, Indian, and Dutch—but, as he pointed out, "Thank God, no Anglo-Saxon"—he attended Fisk University and the University of Berlin before receiving three degrees at Harvard and becoming the first black to earn a Ph.D. in 1895. Although his dissertation was historical in nature ("The Suppression of the African Slave Trade"), he announced two years before his graduation that he planned "to make a name in science, to make a name in literature, and thus to raise my race." Impressed by Du Bois, Washington tried to recruit him as a close supporter, but this effort failed, according to historian Benjamin Quarles, because Du Bois' "ambition and abilities, plus his haughtiness, made him unsuitable as a subordinate." Just how unsuitable became apparent in 1903 when Du Bois openly attacked Washington's policies. While he may not have liked Washington's self-assumed role as a national leader of blacks, which was accepted avidly by whites, he particularly came to believe that the Tuskegee educator, and his "machine," were "leading the way backward."

The assault came in Du Bois' book *The Souls of Black Folk,* a collection of essays. He charged that Washington's position implied that blacks were inferior and encouraged them to forego political action and not agitate for more civil rights. Instead, he said, Washington wanted them to "concentrate all their energies on

industrial education, the accumulation of wealth, and the concili-
ation of the South." Finally, he claimed Washington, with his
stress on vocational training, was hostile to black liberal arts col-
leges and their graduates, whom Du Bois labeled "The Talented
Tenth" because he felt they would have significant leadership roles
in the future rise of blacks. This assertion understandably attracted
the attention of blacks with college training, and many of them
immediately began deserting Washington and his program. Looking back in 1947 in a column in the *Chicago Defender,* Du Bois still
recalled his disagreement with Washington over education:

> I have always advocated training in industries; I said in 1903: "So
> far as Mr. Washington preaches Thrift, Patience, and Industrial
> Training for the masses, we must hold up his hands and strive
> with him, rejoicing in his honors and glorifying in the strength
> of the Joshua called of God and of man to lead the headless host."
> I vehemently opposed our training to industrial skills. As I said 35
> years ago, "The object of Education is not to make men carpen-
> ters; it is to make Carpenters, Men." The mass of men cannot
> learn to read and write, make shoes, build houses and work steel,
> unless also the group has trained teachers, good physicians, hon-
> est lawyers, moral clergymen and skilled engineers.

Du Bois was not the only one to attack Washington in 1903.
William Monroe Trotter and George Forbes, who published the
black *Boston Guardian* and continually attacked Washington and
his program venomously, questioned him at a Boston speech
about black education and voting. Du Bois claimed that this led to
"a disturbance," while the white daily newspapers called it "a
riot." Whatever occurred, Trotter and Forbes were arrested and
sent to jail for a short time. "Many white Americans thus realized

that not all Negroes followed the leadership of Booker T. Washington," noted historian Rayford W. Logan.

Then, in 1905, motivated by Trotter's and Forbes's open attack on Washington, Du Bois launched what became known as the Niagara Movement, after its first meeting in Niagara Falls, Canada. While there was no open criticism of Washington by the twenty-nine members of "The Talented Tenth" who were in attendance, they issued a manifesto calling for such things as freedom of speech and freedom of the press as well as an end to discrimination because of race or skin color. Unless they got those rights, which belonged to all Americans, they said, they would continue to protest "and to assail the ears of America with the story of its shameful deeds toward us." The movement convened once a year, and at its second meeting at Harpers Ferry, West Virginia, Du Bois stated unequivocally what would constitute equality for blacks, which most decidedly was not accepting Washington's program that made them a minority in a society dominated by whites: "We will not be satisfied to take one jot or tittle less than our full manhood rights. We claim for ourselves every single right that belongs to a freeborn American, political, civil and social; and until we get these rights we will never cease to protest and assail the ears of America." The Niagara Movement had about thirty branches around the country and achieved several local victories against discrimination before dying out in 1910, partly because of opposition by Washington, which caused only a small number of "The Talented Tenth" to actually join the organization and resulted in whites being reluctant to donate money to it. There also were those who thought Du Bois was arrogant.

But although the Niagara Movement lasted only five years, it had a significant impact. Not only did it bring wider attention to injustices against blacks, but it helped lay the foundation for what became one of the country's most important black organizations, the National Association for the Advancement of Colored People. Formed in 1909 basically to eliminate discrimination, the NAACP said its goal was "to make 11,000,000 Americans [blacks] physically free from peonage, mentally free from ignorance, politically free from disfranchisement, and socially free from insult." Despite fear by some of the organizers that Du Bois would use the NAACP to make even more strident attacks upon Washington, he was named the director of publications and research, a position he would hold until 1932. In 1910, he started the organization's magazine, *The Crisis,* but perhaps because of restraints placed upon him by the NAACP's directors, he attacked Washington in it less than he had in the *Horizon,* a magazine that he had founded and edited from 1907 to 1910. But that did not mean that he had given up on the goal of total equality for blacks that he had stated so eloquently at Harpers Ferry, and *The Crisis* would have an enormous impact on the black press's views on discrimination in the final year of World War I.

In the midst of this maelstrom, Robert Abbott, who would become one of the most remarkable individuals in black newspaper history, founded the *Chicago Defender.* The route that he took to become a publisher was circuitous—and somewhat painful. Born in 1868 to former slaves and raised in Savannah, Georgia, his dark skin color haunted him for his entire life because he quickly found that local blacks prized light complexions. Thus, he continually fought racial discrimination, according to his biographer, "not because he felt himself different, but because he wanted to be similar and was forcibly held to be different—not only by whites, but by the mulattoes of his own group." Roi Ottley continued:

He came to hate the color black—indeed, I suspect he was afflicted with a case of self-hate. He avoided black as a color for clothes and rarely appeared in public accompanied by a black woman. He even had an aversion to the term "Negro." He was, however, fiercely loyal to any man who was black, as distinct from those who were brown or fair of complexion. He kept notoriously incompetent black workers in his employ simply because he felt society offered them no social mercy. He once retreated sufficiently to observe: "Black isn't a bad shade; let's make it popular in complexions as well as clothes." His eccentricities about color made him object to the use of the term "blackball" by Negro fraternities, and urge instead the use of "whiteball," as a term for denying aspirants membership. Thus the slogan emerged: "Blackballs elect; whiteballs reject!" This preoccupation often produced constructive ideas, such as his campaign, "Go to a White Church Sunday."

Another result of his background, according to historian Martin Terrell, was that he continually stressed the "aspirations, fears, and grievances" of ordinary blacks while shying away from intellectuals, such as Du Bois, who had aristocratic tendencies. At the same time, however, he opposed Washington's conciliatory approach.

After briefly attending Beach Institute in Savannah and Claflin University in Orangeburg, South Carolina, Abbott entered Hampton Institute in 1889, six days before his twenty-first birthday. He ended up spending seven years there, training to be a printer and constantly experimenting with type so that, as he put it, "none of the minute details of the trade might escape my observation." While on a school trip to Chicago in 1893, he wrote his mother: "Tell father if he will back me, I will come home and run a paper. If not, I will stay out here in the west and try to make a fortune. Let me know his intentions before I begin to make up my mind as to what steps to take." Thus, undecided what to do upon graduation in 1896, he returned to Savannah, where he worked part time as a printer, helped his father publish a small paper, and taught school on a plantation. A year later, after a light-skinned black woman followed her parents' wishes and refused to marry him because his skin was too dark and he had virtually no money, he entered the Kent College of Law in Chicago and graduated in 1899 as the only black in a class of seventy. But once again he came away discouraged. He sought out a prominent fair-skinned black attorney for counsel on where to practice law and was informed that he was "a little too dark to make any impression on the courts in Chicago." After unsuccessfully trying to establish a law practice in nearby Gary, Indiana, and being told that he would not do any better in Kansas, he returned to Chicago and became a printer. "Things are beginning now to look bright for me," Abbott excitedly wrote his mother, because he could now earn $20 a week. But the reality was that things were not as "bright" as he claimed. Looking back, he recalled: "It was not often I found work. I would go hungry and probably would have starved to death but for the generosity of some folk who would loan me a dime now and then. Even when I did work, I did not earn enough money to pay back rent, repay loans and eat three meals, too. Consequently, I was always broke. Such was my experience during the early days of struggle in Chicago."

Realizing that he would never make much money as a printer and it would not give him the status that he sought, Abbott decided to do something that he had been talking about for five years: start a newspaper. Even though he had little money, it was a natural direction for him to go; as a friend recalled, he had "a burning, consuming" desire to do this because he wanted "to express his views on the race question." Nevertheless, his friends doubted whether he could succeed, not only because his grammar was not good, but because there were already three newspapers for Chicago's 40,000 blacks—the *Broad Ax,* the *Illinois Idea,* and the *Conservator*—and two other black papers from Indianapolis and New York City that were well read and influential. Undeterred, he rented an office, moved in a folding card table and a borrowed kitchen chair, and spent 25 cents on notebooks and pencils. As for a staff, he started with no one except his landlady's teenage daughter, who helped him after school let out. At the start, he wrote out the paper in long hand and took it to a printer, who agreed to let him pay after the paper was sold, rather than in advance, because Abbott had no money. Finally, after it was printed, he had to sell it himself—regular newsstand sales of the paper did not begin until 1912—and at nights he visited places where blacks congregated, gathering news and soliciting advertising.

Named the *Defender* because of Abbott's pledge to be a defender of blacks, the four-page weekly paper appeared for the first time on May 5, 1905, with a printing of 300, which cost him $13.75. He charged 2 cents an issue, or a yearly subscription could be purchased for $1, which was a saving of 4 cents. The paper almost failed in the first few months for lack of money. His printer threatened to quit unless Abbott paid his bills, Abbott was forced to live on fish sandwiches and soda pop for lunch every day because that was all he could afford, and he had to give up his office and move into the dining room of his landlady, Henrietta Plumer Lee. "She not only underwrote office space, but she actually fed Abbott, frequently supplied him with carfare, often patched his shabby clothes, and gave him encouragement," wrote Ottley, noting that over the next four years Abbott was able to make only "token payments" to her for rent and food. Slowly, however, the paper began catching on, and within several years circulation was up to 1,000 copies for each issue as Abbott adopted the slogan, "If You See It in the *Defender,* It's So!" While the paper had much in common with other black papers, focusing on local gossip and special-interest stories, it slowly began running more articles that uplifted and educated readers. Occasionally, it also was sensational. An early example appeared in a *Defender* campaign against prostitution when it ran a headline, "MOTHER TAKES INNOCENT DAUGHTERS TO HOUSES OF ILL FAME," and then underneath in small letters was a subhead, "To Play Piano."

By 1910, with the *Chicago Defender*'s annual subscription rate still $1 (it would be increased to $1.50 a year in 1912 and then $2 in 1918), its circulation was rising steadily and it finally was on firm financial ground, although profits were minimal. Around this time, the paper began running a slogan in its masthead that became famous, "World's Greatest Weekly," which was a takeoff on the *Chicago Tribune*'s boast, "World's Greatest Newspaper," and it explained in a front-page promotion on May 14, 1910, why the paper was a good buy for blacks: It was not a "lifeless, spineless, inorganic thing of mere ink and paper, made just to sell, but the living, breathing, pulsating embodiment of all that is nearest the heart and most welcome to the mind of the American." While such puffery made for a good promotion, the reality was that Abbott needed to continue to increase circulation in order to make more money, since advertising revenue was as limited at the *Defender* as it was at all black newspapers.

On the positive side, however, it was becoming easier to increase circulation; black illiteracy had dropped from 44.5 percent in 1900 to 30.4 percent just ten years later, black incomes were rising, and black newspapers now rivaled black churches in influence. Furthermore, black newspapers were a necessity if blacks wanted to read about themselves, because white newspapers continued to largely ignore them unless a story involved criminal activity. Thus, by 1910 a survey showed there were 288 black newspapers in the country, with a combined circulation of about 500,000, and at least one paper was published in every city with a sizable black population. Ottley noted that the number of readers, however, was unquestionably far more than half a million. "Every literate Negro read at least one Negro publication," he wrote. "The millions living in poverty, rural isolation and illiteracy in the South often had one person read a paper aloud in places like barbershops and churches and followed this with group discussions. Papers frequently were passed from hand to hand." As for the *Defender,* it has been estimated that each copy was read by five to seven people, and the number might have been even higher if copies had not become worn out.

It was at this point that Abbott made a decision that would change black newspapers forever. He decided to model the *Chicago Defender* after the sensational Yellow Journalism that William Randolph Hearst and Joseph Pulitzer had popularized in New York City beginning in the 1890s but which now was on the wane. Historian Rodger Struitmatter explained:

> Instead of filling his pages with the tepid community news— religious items mixed with announcements of local births, weddings, and deaths—that was the staple of black journalism of the era, he began serving up spicier fare. Political cartoons lampooned racist government officials, and shrill editorials denounced black oppression. Most noteworthy of all were the front-page banner headlines, many of them printed in bright red ink and each one larger than the one before—"White Man

Rapes Colored Girl," "Aged Man Is Burned to Death by Whites." Critics called Abbott's approach to the news sensationalistic, but circulation and advertising revenue soared.

But even as the *Defender* changed, causing other black newspapers to quickly emulate it when they saw how readers liked the new look, it remained the same in one important way: It was biased toward blacks. While white journalists were beginning to discuss and move toward objectivity in the late nineteenth and early twentieth centuries, Abbott was adamant that although the paper must be accurate, there would be no objectivity, because this was an advocacy press. Ottley succinctly summed up the *Defender* as "an organ of racial propaganda."

Searching for higher circulation and thus more money, which Abbott realized was clearly limited if he did not look outside Chicago, he understandably turned to the South. Not only did 90 percent of the country's 10 million blacks live there, but injustices were rampant. The southern states, obviously encouraged by the end of Reconstruction in 1876 and then the *Plessy v. Ferguson* case of 1896, had made the most of their opportunities to keep blacks second-class citizens. Streitmatter wrote: "[Blacks in the South were] prohibited from voting or holding public office and denied political and economic control over their own lives. Most black men and women worked from dawn to dusk as field hands, paid whatever paltry sum their white employers chose to give them. Enduring a virtual feudal system in which even the most basic of human rights did not exist, women and girls were forced into sexual servitude by white overlords who kept black men demoralized and in a constant state of intimidation."

So, Abbott began encouraging southern blacks to move to the North in what he called the "Great Northern Drive." It was not a novel idea, since blacks had been migrating either outside of the United States or to other parts of the country for almost a hundred years. Beginning in 1816, the American Colonization Society had begun settling blacks in Africa, and by the end of the Civil War, as many as 25,000 had gone there as well as to Haiti and elsewhere. Meanwhile, even before the war, blacks moved west into new western states or Indian territory, doing various types of work, including being farmers, miners, and cowboys. One of the latter who became famous was Nat Love, who in 1876 became known as "Deadwood Dick" after winning a riding and marksmanship competition at Deadwood in Dakota Territory. The first large exodus after Reconstruction was in 1879, when more than 7,000 southern blacks, spurred on by crop failures of the previous year, headed to Kansas, with smaller numbers going to Missouri, Nebraska, and Iowa. The wisdom of this migration was debated. Richard T. Greener, the first black graduate of Harvard and dean of the law school, argued that everyone was better off because of it—those who left would get better jobs, and there would be more jobs for those blacks who stayed in the South. Frederick Douglass, the country's most influential black, was against the "exodusters," however, claiming that the blacks who left were unwise for moving where they did not have a virtual monopoly on labor as they did in the South.

The migration continued slowly and sporadically over the years, but it was a trickle compared to what occurred in the 1910s, when at least 500,000 blacks moved from the South to the North. New York City, Detroit, and Philadelphia each had their black populations increase significantly, but Chicago experienced the most growth. According to the 1920 U.S. Census, the city had a 148 percent increase in blacks from 1910 to 1920, going from 44,103 to 109,458. The biggest jump was from 1915 to 1919, when about 61,000 blacks migrated to Chicago. They came in every conceivable way: taking trains, riding on horses and mules, and being pulled in carts. And some even walked barefoot, noted Ottley, "bringing goats, pigs, chickens, dogs and cats, wearing overalls and housedresses."

A number of factors accounted for the sudden increase in migration in the 1910s to various northern cities. An obvious one was the continued intolerable conditions for blacks in the South, which included a rise in the number of lynchings at this time. Just how grateful they were to escape this oppression was shown by migrants on trains traveling from Mississippi to Chicago. When they crossed the Ohio River, they would stop their watches, kneel to pray, and sing a gospel hymn, "I Done Come Out of the Land of Egypt with the Good News." As if southern injustices were not enough to drive them north, blacks lost jobs because of floods in Oklahoma, an infestation of boll weevils in Georgia, and sugar industry problems in Louisiana. But the major reason for the increased internal migration was a decline of immigration from abroad from 1.2 million in 1914 to only 110,000 in 1918, which created an instant demand in the North for black labor. Related to this was increased production in northern factories when the United States entered World War I in 1917 and the fact that many white workers went into the service, both of which created substantial job openings. And many of those who got these jobs eagerly told their friends in the South how much better things were and encouraged them to head north. "I work in Swifts packing Co. in the sausage department," a recent Chicago migrant wrote his sister in Louisiana. "My daughter and I work for the same company—We get $1.50 a day and we pack so many sausages we dont [sic] have much time to play but it is a matter of a dollar with me and I feel that God made the path and I am walking therein. Tell your husband work is plentiful here and he wont [*sic*] have to loaf if he want [*sic*] to work."

It was not surprising that Chicago particularly became what Streitmatter called "a racial magnet." Industrial jobs, as well as work in the growing stockyards, were plentiful, mainly because 350,000 Illinois men enlisted or were drafted into World War I. As a result of the critical labor shortage, the large packinghouses, steel mills, and foundries began encouraging blacks to come to Chicago. In addition, wages were high compared to the South, where black tenant farmers made 50 cents to $1 a day, and for the first time since slaves had arrived in the colonies in the 1600s, blacks were employed in large numbers as semiskilled and skilled industrial workers. Equally important was that the city was a terminus for two major railroads coming out of the South—the Illinois Central and the Gulf, Mobile, and Ohio—which funneled blacks to Chicago from Mississippi, Louisiana, Alabama, Texas, and Arkansas.

And then there was the *Chicago Defender.* Ottley stated that "[s]ingle-handed, Abbott . . . set the great migration of the Mississippi Valley in motion." That is clearly an exaggeration. As historians know, nothing ever happens in history for only one reason. More correctly, Streitmatter noted that numerous persons studying the migration in the 1910s considered the newspaper to be a "key" reason for the size of the migration. One of those was Chicago newspaperman Carl Sandburg, who credited the paper with reaching hundreds of thousands of blacks every week as it agitated with its "propaganda machine." "The *Defender,* more than any other one agency, was the big cause of the 'northern fever' and the big exodus from the South," he wrote. A historian credited the paper with giving Chicago the image of being "a northern mecca," which attracted southern blacks, and another said the

paper was "one of the most potent factors in a phenomenal He-
gira that began to change the character and pattern of race relations
in the United States."

The first article to appear in the *Defender* about blacks leaving
the South seems to have been on March 2, 1911. It noted that
thousands of blacks would be coming in the summer to Chicago,
as well as to the states of Wisconsin and Michigan, to enjoy a few
months of freedom. The paper also began running what would become a staple in its migration campaign: editorial cartoons. In
1915, for example, a drawing labeled "The Exodus" showed a
black man hanging from a tree while a group of blacks in the background marched north. But the paper did not begin hammering
away at the South in earnest until 1916–1917, when its migration
articles, editorials, cartoons, and photographs focused on two
strategies: extolling the positive aspects of the North and pointing
out the negative aspects of the South. This developed into "the
most ambitious project ever undertaken" by the paper, according
to Ottley: "Abbott did everything to aid and abet the migration.
He argued, pleaded, shamed and exhorted Negroes to abandon the
South. He inspired the formation of clubs composed of ten to fifty
persons for the purpose of migrating, and arranged 'club rates' with
the railroads so the fare could be brought within the reach of many.
Even schedules were set up—usually the dates for leaving were
Wednesday and Saturday nights, following pay days. The conges-
tion at Chicago's terminal points testified to how faithfully these
plans were observed. The plans were so cleverly carried out that
the migration assumed proportions never envisioned by Abbott."

By 1916, two-thirds of the paper's sales occurred nationally in
seventy-one towns and cities outside Chicago, mostly in the
South. With this burgeoning prestige and circulation, Abbott
began running stories about how blacks were better off in the

North. He believed a larger population of blacks in the North would decrease racial prejudice there. "Only by a commingling with other races will the bars be let down and the black man take his place in the limelight beside his white brother," the *Defender* proclaimed in 1916, adding "Contact means everything." One series about life in Chicago resulted in the city's Urban League receiving 940 letters from blacks who wanted to come north, and 417 of the 520 letters that were legible came from five southern states—Alabama, Florida, Georgia, Louisiana, and Mississippi. The paper also offered incentives for blacks to migrate by noting that workers who had come north were making enough money to send some of it to relatives and friends still in the South. In one example, a group of workers from Hurtsboro, Alabama, sent $2,000 back home in two months.

In constantly bludgeoning the South, the paper had a number of favorite targets, and one of them that it made "squirm under the lash" of editorial invective was white southern men, whom the paper called "the crafty paleface" and "crackers." That was mild, however, compared to what one of the paper's columnists wrote in 1916 about southern white leaders. He labeled them "looters, grafters, lazy sinecurists, general 'no-accounts,' persecutors, KILLERS OF NEGRO MEN, seducers, RAVISHERS OF NEGRO WOMEN." With such outspokenness, which one historian has noted was important because it convinced southern blacks that the paper was a fearless champion for them, it was not surprising that on October 7, in a story titled "Farewell Dixie Land," the *Defender* encouraged every southern black man, "for the sake of his wife and daughters," to leave, even if it was a financial hardship, because he was worth nothing in the South. "We know full well," the paper said, "that this would almost mean a depopulation of that section and if it were possible we would glory in its accomplishment." A month later, the *Defender* returned to the same theme in "Getting the South Told." The article was notable for its bluntness: "The real reason for the present exodus of blacks [the *New Orleans Times-Picayune* claimed it was 250,000] . . . is he is isolated, ostracized, humiliated, proscribed, discriminated against, practically outlawed, and is the negative force in every equation. . . . Small wonder that he leaves the south. . . . Dogs, horses, monkeys, pets of all kinds, receive more thoughtful consideration at the hands of indulgent masters than does he. . . . We daily see our women . . . prostituted, enslaved, insulted, debauched, and not a hand outstretched to save them. The black man who does becomes an outlaw."

By the end of 1916, with circulation continuing to rise, the migration increasing, and southerners complaining bitterly about their labor losses, Abbott became even more aggressive as he firmly solidified his reputation for being at the forefront of the movement to the North. He felt that it was time for the paper to take a stand, and the result, on December 2, was an extraordinary list of sweeping demands that he presented to the South. He labeled them, dramatically, "The Race's Magna Charta":

> Before the *Defender* will discourage [blacks] from coming north the following conditions must be met.
>
> That all Jim Crow street cars be put out of commission no later than Jan. 1, 1917.
>
> That all plantations be equipped with modern schooling facilities, where the children of the tenants will be able to get educated to what will be equivalent to the eighth grade.
>
> That railroad privileges be accorded our people in the South equal to that accorded them in the North.

That all white men living in open adultery with women, and that all white men who ruin our young girls be made to marry them so that the illegitimate children of them will have lawful names, thus assuring them of the legal support of their fathers.

To force the Negro-baiting police to treat prisoners with black skins the same as the prisoners with white skins are treated.

That lynchings will be stopped, so that even though it is impossible for the Race man to get justice in the courts he will at least have a chance to stand trial.

That all steamboats and ships give equal accommodations to the Race, as the paying of the same fares that the whites pay should justify.

That they give the Race men and women their legal right of franchise so that they may vote as the great Lincoln intended.

Early in 1917, the *Defender* announced that it had arranged with the Illinois Central to have railroad cars leaving the South on May 15 filled with blacks, who would get a discounted fee to Chicago. The paper hyped this in advance with photographs, editorial cartoons, and even a poem: "Some are coming on the passenger [train]/Some are coming on the freight/Others will be found walking/For none have time to wait." Abbott also played up the special day by writing, "Anywhere in God's country is better than the Southland. . . . Come join the ranks of the free. Cast the yoke from around your neck. . . . When you have crossed the Ohio River, breathe the fresh air and say, 'Why didn't I come before?'" For whatever reason, the special day never materialized, but it caused such excitement that hundreds of southern blacks boarded trains anyway and headed north to Chicago and other northern cities at their own expense. In the words of the *Defender,* they were headed for the "Promised Land." Such biblical imagery was used over and over by the paper in reference to the migration as it ran such headlines as: "The Flight Out of Egypt," "Going into Canaan," and "Beulah Land."

As the paper's campaign continued at a dizzying pace, with numerous editorials and testimonial letters from blacks appearing on how much better life, work, and wages were in the North, Abbott as well as the Urban League became concerned about the migrants' behavior, morals, and dress. He felt that blacks were "on trial" before whites and that it was important for them not to embarrass themselves and damage the reputation of all blacks. Furthermore, according to Terrell, he did not want to be "made a fool in the eyes of 'the enemy' [whites] by the raucous behavior of other blacks." Thus, he believed he had an obligation to help them adjust to the North.

Because Abbott viewed the black migrants as somewhat like untrained children, he lectured them in the *Defender* on how not to act and dress, both at work and elsewhere, feeling that this might soften the rapidly growing white opposition to them in the North. His advice appeared, for example, on October 20, 1917, under the headline "Things That Should Be Considered:"

> Don't use vile language in public places.
>
> Don't act discourteously to other people in public places.
>
> Don't allow yourself to be drawn into street brawls.
>
> Don't use liberty as a license to do as you please.
>
> Don't take the part of law breakers, be they men, women or children.
>
> Don't congregate in crowds on the streets to the disadvantage of others passing along.

Don't spend your time hanging around saloon doors or pool rooms.

Don't make yourself a public nuisance.

Don't encourage gamblers, disreputable women or men to ply their business any time or place.

Don't live in unsanitary houses, or sleep in rooms without proper ventilation.

Don't violate city ordinances, relative to health conditions.

Don't allow children to beg on the streets.

Don't allow boys to steal from or assault peddlers going their rounds during the day. . . .

Don't abuse or violate the confidence of those who give you employment.

Don't leave your job when you have a few dollars in your pocket.

Don't work for less wages than being paid people doing the same kind of work.

Don't be made a tool or strike breaker for any corporation or firm. . . .

Don't allow children under fifteen years of age to run the streets after 9 o'clock P.M.

Don't get intoxicated and go out on the street insulting women and children and make a beast of yourself—someone may act likewise with your wife and children.

Don't undermine other people by taking them from their work.

Don't appear on the street with old dust caps, dirty aprons and ragged clothes.

Don't throw garbage in the backyard or alley or keep dirty front yards. . . .

>Don't forget street car conductors are bound by rules of the car company which the law compels them to obey.

>Don't oppose police officers in the discharge of their duty; you should be the one to assist in keeping the peace.

While this was good advice, it did nothing to help blacks still in the South, where the increase in the migration in the 1910s was viewed as a disaster. For example, in 1916, the *Macon Telegraph* said that the departure of black workers from Georgia was the biggest problem facing the state, and Alabama's *Montgomery Advertiser* complained bitterly, "Our very solvency is being sucked out from underneath us." Ottley bluntly summed up the southern view: "[T]he South had dark visions of empty kitchens and empty fields." With that attitude, which was shared by numerous whites in other southern states, it was not surprising that the atmosphere for blacks became hostile and sometimes dangerous if it became known that they were considering leaving. Some blacks found it difficult, if not impossible, to sell their property, there was a fear that local banks would foreclose on mortgages, and occasionally whites attacked blacks or destroyed their homes or businesses. In Mobile, Alabama, 648 men formed a club in 1917 and raised $1,050.53 to go north. The group's leaders were arrested and beaten, and their money was confiscated by police because, according to the *Defender,* "club members were beating people out of their money." There also were instances in which blacks heading north to Chicago were refused train tickets or were beaten if they even came near a station with a suitcase. Some were arrested for being vagrants as they waited for trains, and not all railroad lines were willing to carry them. Consequently, the *Defender* received hundreds of letters from southern blacks interested in heading north who asked not to be identified and instructed the paper not to publish their letters. Abbott always complied with their wishes.

Some white newspapers in the South admitted that the migration was the result of the region making mistakes. The *Atlanta Constitution,* for instance, blamed the state for its "indifference in suppressing mob law," noting correctly that the heaviest labor losses had occurred in counties where blacks had been most mistreated. The *Savannah Morning News* also linked the migration to the way blacks had been treated: "Another cause is the feeling of insecurity. The lack of legal protection in the country is a constant nightmare to the colored people. . . . There is scarcely a Negro mother in the country who does not live in dread and fear that her husband or son may come in unfriendly contact with some white person as to bring the lynchers or the arresting officers to her door which may result in [the] wiping out of her entire family. . . . It must be acknowledged that this is a sad condition."

However, many southerners basically ignored other causes for the migration and solely blamed the *Defender,* which not only had publicly stated it would "glory" in the depopulation of blacks in the South but had a wide circulation in that part of the country. Thus, they were well aware of—and extremely irate at—its influence with blacks. One historian noted that the Bible was the only publication that was more influential than the *Defender* with the black masses. The influence of the paper stemmed from the fact that it was a "herald of glad tidings" to southern blacks, according to historian Richard B. Sherman. He noted that a black man was considered "intelligent" in Gulfport, Mississippi, if he read the *Defender,* and in Laurel, Mississippi, old black men who did not know how to read carried the paper around anyway because it was regarded as such a "precious" possession. In a further example of the paper's influence and popularity, a government investigator was told that a "reputable" black in Louisiana had said of the *Defender:* "My people grab it like a mule grabs a mouthful of fine fodder." In Laurel, a black leader noted the same reaction—"[P]eople would come for miles running over themselves, to get a *Defender"*—and in New Orleans, a black woman said she would "rather read it than to eat when Saturday comes, it is my heart's delight." Perhaps the major reason for this, as Terrell noted, was that "the paper addressed issues that its readers dared not speak of openly, or actively oppose. . . . Whenever black folk assembled with some distance and privacy from white ears, they eagerly read and discussed their 'race papers.'" But these were not the black papers published in the South, which were acutely aware of the racial boundaries and afraid to step over them. A northern minister noted in 1918, "[T]he Negro pays more attention to the northern [black] press because of the suspicion that the local Negro press [in the South] can be influenced by the white community."

In this highly charged environment, whose electricity was amped up by Abbott's sensational front-page headlines—one said "When the Mob Comes and You Must Die, Take at Least One with You" and another one advised blacks to "Call the White Fiends to the Door and Shoot Them Down"—it was inevitable that the South would take action against the paper. In several cities, whites confiscated the *Defender,* as well as other black papers, that were sold on the street and in stores. That resulted in black subscribers getting it delivered in the mail instead, and there were even reports of the paper being hidden in packages that were shipped containing other merchandise. In addition, the Ku Klux Klan threatened those who were seen with the paper. Two Texas distributors of it were killed by the Klan, and an agent of the *Defender* in Yazoo City, Mississippi, was forced to leave after the Klan threatened to kill her. Also in Texas, whites flogged a black teacher in public who had written about a lynching for the newspaper. Some southern towns also passed ordinances prohibiting the sale or distribution of black papers in their city limits, and Tennessee enacted a law that declared it illegal to read "any black newspaper from Chicago." In a novel approach, a judge in Pine Bluff, Arkansas, issued an injunction prohibiting the circulation of the *Defender* in the city or the county after the mayor complained about the paper running a story on a black man who was killed there. "The *Defender*'s account of the affair portrayed Vicks [the man killed] as defending his home, his liberty and his person," said the Associated Press article, "and was held to be false in its entirety by the court." No attention apparently was paid to whether such ordinances and injunctions were a violation of free speech and a free press guaranteed by the First Amendment.

Abbott, never one to shy away from a challenge, fought back against the southern ordinances by ingeniously using the railroads' Pullman car porters. Terrell noted their prestige:

> The Pullman porter was the perfect emissary for the *Chicago Defender*. He worked in a world of luxury and elegance that gave him a special cachet among many members of the black population, most of whom rarely traveled and then did not go first class. Some of the better educated and wealthier blacks may have disdained the porter, but to many of America's blacks the Pullman porter was a man of means and respect. . . .
>
> As a group, Pullman porters came into contact with 35 million passengers yearly, and literally hundreds of thousands of blacks throughout the South. Everybody listened to the porters because they knew they had been places and seen things most of them would never experience.

Abbott began currying the favor of the porters as early as 1910 by running a regular railroad column that contained anecdotes about individual workers, and then he vigorously supported their demand for higher wages with a year-long campaign in the paper. This successfully culminated in 1916 with the Federal Industrial Relations Commission ruling that porters should receive a 10 percent raise. Meanwhile, prior to the passage of southern ordinances banning black newspapers, one of Abbott's many circulation-building ideas was to pay the porters to pick up bundles of the *Defender* at cafes and hotels, put them on their trains, and then drop them at stations throughout the country, where they would be collected and sold on the street or at newsstands or delivered to subscribers' homes. The porters even sometimes gave the paper away to blacks in towns they were visiting for the first time. Furthermore, many of the porters worked as correspondents for the paper, reporting any injustices to blacks that they heard about on their trips, and the paper promptly gave these stories national play. Then, when the ordinances appeared, Abbott had bundles of the papers taken to the porters in the Chicago train yards. They hid them on the trains, and as they rolled south, they would step between cars and throw the papers off at prearranged sites outside city limits, where distributors would pick them up and hand them out. Thus, it was impossible to stop the *Defender,* which made southerners even angrier.

Their anger was not unnoticed or discounted by the federal government, which had become alarmed in the fall of 1916 by what it considered inflammatory and inaccurate reporting of racial issues by the *Chicago Defender.* Its concern was sparked by a reporter from the white *New Orleans Times-Picayune,* who had looked into allegations that the *Defender* was inciting blacks against southern whites. He reported his fears to the local office of the Bureau of Investigation, which began reading the paper weekly to determine whether any federal laws had been broken. The problem came under the bureau's jurisdiction because the paper was shipped through the mail. The special agent in charge told Washington that he felt the paper's articles tended to "incite murder," but the bureau, busy with looking for possible German spies, turned the case over to the post office inspector in New Orleans, and nothing was done.

However, on April 9, 1917, only three days after the United States entered World War I, the Bureau of Investigation (which would be renamed the Federal Bureau of Investigation, or FBI, in 1935) ordered its Chicago office to investigate the paper. Four days later, an agent talked to Abbott about the sensationalistic nature of his paper and wrote Washington, noting, "Abbott in his zeal for the betterment of his people may have overstepped the bounds of propriety." Meanwhile, the government was quickly barraged with letters from southerners complaining about the paper. A Little Rock man, for example, urged the government in July to declare the *Defender* unmailable because it was causing blacks to behave "badly." He also suggested that it was contributing to German propaganda, concluding, "[N]o more insidious and ingenious plan could be adopted for crippling the South and its resources." Such comments from southerners about the *Defender* continued throughout the war, and some of the most noteworthy were from congressmen. Senator John Sharp Williams of Mississippi called it "a Negro paper with a tissue of lies, all intended to create race disturbance and trouble"; Representative M. D. Upshaw of Georgia said the paper was "very inflammatory in stirring up race prejudice [and] publishing wild and exaggerated statements about white crimes"; and Senator Edward Gay of Louisiana said the paper's articles were "highly inflammatory" and led to the "unrest at present evident among the negroes [*sic*] of the South."

In the midst of this, Congress passed sedition legislation, which had an enormous impact on all of the press in both World War I and World War II. President Woodrow Wilson was not in favor of a severe measure but merely one that would restrict those "who cannot be relied upon and whose interest or desires will lead to actions on their part highly dangerous to the nation in the midst of a war." The result was the Espionage Act of June 15, 1917. This legislation made it unlawful to make false statements that interfered with the military; to attempt to cause "insubordination, disloyalty, mutiny, or refusal of duty" in the military; or to obstruct military recruiting or enlistment. Those found guilty could be fined up to $10,000 and/or jailed for up to twenty years. In addition, the postmaster general could refuse to mail anything that he felt violated the law, and he could take away a publication's second-class permit, which was needed in order to mail bulk items profitably. Then, in 1918, feeling that even stricter measures were necessary, Congress passed the most severe limitation on freedom of speech and the press in the country's history. The Sedition Act of May 16 added nine new offenses to the Espionage Act, including speaking, writing, or publishing any "disloyal, profane, scurrilous, or abusive language" about topics ranging from the government to the flag and the armed forces. In addition, writings or statements were prohibited that were intended to result in "contempt, scorn, contumely, or disrepute" of the government, the Constitution, the flag, and even the armed forces' uniforms. By the end of the war in November 1918, the Post Office had taken action against more than 100 newspapers and magazines, and between 1917 and

1921, the Justice Department prosecuted 2,168 persons under the two acts and 1,055 were convicted.

The government moved against only two black publications during this witch hunt. The first time was in late 1917 after a Houston riot killed fifteen persons following an assault on a black woman by a white policeman. The Army hanged thirteen black soldiers who were involved and sentenced forty-one others to life imprisonment. Before the hangings, the black *San Antonio Inquirer* published a letter from C. L. Threadgill-Dennis, a black Austin woman, who told the soldiers to "rest assured that every [black] woman in all this land of ours . . . reveres you, she honors you." She continued:

> We would rather see you shot by the highest tribunal of the United States Army because you dared protect a Negro woman from the insult of a southern brute in the form of a policeman, than to have you forced to go to Europe to fight for a liberty you can not enjoy.
>
> Negro women regret that you mutinied, and we are sorry you spilt innocent blood, but we are not sorry that five southern policemen's bones now bleach in the graves of Houston, Tex.
>
> It is far better that you be shot for having tried to protect a Negro woman, than to have you die a natural death in the trenches of Europe, fighting to make the world safe for a democracy that you can't enjoy. On your way to the Training Camps you are jim-crowed. Every insult that can be heaped upon you, you have to take, or be tried by court-martial if you resent it.

While she said she was sorry that innocent people were killed in the riot, she praised the condemned soldiers for dying for "the most sacred thing on earth to any race[,] even the southern white man, his daughter's, his wife's, his mother's[,] his sister's[,] his neighbor's sister's protection from insult." Although the *Inquirer*'s editor, G. W. Bouldin, was not in San Antonio when the letter appeared, he was charged under the Espionage Act for running it because it made "an unlawful attempt to cause insubordination, disloyalty, mutiny, and refusal of duty in the military forces." He was sentenced to two years in a military prison, and a federal appeals court refused to overturn the conviction.

The other black publication that was moved against by the government was *The Messenger,* a socialist monthly magazine published in New York City. Not only was it against the war, as well as black participation in it, but it applauded Russia's Bolshevik revolution and suggested that "such an upheaval might be good for America." It also demanded government action "to ensure civil liberties and protections, guarantee absolute social equality including intermarriage, and protect the rights of blacks to arm themselves in their own defense." Then, in July 1918, it ran an unsigned editorial noting that the government suspected a link between German propaganda and black discontent. However, it said the real reason for the discontent was that blacks faced "peonage, disfranchisement, Jim-Crowism, segregation, rank civil discrimination, injustice of legislature, courts and administrators." It concluded by suggesting that a government investigation might find that blacks "are still so absorbed in suppressing American injustices that their minds have not yet been focused upon Germany." While one of the editors felt this was merely "satirical and sarcastic," the postmaster general disagreed. He promptly revoked *The Messenger*'s second-class permit, which made it unprofitable to mail, but the magazine continued to publish for three years until the permit was restored in 1921.

The virtual lack of action against black publications by the government, however, did not mean that they were not under surveillance. In fact, the Bureau of Investigation, the Post Office, and Military Intelligence heavily investigated them—the latter, for example, looked at forty-seven black publications from 1917 to 1921—and probably no newspaper was read more closely by these agencies than the *Chicago Defender*. The problem with the *Defender* was that it refused to soften its campaign to lure blacks north after the United States entered the war. Since this campaign included numerous sensational articles about injustices to blacks, the government was worried that blacks would not support the war because of their discontent about the way they were treated.

One area that the *Defender* continued to harp on was white violence against blacks; this was particularly evident in the number of lynchings, which rose from thirty-five in 1917 to sixty a year later. In reporting white violence, no matter what type, Abbott frequently spared none of the gory details. This was particularly evident on December 8, 1917, in one of the paper's most famous articles. It was about the death of Lation Scott in Dyersburg, Tennessee:

> Bound to an iron post by the most savage fiends on the face of the globe or even in the depths of hell below, Scott stood one-half hour, while men heated pokers and s[m]oothing irons until they were white with heat and were as fiery as the flames that heated them. Scott lay flat on his face beneath the yoke of the iron post. Children on the outskirts of the mob played merrily on and their voices could be heard above the hubbub of the mob.
>
> Then a red streak shot out and the holder began to bore out the prisoner's eyes. Scott moaned. The pokers were worked like an auger, that is, they were twisted round and round.

> The smell of burning flesh permeated the atmosphere, a pungent, sickening odor telling those who failed to get good vantage points what their eyes could not see: Smoothing irons were searing the flesh.
>
> Swish. Once, twice, three times a red-hot iron dug gaping places in Lation Scott's back and sides.

Then, while Scott was still alive, men, women, and children piled up wood around him, lit a fire, and continued to throw on more wood until he was "a heap of charred ashes and bones."

Because of such articles, historian Lee Finkle labeled the *Defender* "the most militant black paper" of the World War I period. But while it constantly attacked a wide variety of injustices, even Abbott occasionally realized that he had gone too far. One instance was when he carried an editorial cartoon that depicted black soldiers fighting Germans while white U.S. troops were shooting the blacks in their backs. This resulted in Abbott coming close to being jailed, and he only avoided it by buying government war bonds and carrying an article that encouraged readers to do the same. While such occasions encouraged even more surveillance, the Justice Department refused to take the paper to court. Historian Theodore Kornweibel Jr. noted that the officials considered the *Defender* "innocuous" compared to other publications that opposed the war. Furthermore, an investigation by the Chicago office of the bureau came to the conclusion that the paper was "loyal to the core. . . . There is nowhere connected with it the slightest evidence of German influence."

Nevertheless, the *Defender,* as well as two other black newspapers, the *Baltimore Afro-American* and the *St. Louis Argus,* were warned by the government in 1918 that they should be careful in what they ran. In May, Abbott was visited by Major Walter H.

Loving of Military Intelligence. Considered the Army's most dependable black investigator, he was a conservative member of "The Talented Tenth" who felt that if blacks were loyal, sacrificed themselves, and displayed public patriotism at home, they would be rewarded after the war with more rights and privileges. Because he believed the *Defender* was "the most dangerous of all Negro journals," he told his superiors that he threatened Abbott, telling him that "he would be held strictly responsible and accountable for any article appearing in his paper in the future that would give rise to any apprehension on the part of the government." He added, "I have . . . informed him officially that the eye of the government is centered upon his paper, and caution should be his guide."

Clearly concerned that he might become a victim of government suppression, Abbott wrote Loving several days later to assure him of his paper's patriotism: "You know through your reading of the *Defender* the attitude of this paper towards the government. I say with absolute certainty, that without a doubt, it has never at anytime spoken disloyal, and is entirely guiltless of the attack centered on it. . . . I have more than once advised my staff writers to refrain from expressing their views on problems that would precipitate national strife, or inculcate in the heart of any member of my race the spirit of revolt against the laws of the national or state governments." After receiving this letter, Loving filed a report noting that "the tone of this reply is all that we can expect, if the writer lives up to it, and I shall endeavor and try to see that he does."

On June 13, Abbott received another severe warning, this time from Solicitor William Lamar of the Post Office. It stemmed from a June 8 article in the *Defender*, "Southern Stunts Surpass Hun," which noted that a black man had been decapitated by a train after a white mob had tied him to a railroad track. As a historian noted, such articles showed why whites and blacks disagreed on what it was permissible to print: "What they [whites] viewed as promotion of race hatred black editors would have described as the righteous exposure of racial injustice. . . . In short, what blacks regarded as truth telling, whites considered likely to provoke disaffection, and the government clearly had legal authority to suppress disaffection." Lamar wrote Abbott that while one article inciting race hatred was not enough to bring an Espionage Act indictment, it could interfere with the government's war effort. He said anything that caused "friction" between whites and blacks, and made blacks think they had no part in the war against Germany, "tends to interfere with the cause of the United States in the war . . . and should have no place in a loyal newspaper." He pointed out that he was not questioning Abbott's loyalty, but only saying that he should run his paper in a patriotic fashion.

Six days later, Abbott and Du Bois, the editor of the NAACP's *The Crisis,* were among forty-one black leaders, including thirty-one journalists, who attended a three-day Washington conference hosted jointly by the War Department and the Committee on Public Information, the main government wartime agency working with the press. The meeting was suggested by two blacks in the government who felt that the black press was in danger of being suppressed and needed to meet face to face with government officials, who perhaps could abolish some of the injustices facing blacks. At the same time, they hoped that the editors would become boosters of the war effort; thus, the conference would stress "the fact that we are at war and that Negro public opinion should be led along helpful lines rather than along lines that make for discontentment and unrest."

At the meeting, the participants agreed that defeating Germany was extremely important, and they promised in a statement drafted by Du Bois to try to keep blacks' opinions "at the highest pitch, not simply of passive loyalty but of active, enthusiastic and self-sacrificing participation in the war." However, they pointed out that blacks needed government help: "We believe today that justifiable grievances of the colored people are producing not disloyalty, but an amount of unrest and bitterness which even the best efforts of their leaders may not be able always to guide unless they can have the active and sympathetic cooperation of the National and State governments." Therefore, they asked the government for three things: a statement from President Woodrow Wilson condemning lynchings and the passage of legislation that would stop it; an end to discrimination against blacks who wanted to work in the Red Cross and in government agencies; and a halt to the railroads' discrimination against blacks.

The editors were pleased when some of their demands were met in July. The War Department ordered the Red Cross to hire black nurses, and Wilson issued a statement about lynchings, saying "every American who takes part in the action of a mob or gives it any sort of countenance is no true son of this great Democracy, but its betrayer." Historian William C. Jordan noted that it is unknown whether the president was influenced in what he said, either directly or indirectly, by the black editors. Those at the conference also requested "[s]ystematic getting and dissemination of news of Negro troops at home and abroad." In response, the Committee on Public Information named Ralph Tyler of the black *Cleveland Advocate* as the first black war correspondent, and he covered the final two months of the war in Europe, with his stories about black troops appearing in numerous black newspapers.

In some ways, what occurred at the Washington conference

was stunning. Not only did it represent an "abject . . . surrender" by the black journalists to the government, but as Kornweibel pointed out, Abbott's presence at the meeting "amounted to a public profession of loyalty." Yet another "surrender" occurred in July in *The Crisis*. After the United States entered the war, Du Bois became highly critical of the government in the magazine. The January 1918 issue carried a typical editorial: "We raise our clenched hands against the hundreds of thousands of white murderers, rapists, and scoundrels who have oppressed, killed, ruined, robbed, and debased their black fellow men and fellow women, and yet, today, walk scot-free, unwhipped of justice, uncondemned by millions of their white fellow citizens, and unrebuked by the President of the United States."

Military Intelligence became tired of such comments by June and wrote the NAACP that the magazine might be suppressed because of a large number of complaints. "[The government] can not tolerate carping and bitter utterances likely to foment disaffection and destroy the morale of our people for the winning of the war," it said. The NAACP board immediately told Du Bois to confine himself to "facts and constructive criticism," and he changed completely, writing a famous "Close Ranks" editorial in the July issue. It said: "We of the colored race have no ordinary interest in the outcome. That which the German power represents today spells death to the aspirations of Negroes and all darker races for equality, freedom and democracy. Let us not hesitate. Let us, while this war lasts, forget our special grievances and close our ranks shoulder to shoulder with our white fellow citizens and the allied nations that are fighting for democracy. We make no ordinary sacrifice, but we make it gladly and willingly, with our eyes lifted to the hills."

While Military Intelligence found the editorial "very satisfactory," the major black newspapers attacked Du Bois for not only abandoning the NAACP's traditional fight against discrimination but also because critical articles were the only outlet for black frustration and led to circulation gains. But he would not back down, and in the September issue of the magazine he discussed his new position:

> This ["Close Ranks"] editorial seeks to say that the first duty of an American is to win the war and that to this all else is subsidiary. It declares that whatever personal and group grievances interfere with this mighty duty must wait.
>
> It does not say that these grievances are not grievances, or that the temporary setting aside of wrongs makes them right. . . .
>
> *The Crisis* says, first your Country, then your Rights! . . .
>
> God knows we have enough left to fight for, but any people who by loyalty and patriotism have gained what we have in four wars ought surely to have sense enough to give that same loyalty and patriotism a chance to win in the fifth.

Du Bois' concession would not be forgotten by the black press in World War II.

As Du Bois was backing down, the government ended its investigation of the *Chicago Defender* in September 1918. There were several reasons for this turn of events. Abbott had been under constant pressure from the Bureau of Investigation, Military Intelligence, and the Post Office, and he realized that his financial survival depended upon showing discretion in what he printed. So, while he continued to promote migration from the South, publicize black injustices, and criticize government officials who treated blacks unfairly, he now was more temperate in what he wrote. "The federal intelligence system had accomplished its goal," said Kornweibel, "not to halt all criticism, but to ensure that criticism be sufficiently moderated so that it would not impede the prosecution of the war."

A year later, Abbott abruptly ended his migration campaign. Not only was Chicago, as well as other northern cities, becoming too populated with blacks, but crime had increased, schools and housing had become inadequate, and health problems had erupted. An even larger issue, however, arose when white soldiers began returning home from the war. Their former jobs were now filled by blacks, who also had moved into their neighborhoods and were in no mood to leave. In July, a four-day race riot erupted in Chicago, leaving fifteen whites and twenty-three blacks dead and more than 500 wounded, and by the time the summer was over, twenty-two riots had occurred nationwide. In the wake of the Chicago riot, the Illinois governor formed a Commission on Race Relations to examine the reasons for it. The commission concluded that the riot had stemmed from "a symptom of serious and profound disorders" between the races in the city. Turning specifically to the *Defender,* the commission praised its editorials for their careful writing and balance even though they were sometimes critical, but the paper was urged to be more accurate in reporting racial incidents. It also urged all black newspapers to abandon "sensational headlines and articles on racial questions" and to spend more time "educating Negro readers as to the available means and opportunities of adjusting themselves and their fellows into more harmonious relations with their white neighbors and fellow-citizens."

Streitmatter noted that the Chicago riot had a profound effect on the Defender's publisher. "Abbott could no longer, in good conscience, portray his adopted city as the Promised Land," he wrote. "Like the rest of his race, the editor came to see that many of the same problems that existed in the South would persist in the

North. Chicago and other industrial cities became yet another lo-
cation where the Black American Dream was ultimately de-
ferred." So, the Chicago Defender became less strident and sensational, and while it continued to be a place for blacks to read about
themselves, it no longer defied whites as rigorously as it had before. However, Streitmatter emphasized, the change in the paper
in 1919 did not mean Abbott's migration campaign had been a
"failure":

> [T]he mass exodus that the dissident newspaper spearheaded . . .
> was a glorious triumph. . . . The flight out of the South did not
> merely mark a demographic shift. It also signaled the death knell
> for the feudal existence that most African Americans had been
> forced to endure, thereby giving them a glimpse, for the first
> time, of a modern and civilized way of life that was defined by
> personal as well as racial freedom. . . .
>
>   Robert S. Abbott's successful effort to transform the lives of
> half a million people—not to mention the lives of their children
> and their children's children—was so remarkable that his leader-
> ship of the mass movement has assumed legendary status. Schol-
> ars who have studied the 3,000 African American newspapers that
> have been published during the last 200 years have repeatedly sin-
> gled out the *Chicago Defender*'s role in the Great Migration as the
> most extraordinary achievement in the entire history of this most
> prolific of advocacy presses.

Certainly the campaign was not a failure financially for Abbott,
who became one of the country's first black millionaires. From a
circulation of 33,000 in early 1916, according to James R. Grossman, his paper jumped to about 50,000 by the end of the year,
about 90,000 a year later, 125,000 in 1918, and 130,000 by the time

the campaign ended in 1919. And it may have been even higher. Ottley, in his biography of Abbott, said the *Defender* reached a circulation of about 180,000 by 1918 and more than 230,000 in 1919. In 1920, in a promotion pamphlet, the paper claimed to have a circulation of 283,571. Whatever the correct figures, it was clearly the country's largest black newspaper up to that time.

Between the two world wars, the black press would become even larger and more powerful, and while the *Chicago Defender* would remain influential, a new giant would arise to equal it, and in some ways surpass it, becoming one of the two most important newspapers in black press history. At the same time, the Bureau of Investigation would continue to heavily investigate black newspapers, guaranteeing that there would be a clash between the government and the press if another war occurred.

═══════════════◇═══════════════

FIVE

BETWEEN THE WARS

The Negro seems . . . to have realized the extraordinary power of his press.
    —Robert T. Kerlin, *The Voice of the Negro* (1919)

On the night of June 2, 1919, nine explosions rocked government buildings and the homes of political and business leaders in eight U.S. cities. Two of the bombs were set in Pittsburgh; the others were in New York City, Boston, Philadelphia, Washington, and the smaller cities of Paterson and East Orange in New Jersey and Newtonville in Massachusetts. A tenth was successfully defused in Cleveland. Police found identical handbills, headlined "Plain Words," at each bombing site. They said, in part: "The powers that be make no secret of their will to stop here in America the worldwide spread of revolution. The powers that be must reckon that they will have to accept the fight they have provoked. A time has come when the social question's solution can be delayed no longer; class war is on, and cannot cease but with a complete victory for the international proletariat. . . . There will have to be bloodshed; we shall not dodge; there will have to be murder; we will kill; . . . there will have to be destruction; we will destroy. . . . We are ready to do anything and everything to suppress the capitalist class—The Anarchist Fighters."

The Washington explosion occurred at 11:15 P.M. just as Attorney General A. Mitchell Palmer and his wife had gone into an upstairs bedroom of their fashionable home in Georgetown. They heard a strange thump at their front door and then an enormous explosion shook the house, shattering the front of it, blowing out windows, and damaging nearby houses. While Palmer and wife were not injured, the dynamite blast killed the two unidentified anarchists and flung parts of their bodies up to a block away.

Historian Jay Robert Nash noted that the actions of the bombers, called the "Red Menace" in reference to their sympathies with the Russian Revolution, "caused a national panic and created political pandemonium." No one was more aware of that than Palmer. He told a Senate investigating committee what it was like on the morning after the explosion: "I stood in the middle of the wreckage of my library with Congressmen and Senators, and without a dissenting voice they called upon me in strong terms to exercise all the power that was possible . . . to run to earth the criminals who were behind that kind of outrage." He moved quickly to comply with their wishes. Within forty-eight hours, he made several key Justice Department appointments designed to accelerate the investigation and prosecution of radicals that had already begun in World War I. Then, on August 1, he created the General Intelligence Division, with twenty-four-year-old J. Edgar Hoover as its head. The GID, as it was commonly called, was ordered to gauge the extent of subversive activities in the country and decide who should be prosecuted under federal law. Because Hoover was to receive all information about radicalism gathered by Bureau of Investigation agents, the GID was often referred to as the Anti-Radical Division of the Justice Department.

Hoover's new position launched him on a stunning career in which he would become the most feared person in America, mainly because of the secret information stored in the famous FBI files, and which would only end when he died in 1972 after forty-eight years as director of the bureau. But well before he took over the bureau in 1924, he already was convinced that the black press was dangerous and should be investigated heavily, and this belief never changed. He was a dangerous enemy, lurking in the background and ready to strike, as black newspapers reached new heights of circulation as well as of influence and power between the two world wars.

The selection of Hoover to head the GID was not surprising—he had been on a fast track at the Justice Department for several years. After getting a law degree at George Washington University in 1916 and a master's in 1917, when he was admitted to the bar, he joined the department as a clerk. Less than six months later, when a national "Hun scare" in World War I resulted in a work overload, he was placed in charge of an enemy alien registration section. Nash noted the zeal with which he pursued his new position: "Hoover worked tirelessly at his job. His chance to prove his integrity and ingenuity had arrived. With him it was not a case of 'rounding up the usual suspects.' He worked day and night rooting out would-be spies, saboteurs, and slackers who had not responded to the draft. . . . By 1919, Hoover had . . . acquired a reputation for dedication to duty."

As head of the GID, Hoover exhibited a tireless enthusiasm, and one reporter described him as a "slender bundle of high-charged electric wire." He quickly read extensively from the works of Karl Marx, Friedrich Engels, Leon Trotsky, and V. I. Lenin, which convinced him for the rest of his life that communism was a serious threat to the United States. He also began collecting massive amounts of information on radical individuals, publications, and organizations. In Hoover's first hundred days on the job, the GID collected data on 60,000 radicals, and in less than a year and a half the card catalog grew to include more than 450,000 people. Who was in the files, and the accuracy of the information, was largely unknown, since the files were classified and not available to the public. Hoover would only tell the Senate that they included persons "showing any connection with an ultraradical body or movement," especially "authors, publishers, editors, etc." The mention of journalists was not surprising. GID officials regularly read 625 "radical" newspapers, 251 of which were considered ultraradical.

Black publications, both magazines and newspapers, were among those watched closely by Hoover. In September 1919, he noted that both the NAACP's *The Crisis* and the socialist magazine *The Messenger* were "well known" to him. He added, "[I]f possible something should be done to the editors of these publications as they are beyond doubt exciting the negro [*sic*] elements in this country to riot and to the committing of outrages of all sorts." However, as Hoover discovered, the government was not eager to prosecute them. An assistant attorney general explained to a South Carolina congressmen in September 1919 that the Justice Department only went to court against publications "when it is reasonably satisfied that a conviction can be secured, as it is believed that the loss of such cases does more harm than good."

Thus, throughout the fall of 1919, the Justice Department considered moving legally against some of the most outspoken black publications, but it shied away because it was not sure that it could win in court. As a U.S. attorney pointed out in December 1919, referring to *The Messenger:* "The purpose and object of the publication is to prevent the lynching of negroes [*sic*] and their oppression and discrimination against them. . . . If the purpose stated be the true and be the sole purpose for which the magazine is published, there is nothing unlawful in its publication."

Thus, with the feeling that there was little chance of success against the black press under existing laws, Palmer and Hoover decided to push for the country's first peacetime sedition law since the Alien and Sedition Acts of 1798–1801. Hoover wrote two lengthy reports linking blacks with communism, and Palmer sent them to the Senate in November 1919 and the House in June 1920. The initial report, entitled "Radicalism and Sedition among Negroes as Reflected in Their Publications," said: "Among the most salient points to be noted in the present attitude of the Negro leaders are . . . the identification of the Negro with such radical organizations as the I.W.W. [Industrial Workers of the World] and an outspoken advocacy of the Bolsheviki or Soviet doctrine. . . . The Negro is 'seeing red,' and it is the prime objective of the leading publications to induce a like quality of vision upon the part of their readers." The report added that "the number of restrained and conservative [black] publications is relatively negligible." Palmer also told Congress that the typical black publication was "always antagonistic to the white race, and openly defiantly assertive of its own equality and superiority." He pointed out that a common theme in the publications was the pride that blacks showed in fighting white rioters. "Defiance and insolently race-centered condemnation of the white race," he stated, "is to be met with in every issue of the more radical publications."

Hoover pounded these points home by sending Congress numerous examples that he considered objectionable from black newspapers and magazines. These particularly focused on *The Messenger,* which the GID called "the most able and the most dangerous of all the Negro publications." The two editors of *The Messenger* promptly ran the statement about being "the most dangerous" in each issue because they considered it a compliment.

The Justice Department's attack angered the black press. Robert Vann, publisher of the *Pittsburgh Courier,* wrote in the paper on October 25, 1919: "[T]he only conclusion therefore is: As long as the Negro submits to lynchings, burnings and oppressions—and says nothing, he is a loyal American citizen. But when he decides that lynchings and burnings shall cease even at the cost of some human bloodshed in America, then he is a Bolshevist." Despite such criticism, Hoover's report to the Senate helped to generate action, and in late 1919 and 1920, seventy peacetime sedition bills were introduced in Congress. The final House version called for a $10,000 fine and/or twenty years in prison for anyone who sought to overthrow, destroy, or delay the government. The Senate version passed quickly and was sent to the House, where the two bills were combined and committee hearings began. However, public sentiment quickly solidified against the bill, and the press angrily attacked it as a danger to free speech and a free press. Faced with such opposition, Palmer admitted the bill was too strong and should be modified, and when the House committee reported back unfavorably on the bill in 1921, no action was taken.

Finally, black mainstream publications, which had feared that a sedition act would silence their complaints about lynchings and disenfranchisement, did not have to worry about being suppressed by the federal government for the first time since 1917. However, as historian Theodore Kornweibel Jr. noted, the *Chicago Defender* probably never fully realized how heavily it had been investigated from 1919 to 1921 by four agencies—the Justice Department (which included the Bureau of Investigation), the Post Office, Military Intelligence, and the Office of Naval Intelligence—and how close the government had come to taking legal action against it. And yet it survived untouched, as did the other black newspapers. Part of the reason, Kornweibel pointed out, was the nature of the black newspapers, which were different from many black magazines, such as *The Messenger*:

> While weekly "race papers" argued for the rights and privileges that were due African Americans, they were business ventures and not primarily vehicles for protest [as were black magazines]. Without advertising and subscriptions their precarious financial situation would become hopeless. Economic survival demanded editorial positions in the mainstream. None of the papers' publishers embraced Bolshevism or socialism because they themselves were capitalists and businessmen. But as black businessmen they did not shy away from criticizing the government and white society for mistreating African Americans. So the newspapers' "sin" was their alleged cultivation of "race hatred." But in fact they hated only white racism, not white people. . . . The newspapers simply carried on a venerable journalistic tradition, harking back to Frederick Douglass's *North Star,* by providing a predominantly black readership with a mixture of racial news, racial defense, and racial advocacy.

But even as the federal government backed away—albeit somewhat reluctantly—from taking action in 1919–1921, black newspapers as well as black magazines experienced some final angry convulsions in the South. In Mississippi, the legislature passed an act in 1920 making it illegal "to print or publish or circulate printed or published appeals or presentations of arguments or suggestions favoring social equality or marriage between the white and Negro races." Historian Frederick G. Detweiler said the law undoubtedly was aimed at the *Chicago Defender* and *The Crisis.* Later in the year in Mississippi, a black minister who had given away several copies of *The Crisis* on a train was mobbed because of it when he got off at a small station. He fled to a swamp, eluded angry whites hunting him in a field that night, and after hiding there during a thunderstorm went back to town and asked for help from a justice of the peace. The official threw him in jail and quickly sentenced him to serve time on a chain gang. A lawyer who came to defend him was threatened with being lynched if he did not leave, and both the governor and lieutenant governor refused to step in to help the minister, saying he got off easy. Meanwhile, in Texas, the *Houston Informer* not only had advertisements withdrawn on three occasions by white businessmen because of articles they disliked, but its printing office was raided one night in 1921, and the newly printed paper was stolen along with its subscription and advertising lists.

But more often, there were merely threats against the black press. In 1919, a black weekly in the North, which was edited by a southern black, noted the situation in Somerville, Tennessee: "White people of this city have issued an order that no 'colored newspapers' must be circulated in this town, but that every 'darkey,' the petition reads, must read the *Falcon,* a local white paper edited by a Confederate veteran. The whites stated that step was being done in order to keep the 'nigger from getting besides himself, and to keep him in his place.' Since the invasion made in this city by newspapers of our race, people have been leaving by the wholesale, seeking better opportunity and development in northern cities. The edict was issued against the newspaper when white men were forced, because of the lack of help, to plow the fields." Two years later, the *Dallas Express* received an anonymous letter from the Ku Klux Klan predicting that there would be "a Negro massacre" unless the paper toned down and stopped inciting trouble between blacks and whites. The letter concluded, "We've been Coon hunting before—Yours for Law & Order even though it takes Death."

But the South could not stop the black newspapers, whose popularity and growth had been fanned like a wildfire in the 1910s by the *Chicago Defender* and by the 1920s were a potent force to be reckoned with. Thus, in 1922, it may not have been an exaggeration when Detweiler claimed that "every Negro who can read does read a race paper." Certainly black readers had a lot of papers from which to choose. In 1910, a university survey identified 288 black papers; there were 492 by the summer of 1921 in thirty-eight states, with 76 of them located in the country's twelve cities with populations of 500,000 or more. Overall, 310 of the papers (63 percent) were in towns with at least 10,000 people, and Detweiler speculated that the decrease in black illiteracy from 30.4 percent in 1910 to 22.9 percent in 1920 was due to the increasing number of papers and their growing circulations, which totaled more than 1 million.

But that did not mean the existence of the papers was widely known by anyone other than blacks. Journalist Ray Stannard Baker had noted in 1916 that few whites realized there were more than 450 black newspapers and magazines, and that alarmed him. "The utter ignorance of the great mass of white Americans as to what is really going on among the colored people of the country is appalling—and dangerous," he wrote ominously. One white who was familiar with the black press, and appreciated its potential, was Ohio Senator Warren G. Harding, who became president in 1921. In the previous year, he found it "pleasing" to see the growth in black publications because this meant that blacks would show "educational advancement and intelligent enlightenment," which he labeled progress. And he predicted accurately that black publications would become "the greatest weapon of all in furthering the cause of the Colored people of the United States."

Despite the growing number of black newspapers, their presence in more communities nationwide, and their burgeoning circulations, they remained unchanged in one significant way: They were virtually all weeklies. While the country's first daily black paper appeared in 1864, lasting five years, only two dailies— the *Washington Colored American* and the *Richmond Colored American*—were published in the early 1920s. The black *Brooklyn and Long Island Informer* editorialized in 1921 that a daily black paper was needed in New York City just as much as a black-owned bank, but it pointed out that it would have a problem competing with large daily white papers in the city "in point of capital, organization and literary efficiency." About the same time, an investigation in Chicago into whether to have a black daily concluded that it was unwise to establish one because such a paper could not provide "any part of the public with news from day to day." Nevertheless, Detweiler felt the daily black papers in Washington and Richmond fulfilled a "special," valuable role because they could be "posted on the wall, in a barber-shop for example, where individual reading may be followed by group discussion."

However, all of the black papers, even the weeklies, were "special" because they rendered a unique service to black readers. A 1921 letter from a Kentuckian in the *New York Age* noted the nature of that service: "I feel that this [black newspapers] is the only source from which we can learn of what good Negroes are doing. The white press just will not publish anything good of us. All we can see from their papers is the bad side." It is true that blacks usually showed up in white papers only if it appeared they might have committed a crime, although black athletes and those in the entertainment field were covered occasionally. Such selectivity in coverage increased the importance of the black papers, as black journalist Vernon Jarrett recalled in 1999. "We didn't exist in the other papers," he said. "We were neither born, we didn't get married, we didn't die, we didn't fight in any wars, we never participated in anything of a scientific achievement. We were truly invisible unless we committed a crime. But in the black press . . . we did get married, they showed us our babies being born, they showed us graduating, they showed our Ph.D.s."

Thus, ironically, by basically ignoring blacks except when they appeared in a negative light, the white press unwittingly strengthened black papers by encouraging blacks to read them if they wanted news about themselves. This had several consequences. It drove circulations upward, resulting in black papers unquestionably becoming the most powerful and influential elements in black communities. "The Negro seems . . . to have realized the extraordinary power of his press," researcher Robert T. Kerlin wrote in 1920. "Mighty as the pulpit has been with him, the press now seems to be foremost. It is freer than the pulpit, and there is a peculiar authority in printer's ink. His newspaper is the voice of the Negro. . . . It is in them the Negro speaks out with freedom, with sincerity, with justice to himself, for there he speaks as a Negro to Negroes." And principal among those speaking out on the black newspapers were reporters and columnists, whose by-lines made them "stars" in the black community, according to black journalist Edward "Abie" Robinson. Another black journalist, Phyl Garland, recalled the same thing: "Being an entertainer or an athlete was about the only thing more glamorous than being a member of the black press with your byline out there so people could see you. Everyone knew them. 'Here comes so and so.' When they walked into a club or a restaurant, everyone was excited, and this was heady stuff."

But the influence of the black papers, and the celebrity status of their reporters, could not hide the fact that they had problems. Still, as the *Baptist Vanguard,* a black paper in Little Rock, Arkansas, noted in 1921, their problems were far outweighed by their contributions:

> The value of our newspapers in the course of our race progress can hardly be estimated. They don't always come out on time, they are not always brim full of news, and they don't always wield the best of influence in times of heated excitement. But in spite of that they are generally there with the goods and usually furnish the whistle for the race to keep up its courage. They contend for that which is right for the race and their voice is usually heard whether everybody says so or not. The influence of the Negro newspaper is saying something and doing something for the most ignorant Negro in the fartherest [*sic*] off backwoods. But the tragedy of Negro journalism lies in the fact that it is more often found casting pearls before swine. . . . The Negro race ought to wake up and give the most liberal sort of support to the Negro press.

Not unexpectedly, leading the way among black newspapers in the 1920s, both in circulation and influence, was the *Chicago Defender,* but it was not the same paper that it had been in the 1910s. Concerned about criticism that he was a "yellow journalist" and possibly stung by the Commission on Race Relations' comments about the paper following the Chicago riot of 1919, Abbott slowly and subtly changed the focus of the paper editorially and adopted what his biographer Roi Ottley called "a policy of gradualism."

The protests against black inequities continued, but he now urged readers to have patience; fewer articles appeared about violence, and black achievements were emphasized more. Abbott also adopted a "somewhat philosophical vein of the elder statesman," noted Ottley, by running his personal advice in a nonracial manner at the top of the editorial page. Examples included: "Our children should be taught that they are Americans first, everything else afterwards"; "Sown seeds often sprout where least expected"; and "It's not how much you work, but how much you think while you're working that counts." All of these changes were signs, wrote Ottley, that Abbott, as a leader of blacks with a lot of responsibility, realized he was now considered a "substantial citizen," which pushed him to be positive and encouraging. "If there ever was a time in our history when every mother's son of us should be up and doing, that time is now," he wrote. "Many of the larger opportunities we have sought, and for which we have fought, now are open to us. The question we must ask ourselves is, 'Are we prepared to take advantage of these opportunities, and are we fully alive to the fact that they are ours for the asking?'"

While it was true that there were great opportunities in the North for blacks in the 1920s, those rapidly disappeared with the onset of the Depression in October 1929. Yet, with the increasingly abysmal labor conditions in the South, which stemmed from problems with soil erosion and boll weevils as well as from a shift in cotton cultivation to the Southwest, more blacks began streaming north into not only Chicago but also New York, Detroit, and St. Louis. And where there had been only two northern cities before 1930 with at least 100,000 blacks, by 1935 there were eleven. With Chicago hard hit in this latest migration, and problems growing with unemployment, crime, disease, and discrimination, as well as an increase in the number of broken homes and out-of-work men deserting their families, Abbott reversed the position that had made his paper famous and him rich—he urged blacks not to leave the South. But while they had listened to him before, now they ignored him. In addition to Abbott's decline in influence, the *Defender,* like numerous other companies caught in the dangerous, swirling economic downturn, suddenly began to falter, and from 1930 to 1932, the paper lost $66,838. For the first time in its history, it had to operate in the red. Circulation also declined. From about 200,000 in 1925, it dropped below 100,000 in 1933, and then two years later to only 73,000. There was a noticeable drop as well in the paper's editorial quality, which Ottley attributed to a decline in Abbott's health and his increasing absences from the office.

As the *Chicago Defender* spiraled downward rapidly, the *Pittsburgh Courier* stepped forward eagerly and brashly and surpassed it, both in influence and circulation. The paper was published by Robert Vann, who had just as remarkable a rags-to-riches story as Abbott. He was born on a farm in North Carolina in 1879 and raised by his mother, Lucy Peoples. Although she made little money as a cook for white families, and could neither read nor write until he taught her how, she was determined he would develop a good "character" and be raised correctly, part of which involved strict discipline. "She wore to shreds many a cedar twig in her efforts to refute the tradition that a woman could not rear a child with any degree of success," recalled Vann. ". . . Whenever I broke her established code of behavior for me, she gave me a sound thrashing and thanked anyone else who performed the function for her." This upbringing made such an impression that he said it took all of his "energy, patience, and courage" when he became an adult to maintain his mother's high standards.

The importance of education also was stressed by his mother.

At age six, Vann began attending a one-room school with sixty other black children between the ages of six and fourteen. After going regularly for six years, he entered a period when he worked some of the time, doing everything from being in the cotton and tobacco fields to digging ditches, splitting rails, or cooking, until he had saved enough money to go for a while to a private Baptist school, Waters Training School, in Winton, North Carolina. When he ran out of money, he went back to work until he could afford to return to school again. Finally, shortly before he turned twenty-two, he graduated in 1901 as the top student.

Vann's valedictory address was a harbinger of the life he would lead. It focused on tenaciously pursuing personal goals and self-realization, as well as the belief continually espoused by Booker T. Washington that blacks could succeed through education and hard work. An accomplished speaker, he proclaimed confidently:

> The voyage of life is great and for its accomplishment the demands are great. In order to prepare for any contingencies, the pilot must plot his course with care for so many wrecks along the way of life today are occasioned solely on the account of deficient preparations. He who builds or ventures upon an infirm foundation is but a failure. . . . Once having found what he was best suited for, the individual should pursue aggressively his goal. Opportunity would then almost inevitably come his way. To every individual there comes as much as once in a life an opportunity which, seized at its flow, leads on to fortune; omitted, all his life is left a spectacle of failure and disgrace, and he together with his once glittering talent soon sinks into oblivion and despair.

Vann immediately put his words about "aggressively" seeking a goal into action. That fall, he entered a prep school in Richmond, and a year later he enrolled at Virginia Union University, where he only stayed one year before accepting a scholarship at the Western University of Pennsylvania at Pittsburgh in 1903. Among his reasons for heading north, according to his biographer Andrew Buni, were the intolerable conditions for blacks in the South. As Vann recalled, he felt "a great discontent, a great restlessness, a great determination somehow to escape." Unquestionably there were far more opportunities for blacks in the North, and he was ambitious, so he turned his back forever on his native region, boarded a train, and joined a black migration that had been going on for decades and would be dramatically accelerated, with Abbott's help, in the 1910s.

While Pittsburgh had a sizable black community, Vann was one of the few at Western University. As a result, the registrar, noticing his light-colored skin, straight hair, and thin nose, suggested that it would be easier for him if he claimed to be an Indian. Vann, however, insisted on being registered as a black. Over the next three years, he waited on tables in order to have enough money for clothes and food, and he worked on the university newspaper for two years, serving in his senior year as the first black editor-in-chief. When he graduated in 1906, which was notable because an average of only one black every two years graduated from Western University between 1890 and 1909, he considered attending the Pulitzer School of Journalism in New York. He quickly changed his mind, however, because he could not afford it, and entered the university's School of Law, where he was the only black student, again waiting on tables, this time on trains, to support himself. He completed his courses in June 1909, studied diligently for the bar exam for six months, during which he sent his fiancée out of town because, as he told her bluntly, "Courting and studying do not mix," and then passed the exam and was sworn in as an attorney that December.

About the time that Vann began practicing law, five local men put out the first issue of the weekly *Pittsburgh Courier,* which consisted of only four pages, on January 15, 1910. Vann wrote both articles and poems for what was billed as "Pittsburgh's Only Colored Newspaper," and then he drew up its incorporation papers in May, when he became the paper's lawyer. Because the owners had little cash, he received ten shares of stock, each worth $5, to cover his fee. The paper, now consisting of eight pages, claimed to have a national circulation, but that was misleading—staff members merely sent free copies to their friends elsewhere in the country. Then, even though the paper only sold about 3,000 copies a week, it said it was read by 10,000 blacks, which was based on the premise that each issue was passed around to three or four people.

But although 25,000 blacks lived in Pittsburgh, the *Courier*'s sales increased slowly, not only because of illiteracy but also because many potential subscribers simply could not afford it. Furthermore, some middle-class blacks deliberately shunned it, as they did other black papers around the country. A journalist at the time explained: "There was a class of Negroes who were proud to say that they never read a Negro newspaper. They thought such newspapers were beneath them, that they were too intelligent and classy to be caught with such a publication around their house. . . . They used to think they could show their intelligence by *not* reading Negro newspapers."

With the paper struggling to gain readership and having enormous financial problems, the editor quit in the fall of 1910, and Vann was offered the position by the remaining partners. He was a logical choice. Not only had he edited his college paper and written regularly for the *Courier,* but he had a rising reputation in the black community because of his law practice. He accepted, even though his only payment at first was $100 of *Courier* stock a year, and became the editor, treasurer, and legal counsel for the paper, positions which he held for the rest of his life.

The paper he took over was struggling just as much as Abbott's *Chicago Defender* in its early years. The only other staff members were a reporter, a sports editor, a secretary, and an errand boy, who also read proof and served as mailing clerk. They produced the paper over a funeral parlor, in a room that had a typewriter, a used desk, and two chairs, and then sent it to a local printer, whose cost amounted to a staggering one-third of the paper's expenses. Because Pittsburgh newsstands would not sell the *Courier,* it had to depend on agents, who were not always dependable, making it a constant struggle to get the paper out. Finally, it faced the same problem that had plagued black newspapers from the beginning: It made little money from advertising and thus had to depend on circulation to survive.

The easy answer to the latter problem was to adopt Abbott's sensationalism, which had quickly become popular with many black papers, but Vann, at least in the *Courier*'s early years, refused to do this. Buni explained why: "He was idealistic about the purposes of his young newspaper, and his middle-class moralistic conscience disliked stories of interracial sex affairs or sordid crimes which catered to the morbid side of the readers' imaginations. Vann was somewhat naïve at this time and did not realize, as he later would, that working-class readers wanted sensational news. Stories of Baptist conventions were fine, but there was nothing like a sex crime to arouse readers' interest."

By the end of 1914, the paper was becoming financially sound and was able to move into new, spacious offices. Vann capped off the year with an editorial in which he noted that the paper had never missed an issue in its first five years. Also, he rededicated it "to the cause of the Negro and all that pertains to his interests." He continued: "We propose to continue our fight for the general advancement of the Negro . . . [and] to abolish every vestige of Jim Crowism in Pittsburgh. . . . Let us leave no stone unturned which will lead toward advancement."

When the United States entered World War I in 1917, Vann enthusiastically backed the country and predicted optimistically in the *Courier* that the war would benefit blacks. "When this war shall have ceased," he editorialized in October, "THE NEGRO WILL HAVE ASSUMED HIS RIGHTFUL PLACE IN THE OPINIONS OF AMERICANS." Believing that blacks would be loyal despite the injustices they faced, he never flagged in making patriotic statements during the war, and this was one reason why the government did not investigate his paper as it did the *Chicago Defender* and others. Then, too, the *Courier* had a small, local circulation and little influence, and Vann was an avid anti-Communist who favored deporting anarchists, a stance that would have impressed Hoover and the GID.

But while the *Courier* had nothing to fear from the government, it still was questionable whether it could survive financially; at the end of 1919, it showed a net profit of only $102.20. Vann wanted to increase the price of the *Courier* but felt he could not do so without persuading Abbott to do the same thing. Abbott was not only the black press's most influential publisher but his paper's campaign during the migration of the 1910s had made him a national trailblazer, and other black publishers felt that making drastic changes without him could be hazardous, even fatal, to the existence of their papers. After extensive correspondence in early 1920 between the two men, Abbott agreed to increase the price of the *Defender* because, like Vann, he had higher newsprint and labor costs, and Vann quickly followed suit in July, going from 5 cents to 10 cents an issue. He knew it was an enormous gamble, and at first the circulation of the *Courier* dropped by one-third, from 12,000 to 8,000. But as the year went on, sales nearly returned to what they had been, and the paper's survival was assured. By 1922, circulation was rising rapidly as the paper slowly became more sensational, which worried Vann. As he told his staff, he was "opposed in principle to sensationalism," although he recognized the potential it held for selling more papers. He continued: "I do not mean that we should by any means surrender our high standards and ideals by making the paper entirely yellow, but that more, or rather some, yellow matter should be printed each week."

As the 1920s rolled on, an example of the new tone of the *Courier* was a series of articles entitled "Aframerica Today," which attracted national attention. It was based on a nine-month trip by columnist George Schuyler in 1925–1926 to every town and city with more than 5,000 blacks in thirteen states: Alabama, Arkansas, Florida, Georgia, Kentucky, Louisiana, Mississippi, North Carolina, Oklahoma, South Carolina, Tennessee, Texas, and Virginia. Besides describing each community's racial conditions and talking about prominent blacks, businesses, schools, and churches, he attacked injustices to blacks with a biting satire for which he had become famous in his column. One example parodied baseball: "For the year 1925, the great state of Florida wins the pennant in the Lynching League of America. There are eight lynchings to the credit (or discredit) of the great commonwealth of real-estate boosters, while closely following it is magnificent Texas with a paltry seven. Then there are our old friend Mississippi with four; South Carolina with three; Arkansas with two; and Georgia, Kansas, New Mexico, Tennessee with one each." By the summer of 1926, when the *Courier* had a national edition and branch offices in Philadelphia and New York City, Vann estimated that Schuyler's series, along with recent circulation drives, had increased the paper's circulation from 40,000 to 50,000. As a reward, Schuyler was made the paper's main editorial writer.

Although the sensationalism in the *Courier* increased throughout the 1920s, with frequently two or three large, sensationalistic front-page headlines on murder, crime, or interracial love, its reputation still rose among whites. At the end of 1928, Eugene Gordon, who made a study of the black press for the *Boston Post,* declared the *Courier* the best black paper in the country— principally because of its improved staff, its writing, and its editorial cartoons—and also the top paper for editorials. He particularly praised its expanding national news coverage, although he felt this also was a weakness because it resulted in less local news than before. Then, two years later, famed *Baltimore Sun* columnist H. L. Mencken called it the "best colored newspaper published." One clear sign of the paper's increasing prominence and financial well-being came in December 1929, two months after the beginning of the Depression, when it opened a new printing plant that cost $104,000. Its presses could print 15,000 papers an hour, in contrast to most black newspapers, which were still contracting out their printing to small shops with limited and sometimes inadequate equipment. Then, by 1930, with the paper increased from sixteen to twenty pages, it had four editions—local, northern, southern, and eastern—and was distributed in every state plus Europe, Cuba, Canada, the Philippines, the Virgin Islands, and the British West Indies.

As the paper slogged through the Depression, being forced to cut staff salaries as much as 40 percent, Vann desperately looked for issues that would increase circulation, which reached 100,000 for the first time in the fall of 1935. This figure put it well ahead of the *Chicago Defender* as the country's largest and most influential black paper. One such issue that paid off handsomely was the paper's coverage of the rise of boxer Joe Louis, who was known as the "Brown Bomber." The paper began covering him extensively in late 1934 and never backed off as he became the heavyweight champion of the world by 1937. The *Courier,* which began referring to itself as the "Joe Louis paper," sometimes grandiosely described him almost like a savior, as when reporter William Nunn called him in 1935 "the answer to our prayers, the prayers of a race of people who are struggling to break through dense clouds of prejudice and . . . misunderstanding, a race of people who, though bowed by oppression, will never be broken in spirit." Readers loved it, and circulation rose to 250,000 by 1937.

Also playing a major role in the paper's enormous circulation increase in just two years was its coverage beginning in 1934 of the Ethiopian crisis. When Italy invaded the African nation in October 1935, Vann began portraying the country's blacks as the victims of European white imperialism, and this struck a strong chord with many of the *Courier*'s readers because of their interest in their African ancestry. To further heighten this interest, Vann sent J. A. Rogers to cover the war. As the only black correspondent on the front lines, simply because most black papers could not afford to send someone to Africa, he played up the war grandly and nonobjectively. He wrote about the Italians' "sex lust" for black women; he referred to Emperor Haile Selassie shooting at the Italians rather than seeking shelter and thus being a "triumphant God, hurling his thunder-bolts from sky-tipped mountain peaks"; and he talked about the Ethiopians "[b]ravely advancing into the barrels of the Italians' death–dealing machine guns." Then, in March 1936, in what was the highlight of the paper's coverage, Rogers became the first reporter to interview Selassie shortly before the war ended. The emperor stated, "The devotion of the Afro-Americans to our cause has touched me and my people profoundly. In the New Ethiopia the colored Americans will find their place." Again, this was a huge hit with readers.

Buni noted the importance of these issues in the mid-1930s for the readers of black newspapers: "The two [Louis and Ethiopia] had much in common in the eyes of black Americans. Both represented the black man's fight for survival and self-respect against seemingly insuperable odds, and both were sources of pride for the black man in a dreary, depressed time. The great contribution of the *Courier* was to cover these events better than any other black publication, in a manner noteworthy for the immediacy of its reportage and the quality of its writing."

The national circulation of the *Courier* quickly slipped from its peak of 250,000 back to about 149,000 for the rest of the 1930s, and its local circulation remained steady at only about 20,000. While these figures still showed its national influence, the paper continually looked for issues to play up that stressed the inequality of blacks. In February 1938, it discovered such an issue   the virtual absence of blacks from the Army—and began campaigning to have the Army made up of 10 percent blacks, which was their proportion in the overall U.S. population. But it had little initial success. At the end of 1939, blacks only made up 1.89 percent of the Army (4,451 black enlisted men and 5 black officers compared to 229,636 white enlisted men and 1,359 white officers).

Thus, in April 1940, the paper increased its campaign every week with front-page stories on the small number of blacks in the Army, along with frequent editorials. In addition, readers were urged to complain to their congressmen and to organize local committees that would hold large protest meetings. An eleven-person committee also was organized and appeared before the Senate Subcommittee on Military Appropriations to request that the Army be made up of 10 percent blacks. Howard University's Rayford W. Logan, who was the group's spokesperson, told the subcommittee that blacks deplored segregation, oppression, and discrimination and insisted "that Negroes be given the opportunity to exercise their rights." Although the Senate refused to act, President Franklin D. Roosevelt signed a Conscription Bill in September 1940 that had a nondiscrimination clause, and two months later the White House released a statement granting what the *Courier* had been promoting for two and a half years: proportional representation to blacks in the Army. However, it also continued the separate but equal status of blacks when it refused to mix whites and blacks in the same regiments. As historian Lee Finkle noted, "It became a national insult to black citizens, and black papers reflected their indignation on every fron [*sic*] page."

Such indignation by the black press about a wide variety of injustices to blacks had caught the attention of the federal government during World War I and the Red Scare period of 1919–1921, and its interest never abated over the next twenty years. As I noted in my 1986 book focusing on the World War II period in the history of the black press:

> The significance of the period from 1917 to 1921 as a forerunner of what would occur during World War II was substantial. The black press came out of the four-year period with a radical reputation. That reputation was not warranted by many black magazines and newspapers, but the government, and particularly Hoover, was in the grip of [a] national hysteria over communism and not in a mood to make fine distinctions among publications.

. . . But a radical reputation based on a connection with communism was not the only legacy that followed the black press into World War II. There was also the government investigation. Once begun on a large scale, it did not end simply because there was no war or no perceived threat to democracy from a different ideology. Documentary evidence strongly suggests—and in some cases confirms—that both the Bureau of Investigation and the army investigated black publications vigorously throughout the entire period between the wars. In the case of the former [agency], the investigation was not unexpected in light of Hoover's belief in the dangerous nature of black publications.

Enhancing the danger of these newspapers for Hoover, who took over the Bureau of Intelligence in 1924 (it was renamed the FBI in 1935), were avid attempts by both the Communists and the Japanese to curry black support throughout the interwar period. Both groups largely failed, but the black papers occasionally praised Japan, and the FBI was quick to put that in its files as if such statements suggested disloyalty or were somehow illegal. In 1939, for example, it noted that the *Baltimore Afro-American* wrote that Japan was "justified" in kicking whites out of the Far East and controlling the region. It also pointed out that the black *Amsterdam News* had written: "If Japan goes down, every black man's right will go down with her." Army Military Intelligence also was busy. In July 1941, it forwarded a report to Hoover claiming that "Japanese and Communist press agents are releasing news in all available negro [sic] publications and in some cases, Communists or Communist sympathizers are employed on the editorial staffs of these papers." Five black journalists, three of whom worked for the *Pittsburgh Courier,* were labeled Communists, Communist sympathizers, or radicals.

The FBI had visited the publisher and the executive editor of the *Courier* in 1940 because of articles that noted the attempts of blacks to vote in the South. The agents complained to several reporters that the articles were "holding America up to ridicule." In the same year, a Savannah, Georgia, citizen complained to the FBI that articles in two issues of the *Chicago Defender* "might possibly hinder the Government in securing registrations from negroes [*sic*] who come within the draft age." Hoover asked the Justice Department if any federal statute had been violated and a month later was told that the articles were not unlawful.

Meanwhile, black newspapers kept infuriating the Army. One example came in the spring of 1941 when Percival Prattis, the executive editor of the *Pittsburgh Courier,* visited thirteen Army camps and wrote about the bad treatment that black troops were receiving. An intelligence officer at a Louisiana camp complained that the articles were "radical" and inaccurate and recommended that the FBI investigate Prattis. The FBI finally responded on November 29, 1941, saying that an investigation had shown that the paper was not "engaged in questionable activities with reference to the national defense program." It also noted a letter that Ira F. Lewis, the paper's president, had written to one of the paper's columnists in June:

> The *PITTSBURGH COURIER* has . . . tried to be decent and reasonably conservative. In short, we have never believed in red, scare-head headlines; we have never believed that the Negro could be helped a whole lot by appealing directly to the prejudice within a Negro. We subscribe to the theory that to appeal

to the prejudice in the Negro is but to heighten the prejudice in a white man.

With the foregoing in mind, we are writing to advise that we think this is a very nice country in which to live. We know that all is not right here for any group; at the same time we believe that we can do better here than we can anywhere else. . . . We are going to continue to intelligently protest, but our basic policy in this emergency will be the policy that will be characteristic of all good Americans—the support of the President and the country's foreign policy.

Although the black newspapers had no way of knowing the extent of the intense federal investigation into what they were writing, black editors by late 1940 agreed with the government that black morale could be a problem if the United States entered World War II. Thus, a committee of black editors studying the papers said they must "do everything possible" to become "a powerful and effective force in maintaining the traditional loyalty of the Negro to his country." As a result, by the summer of 1941, most of the papers were saying that blacks should fight in a future war, but stressing that this did not mean they had to give up the struggle against discrimination in the United States. The civil rights cause remained important to black publishers, partly because of economic realities. Since most of their money came from circulation, not advertising, they could not afford to write anything that would alienate readers—and toning down their complaints against injustices just might do that and result in a fatal drop in the number of papers sold. As the *Courier*'s Schuyler noted, "[The black press] is and must be responsive to the wishes of its readers because it is more dependent upon them than other newspapers."

Prattis and others also felt that the black newspapers' outspokenness was important, reasoning that it actually led to fewer racial problems, not more, because it provided "a release for pent-up bitterness and aggression felt by Negroes."

In 1940, both Abbott and Vann died, but their deaths, while widely noted and tragic, had no effect on the black press, which was growing more and more powerful and influential all the time. When Roosevelt became president in 1933, there were about 150 black newspapers with an overall circulation of around 600,000; by 1940, the number of papers had increased to 210, and the combined circulation had more than doubled, reaching 1,276,000. Finkle attributed the sharp increase in circulation in only seven years to the fact that the black papers were "a vehicle to express the feelings of blacks toward American society and as a means of obtaining information not found in the white press or on the radio." The *Pittsburgh Courier*, which had expanded to twelve branch offices and fourteen national editions that were published from coast to coast, had the largest circulation as the United States came closer to entering the war, at about 141,000, and the *Chicago Defender* was second at about 83,000. But the circulation figures were misleading. Before the war, more than a third of the country's black families subscribed to a black paper, and during the war, between 3.5 million and 6 million of the nation's 13 million blacks read the papers every week.

But the rapidly increasing circulation was not the only thing that concerned the government in 1941. There also was the black newspapers' unabashed lack of objectivity, for which it had no apologies. "The black press never pretended to be objective," noted journalist Phyl Garland, "because it didn't see the white press being objective and it [the black press] often took a position, it had an attitude. This was a press of advocacy. There was news, but the news had an admitted and a deliberate slant." As events would quickly show, such a "slant" could be dangerous during a war; it might negatively affect black morale, which was sure to attract heightened government attention to the black press and possibly result in Espionage Act indictments of publishers. It only would take the Japanese bombs dropping at Pearl Harbor on December 7, 1941, to set all of this into motion.

SIX

———————◇———————

WORLD WAR II

War may be hell for some, but it bids fair to open up the portals of heaven for us.
—Joseph D. Bibb, *Pittsburgh Courier*

On January 31, 1942, less than two months after the United States entered World War II, the *Pittsburgh Courier* ran a letter from James G. Thompson, a twenty-six-year-old black cafeteria worker at the Cessna Aircraft Corporation in Wichita, Kansas. He expressed his feelings on patriotism:

> Like all true Americans, my greatest desire at this time . . . is for a complete victory over the forces of evil which threaten our existence today. Behind that desire is also a desire to serve this, my country, in the most advantageous way.
>
> Most of our leaders are suggesting that we sacrifice every other ambition to the paramount one, victory. With this I agree, but I also wonder if another victory could not be achieved at the same time. . . .

Being an American of dark complexion . . . these questions flash through my mind: "Should I sacrifice my life to live half American?" "Will things be better for the next generation in the peace to follow?" "Would it be demanding too much to demand full citizenship rights in exchange for the sacrificing of my life?" "Is the kind of America I know worth defending?" "Will America be a true and pure democracy after this war?" "Will colored Americans suffer still the indignities that have been heaped upon them in the past?" . . .

I suggest that while we keep defense and victory in the forefront that we don't lose sight of our fight for true democracy at home.

The V for victory sign is being displayed prominently in all so-called democratic countries which are fighting for victory over aggression, slavery and tyranny. If this V sign means that to those now engaged in this great conflict, then let we colored Americans adopt the double VV for a double victory. The first V for victory over our enemies from without, the second V for victory over our enemies from within. For surely those who perpetuate these ugly prejudices here are seeking to destroy our democratic form of government just as surely as the Axis forces.

Thompson's letter, which arguably is the most famous ever run by a black paper, had a huge impact. It resulted in the *Courier* immediately launching a high-profile Double V campaign, which ranked historically in importance with Ida B. Wells's vigorous antilynching crusade and Robert Abbott's extraordinary call for blacks to leave the South. Other black newspapers quickly joined in, continually pushing for a "double victory" for the remainder of the war. This time there would be no controversial "close ranks" editorial by black newspapers like the one W. E. B. Du

Bois had written toward the end of World War I. Blacks wanted more rights, and they wanted them now; they saw no reason to wait until the war was over. And, as events would show, blacks would make enormous gains by the time Germany surrendered in May 1945, followed by Japan three months later. *Courier* columnist Joseph D. Bibb had been right on October 10, 1942, when he had predicted: "When the war ends the colored American will be better off financially, spiritually and economically. War may be hell for some, but it bids fair to open up the portals of heaven for us."

With the bombing of the U.S. Pacific Fleet at Pearl Harbor, which united the country with patriotism and a fervor that had not been seen since the sinking of the battleship *Maine* in 1898, blacks assumed that many discriminatory barriers would vanish quickly in the push to win the war. But they were wrong. When they tried to enlist in the Marines, the Coast Guard, and the Army Air Corps, they were turned away because those services had never had blacks. Meanwhile, the Navy was willing to take them, but only if they agreed to work as messboys in the kitchens, and the Army, which was deliberately 10 percent black to coincide with their percentage in the population, only accepted one black for every nine nonblacks. Furthermore, the extraordinary heroism of a black messboy was tainted by the Navy, at least in the view of the black press, and this escalated black anger. Dorie Miller, who was on one of the ships at Pearl Harbor, had dashed from the kitchen onto the deck during the attack, moved his wounded captain to safety, and then fired a machine gun at the Japanese airplanes until he ran out of ammunition. Learning what he had done, the *Pittsburgh Courier* angrily attacked the Navy's discriminatory policies on January 3, 1942: "Is it fair, honest or sensible that this country, with its fate in the balance, should continue to bar Negroes from service except in the mess department of the Navy, when at the first sign of danger they so dramatically show their willingness to face death in defense of the Stars and Stripes?" The paper campaigned for Miller to receive the Congressional Medal of Honor, and it was not pleased when he was not decorated until May and only then got the Navy Cross, which was that service's highest honor.

Things were no better for blacks outside of the armed services. The Red Cross, for example, refused at first to take blood from blacks. Black newspapers criticized this policy heavily during December 1941 and January 1942, correctly pointing out that scientists had conclusively proven that a certain type of blood from a black was no different than the same type from a white. The Red Cross relented and began accepting blood from black donors, but it still refused to give that blood to whites. In a letter to the *Courier,* one infuriated woman wrote, "I bet the same person who would refuse a transfusion of Negro blood would gladly accept a monkey gland transplanted into his carcass to restore his manhood." At the same time, violence against blacks erupted. After a white policeman struck a black soldier with a club on January 9, 1942, a riot broke out in Alexandria, Louisiana, and twelve black soldiers were shot. But nothing riveted blacks more than what occurred in Sikeston, Missouri, on January 25, when 600 whites seized Cleo Wright, a black who was in jail after being charged with attempting to rape a white woman. They tied him to a car, dragged him at high speeds, and then hanged him before throwing gasoline on his body and burning him. This resulted in a widely noted editorial cartoon in the *Baltimore Afro-American* on January 31 that showed Germany's Adolf Hitler and a Japanese soldier grinning on the other side of an ocean as a white mob lynched Wright. The caption for the drawing said, "Defending America Our Way."

In the midst of this turmoil, which caused the black press to be even more critical of black inequities than it had been before the United States entered the war, the NAACP's *The Crisis* was praised by black newspapers for declaring in its January issue that it was not returning to its "close ranks" position of 1918. *The Crisis* explained its new position as follows:

> *The Crisis* would emphasize with all its strength that now is the time not to be silent about the breaches of democracy here in our own land. Now is the time to speak out, not in disloyalty, but in the truest patriotism, the patriotism with an eye—now that the die is cast—single to the peace which must be won.
>
> Of course, between the declaration of war and the making of a just peace there lies the grim necessity of winning the conflict. To this task the Negro American quickly pledged his fullest support. Be it said once more that black Americans are loyal Americans; but let there be no mistake about the loyalty. It is loyalty to the democratic ideal as enunciated by America and by our British ally; it is not loyalty to many of the practices which have been—and are still—in vogue here and in the British empire. . . .
>
> If all the people are called to gird and sacrifice for freedom, and the armies to march for freedom, then it must be for freedom for everyone, everywhere, not merely for those under the Hitler heel.

This was followed with a prediction by a black journalist in *Common Ground* that any editor who printed a "close ranks" editorial would lose influence with black readers.

Clearly the *Pittsburgh Courier*'s Double V campaign, which began in early February 1942, did not advocate a "close ranks" position, and blacks immediately embraced it wholeheartedly. Over the next six months, the paper received hundreds of letters and telegrams praising the campaign, and by mid-July it had signed up

200,000 Double V members. Part of the reason for this success was the timing. While the campaign expressed nothing radically new, it came at a time when the government was desperately stressing the need for a united home front in order to win the war, and blacks assumed that discrimination against them, particularly in the South, could no longer be ignored and thus would be eliminated. As it turned out, they were only partially correct.

The *Courier* introduced the campaign on February 7 with a drawing that became familiar to readers: It contained an American eagle and the words, "Democracy. Double VV victory. At home—abroad." Then, a week later, in a sign of the commitment that the paper would make to the campaign in the coming months, it allotted five and a half times more space to it. Thompson's theme was restated in a box at the top of page one in an obvious effort to convince whites that the paper was not suggesting blacks should be unpatriotic: "Americans all are involved in a gigantic war effort to assure victory for the cause of freedom. . . . We, as colored Americans, are determined to protect our country, our form of government, and freedoms which we cherish for ourselves and for the rest of the world, therefore, we adopted the Double 'V' War Cry. . . . Thus, in our fight for freedom, we wage a two-pronged attack against our enslavers at home and those abroad who would enslave us. WE HAVE A STAKE IN THIS FIGHT. . . . WE ARE AMERICANS, TOO!"

Accompanying the Double V campaign from the beginning was a torrent of photographs of smiling blacks. Besides a standard pose of one or more blacks making two V's with their fingers, there were pictures of women wearing clothes with a Double V sewn into them, women with two V's woven into their hair (a style known as a "doubler"), a woman holding a Double V quilt, a soldier forming two V's with his hands and two military flags, and children selling war bonds and stamps while flashing two V's. By late March, the *Courier* also began selecting and running pictures of Double V beauty queens. Particularly standing out in the photographs were celebrities who supported the campaign. Among the blacks were singers Marian Anderson and Etta Moten; bandleader Lionel Hampton; New York City Councilman Adam Clayton Powell Jr.; NAACP Assistant Secretary Roy Wilkins; and boxer Joe Louis's wife, Marva. Although their numbers were never large, famous whites also were pictured, including politicians Wendell Wilkie and Thomas Dewey; columnist and broadcaster Dorothy Thompson; novelist Sinclair Lewis; comedian Eddie Cantor; CBS's William Paley and NBC's David Sarnoff; and movie stars Humphrey Bogart, Ingrid Bergman, and Gary Cooper.

Accompanying these photographs were hundreds of letters from across the country congratulating the *Courier* on its campaign and its goals. Some of them were extremely positive while others were strikingly blunt. On March 7, when the paper ran fifteen letters, "a 19-year-old Colored Boy" from Columbus, Ohio, wrote:

If and when the American White Man loses this war, I am wondering if he will think why he did not give the colored man a chance with the white in the Navy? It may be too late for he may not have the Navy himself! He may ask why he did not give the colored man a bigger part to play in the war. He may say, "We could have used the colored man but we didn't. Why didn't I give more jobs in the factories, where he was much needed at the time? We have found that we could have won the war with his aid, that we couldn't win without him. Why didn't we let more of these colored men into the Army and the Marine Corps? Why didn't we let him do more than flunky work? That is all too late now. We were only thinking of ourselves." Your Double V campaign will help to avoid the above situation.

Others letters were equally grim. A Texas woman labeled the campaign important "because many Americans are more dangerous to us [blacks] than some of our enemies abroad." And a Baptist minister in Ohio said the Double V "will teach the Mr. Charlie of the South a new lesson and will shake the foundations of the hypocritical North."

Not content to make its point with just photographs and letters from readers, the *Courier* continually played up the Double V in editorials, editorial cartoons, and columns. Columnist Frank Bolden, noting that the paper would continue the campaign until its goals were reached, summed up his views on discrimination against blacks in capital letters on March 7: "THOSE WHO DO NOT WANT COLORED PEOPLE TO FULLY PARTICIPATE IN THE WAR EFFORT SHOULD BE CLASSED AS TRAITORS TO THE CAUSE OF DEMOCRACY, BECAUSE THEY ARE BLOCKING THE ASSISTANCE OF A POWERFUL ALLY THAT HAS NEVER SHOWN A SHORTAGE OF COURAGE AND SACRIFICE— COLORED AMERICANS!"

While the paper was quite willing to unleash its stable of famed columnists, who were noted for being outspoken and fearless, it nevertheless sometimes countered their tough statements with calmer comments, apparently concerned that whites, particularly those in the government, might become jittery over what was being written. For example, on March 21, the paper said, "The 'Double V' combines . . . the aims and ideals of all men, black as well as white, to make this a more perfect union of peace-loving men and women, living in complete harmony and equality." It also referred to blacks as "the most loyal segment of the American population." Then, three weeks later, it wrapped itself in patriotism with a Double V Creed across the top of the front page in large type: "We pledge allegiance to the United States of America . . . to its all-out victory over the forces of our enemies on the battlefronts in every section of the world. We pledge allegiance to the principles and tenets of democracy as embodied in the Constitution of the United States and in the Bill of Rights. To full participation in the fruits of this victory . . . victory both at home and abroad . . . we pledge our all!"

Meanwhile, the *Courier* was filling as much as 13 percent of its available newshole each week with an amazing variety of Double V events. There were Double V dances, flag-raising ceremonies, gardens, and professional baseball games between black teams, with a drum and bugle corps forming a giant Double V on the field before one of the games. The paper also encouraged readers to form clubs and sold Double V pins for 5 cents apiece. The clubs participated in such activities as writing congressmen to protest poll taxes, which were designed to keep poor blacks from voting; contacting radio networks, asking that two programs popular with blacks, "Southernaires" and "Wings over Jordan," not be broadcast at the same time, so that listeners could hear both; meeting with businessmen to promote nondiscriminatory hiring; and sending such things as books, cigarettes, shoe polish, candy, and cookies to military camps. There was even a Double V song, "A Yankee Doodle Tan," which Lionel Hampton's band performed on an NBC radio national program in May. The paper noted that it was heard by 2 million listeners, and two weeks later, the paper was selling sheet music for the song for 30 cents a copy.

As the campaign roared onward, the *Courier* ingeniously played it up in numerous ways. For example, it began replacing the standard straight rules between articles with two long dashes and a "VV" between them. Suddenly, wherever readers looked in the paper, they were confronted with the Double V. It also started filling small spaces at the ends of stories with a boldface filler: "Fifteen million people with one unified thought, 'Double V;' Victory at Home and Abroad."

But through all the hoopla, the paper never forgot the reason that it had a campaign: the letter written by Thompson. Thus, in April, it sent columnist George Schuyler to interview him. The opening paragraph of the story set the tone by almost breathlessly portraying him as a hero:

> For 900 miles by airplane and train from Pittsburgh to Wichita, Kansas, I had been wondering what manner of person was James Gratz Thompson, whose stirring letter to The Pittsburgh Courier had launched the nationwide "Double V" campaign. I knew that he was young and endowed with unusual gifts of expression. I knew that in his memorable letters he had expressed the feelings of millions of Negroes, young and old, from the Atlantic to the Pacific. It was clear he was a thoughtful young man and his photograph indicated that he was handsome and upstanding. Now, as I pressed the buzzer at the front door of the five-room one-story house the Thompsons own at 1239 Indiana Avenue, my curiosity was to be satisfied. At last I was to see and talk with the Negro youth whose words had thrilled a million COURIER readers.

After pointing out that Thompson had quit working at the cafeteria because he had been denied a five-cent-an-hour raise, Schuyler called him "the idol of Wichita's 6,000 Negro citizens."

With such adulation, it should have surprised no one when the paper hired Thompson two months later as head of its Double V campaign. This led a minister in Hopkinsville, Kentucky, to base a sermon on Thompson and the campaign. "Jesus Christ, our 'Double V' Friend, kissed the idea [of the campaign] when he kneeled and prayed in the Garden of Gethsemane," said Rev. L. S. Grooms. "The idea of 'Double Victory' did not leave the earth, it simply remained silent until the selected person [Thompson] was notified and the time pronounced." Thompson directed the paper's campaign for eight months until he joined the service in February 1943.

Going hand in hand with the Double V was the continuing drumbeat by black newspapers about specific instances of injustices against blacks. One of the frequent targets of criticism was the Army, which on the day after the bombing of Pearl Harbor met with a group of black editors, publishers, and columnists and angered them by saying it was not going to be a "sociological laboratory" and change its racial policies during the war. According to historian John Morton Blum, such "unchanging policies" by the military, particularly the Army, were the reason for considerable black discontent: "Angry about military segregation, blacks detested the harassment they suffered from Military Police, the abuses they suffered from civilians in towns near cantonments, especially in the South, and the Army's endorsement of Jim Crow regulations in cities frequented by troops on liberty. Segregation on Southern trains and buses especially irritated northern blacks in training camps in Dixie."

Black problems at Army camps, which frequently involved black soldiers and white military policemen shooting at each other, were among the stories played up heavily on the front pages of the black papers. From August 1941 until June 1942, there were racial disturbances, and sometimes riots, at Fort Dix in New Jersey, Fort Bragg and Camp Davis in North Carolina, Fort Benning in Georgia, and Mitchel Field in New York. A Military Intelligence report did not blame the black press for the problems, but it complained that some of the black newspapers' articles about racial incidents in the camps, as well as other more general problems in the Army, were "beyond the normal agitational behavior of the press" and were not improving black soldiers' allegiance to the country. One article that angered the Army was from the black *People's Voice* in New York, which managed to sneak a reporter into a barracks at Fort Dix on April 3 to cover a gun battle between blacks and whites. The reporter predicted that more race riots would follow in the Army camps, and he belittled an official statement that the shooting was not racially motivated. Military Intelligence, in noting the influence among black troops of black newspapers, such as the *Pittsburgh Courier* and the five papers in the *Afro-American* chain (of which the Baltimore paper was the largest), concluded: "As long as these papers carry on their efforts for the purpose of racial betterment they cannot be termed as subversive organs. They do, however, at times appear to achieve the same result as outright subversive publications."

That comment from Military Intelligence was at the core of a crucial problem for the government in the first half of 1942. It was not sure that it could win the war without the support of the entire country, and there was a fear that critical articles by the black newspapers, whether justified or not, might harm black morale. If that occurred, blacks, who made up 10 percent of the population, might be persuaded, at best, to ignore the war effort, or, at worst, to become internal saboteurs and do such things as blow up railroad lines or power plants. Such concerns led on May 22 to a discussion at a presidential cabinet meeting of the critical nature of the black press as part of an overall assessment of black attitudes toward the war, which everyone agreed were not good. This conclusion was supported by an Office of Facts and Figures report on the same day noting that many articles and editorials in black newspapers were playing up discrimination and that this was hurting black morale. President Franklin D. Roosevelt suggested to Attorney General Francis Biddle and Postmaster General Frank Walker that they should talk to black editors in order to, in Biddle's words, "see what could be done about preventing their subversive language."

Roosevelt probably wanted to only scare the black press into toning down instead of actually suppressing it under the Espionage Act, which had once again gone into effect when the United States entered the war. After all, he appreciated the important part that blacks had played in his reelection in 1940, and he would not have wanted to offend them by publicly attacking the black newspapers. Furthermore, he was not a racist, and blacks made immense strides during his presidency. But as a politician, he was aware that contact with blacks might offend southern voters, and so he used others to interact with them, such as his wife, Eleanor. When asked whether this practice might still lead to criticism of him, he countered, "I can always say, 'Well, that's my wife. I can't do anything about her.'" Thus, asking Biddle and Walker to see the black editors was characteristic of the way he operated.

There is no evidence that Walker had more than a brief, polite conversation with any of the black editors, preferring instead to have his aides handle something that controversial. But Biddle did not avoid the confrontation, and he came into it with a definite familiarity with the black newspapers and what they were writing. Since early spring, the Justice Department had been heavily investigating the country's print media, and the black newspapers particularly posed a thorny problem. Their articles and editorials clearly were more critical of the government and outspoken about injustices than most of the mainstream white-owned papers, but they were far less so than the radical fascist press. That left the Justice Department with a dilemma—it was unsure of whether it could successfully prosecute the black press under the Espionage Act.

The Justice Department addressed the problem in June 1942 when the Post Office asked if an issue of the *Chicago World,* whose weekly circulation of 28,000 made it one of the country's ten largest black newspapers, could be declared unmailable because of its criticism of the treatment of blacks. "What is tyranny in one imperium should not be a blessing in another," the paper wrote in May. "If segregation is the curse of Hitlerism then segregation is the curse of any nation that indulges in it." The Justice Department said the question was whether a publication could combine "all-out united" support of the war with denunciations of discrimination against blacks, which resulted in criticism of the government. It said it relied generally on a statement by legal expert Zechariah Chafee Jr., who had written: "[I]n our anxiety to protect ourselves from foreign tyrants, [the country should not] imitate some of their worst acts, and sacrifice in the process of national defense the very liberties which we are defending." Applying that principle, as well as others from cases that had been decided by the Supreme Court, the Justice Department concluded that the *World* was "basically neither defeatist nor obstructionist nor divisionist"; instead, it was merely pointing out factually what blacks considered to be unfair treatment. "If such utterances [as in the *World*] do not fall within the traditional constitutional immunities for freedom of speech," it said in declaring what the paper wrote as within the law, "categories long established will have to be formulated anew."

While that was a liberal interpretation of freedom of the press in wartime, which was not surprising because Biddle did not think that First Amendment rights shrunk even if the life of the republic was at stake—a belief that he conveyed to those who worked for him—the black newspapers had no way of knowing that was the tack the Justice Department was taking. Consequently, John Sengstacke, who had taken over the *Chicago Defender* in 1940 when his uncle, Robert Abbott, died and who had quickly established himself as the country's leading black publisher, nervously asked for a meeting with Biddle in June 1942. The reason was simple: The black publishers were worried that the government might try to shut down one or more of the papers, and he hoped to forestall any such move.

Biddle readily agreed to see him, and when Sengstacke was shown into a Justice Department conference room in Washington, he found numerous black newspapers, including the *Defender,* the *Pittsburgh Courier,* and the *Baltimore Afro-American,* spread out on a table. All of them had headlines about clashes between whites and blacks in Army camps. Biddle said bluntly that such articles were hurting the war effort, and if the papers did not change their tone quickly, he was going to take them to court for being seditious. Then, turning specifically to the *Defender,* he said a number of its articles were close to being seditious, and the paper was being watched closely by the Justice Department.

Sengstacke, who was just as tough as Biddle, denied that the black newspapers were detrimental to the war effort. He pointed out that they had been fighting against black injustices for more than a hundred years, and then he said firmly, looking Biddle in the eyes, "You have the power to close us down, so if you want to close us, go ahead and attempt it." However, he continued, there was a possibility of a compromise. More than forty years later, he recalled what he said next:

"I've been trying to get an appointment to see [Henry] Stimson [the secretary of war]. . . . I've been trying to get in touch with everybody else [in the government]. Nobody will talk with us. So, what do you expect us to publish? We don't want to publish the wrong information. . . . We want to cooperate with the war effort. . . . But if we can't get information from the heads of the various agencies, we have to do the best we can."

So, he said, "Well, I didn't know that." I said, "That is correct." . . . He said, "Well, look, I'll see if I can help you in that way. . . . And what I'll do is make arrangements for you to see some of these people." So, he called Secretary [Frank] Knox [of the Navy] and made an appointment for me to see him.

Then, at the end of the hour-long meeting, Biddle executed an abrupt 180-degree turn from the meeting's beginning, almost surely because he had never had any intention of going after the black publishers with the Espionage Act. He promised that none of them would be indicted for sedition during the war if they did not write anything more critical than what they already had carried, and, in fact, said he hoped they would tone down. Sengstacke replied that he could not promise that would be the case, but added that if the black papers could interview top government officials, they would be "glad" to support the war effort.

Sengstacke promptly went out and told other black publishers what had occurred, particularly that there would be no Espionage Act indictments, but none of them ever told their readers, and apparently they told few on their staffs. Bolden, who was a war correspondent for the *Pittsburgh Courier,* recalled that his executive editor told him the news confidentially by the end of the summer of 1942, and he was not surprised at Biddle's decision. "We didn't think we were doing anything unconstitutional," he said. "Of course, that may have been debatable. But we had confidence in our government that it wouldn't do anything silly like shutting down the black press. There was just too much pressure on the government to do that."

Biddle's wish for the black newspapers to tone down presented the publishers with a dilemma: Readers expected them to vigorously attack injustices to blacks, and any paper that stopped doing that would almost surely face severe, possibly even fatal, circulation losses. They solved that problem by becoming far less critical of the federal government and instead focusing on injustices by states and governors and private businesses, and there was no evidence throughout the war that the readers ever noted the subtle shift in coverage. Making this change easy for the publishers was the fact that by the summer of 1942, blacks had made enormous job-related gains. They were in the Marines, the Coast Guard, the Army Air Corps, and the Women's Army Auxiliary Corps for the first time; they were no longer confined to the kitchens in the Navy; and their numbers had grown rapidly in the Army as it had expanded, even though it continued to remain only 10 percent black. They also were being hired in defense plants, not only because of the large number of men who left their jobs to go into the armed services but also because of pressure from the government's Fair Employment Practice Committee, and they were becoming stenographers and secretaries and file clerks in the numerous government agencies, which expanded rapidly because of the war. And many of these jobs paid more than the blacks had ever made before. The publishers played up these important gains, whether they were by men or women, and not to have done so probably would not only have alienated readers but could have angered the government. So many blacks were now working in government jobs that the improvement could not be overlooked.

There also was another major reason for the newspaper publishers to tone down by the summer of 1942: Some of the larger papers were suddenly making substantially more money from national advertising for the first time in black press history. This was the result of Congress passing an excess profits tax in 1940 (which was followed by several related tax rulings by the Internal Revenue Service) in anticipation of corporations making large amounts of money from the war. Using a formula, the government determined what would be classified as "surplus" cash, and then businesses could avoid paying higher taxes on it by plowing the money back into the economy in new ways. This encouraged a number of the large national corporations owned by whites to immediately begin advertising in the black press, although some of them probably did it reluctantly; they had largely ignored the black press as an advertising medium in the past because they felt that blacks did not have enough income to be a reasonable market for their products. But now these corporations noted that blacks' incomes were rising, which gave them more spending power, and they decided to try to boost their profits by advertising in what was basically a new market. Rapidly increasing circulation figures among the black newspapers also made them an attractive venue.

A study of national advertising in the *Pittsburgh Courier* during the war indicated the impact of the excess profits tax on the black newspapers. Whereas nineteen different national advertisers appeared in the paper in 1941, fifty-one appeared in 1944, and over the same period the number of national ads rose from 402 to 709, with health-care products, such as Arrid, St. Joseph Aspirin, Noxema, and Penetro nose drops, averaging between 61 percent and 85 percent of the ads annually. With this increase in ads, and more money suddenly flowing into a number of papers, black publishers would not have wanted to chance losing it by remaining critical and possibly being indicted under the Espionage Act, despite what Biddle had promised.

At the same time that black newspapers were toning down in the summer of 1942, the *Pittsburgh Courier* was cutting back dramatically on its Double V campaign. From the start of the campaign in February until the end of the year, the paper ran 970 Double V items: 469 articles, editorials, and letters; 380 photographs; and 121 editorial drawings. The emphasis on the campaign peaked on April 11, when 13.06 percent of the newshole was filled with Double V material, but then the campaign tapered off gradually, until it seldom occupied more than 2 percent of the editorial space in the final three months of the year. As for the front page, Double V material appeared on page one only seven times in the final thirty-one weeks of the year.

Historian Lee Finkle noted that many southern black newspapers toned down or eliminated the Double V in the summer of 1942 after three prominent white journalists criticized the campaign because the papers did not want to jeopardize their good relationship with southern white liberals. But outside of the South, he wrote, the black press, "aware of its readers' approval, in no way softened its tone as a result of these attacks. . . . The 'Double V' and 'fight for the right to fight' became the wartime slogans of the black press." It was not difficult to see why readers liked the campaign's theme of two victories. The significance of the campaign was evident on March 7, 1942, when the *Chicago Defender* ran a letter that equated the blacks' fight against injustices both home and abroad with Roosevelt's Four Freedoms, which he listed in a speech to Congress in January 1941 ("freedom of speech and expression, . . . freedom of every person to worship God in his own way, . . . freedom from want, . . . [and] freedom from fear"). "[W]ith America trying to spread the gospel of the Four

Freedoms world-wide, why should we cease our fight for them right here at home?" said the writer. "While we 'Remember Pearl Harbor' let's 'Remember Jim Crow' too."

But while the Double V theme continued for the duration of the war, the *Courier* backed off the campaign, according to Bolden, for the same reason that other publishers toned down that summer: the immense gains made by blacks since the beginning of the war. Looking back forty years later, Bolden explained:

> What else could we do? We had knocked on the door and gotten some attention and so the [*Courier*'s] editors said, "Let's concentrate on what the people are doing." For example, why would I want to read about the Double V when people are already working in a war plant down the street? I wouldn't. These gains showed good faith intentions by the government and other people [those who owned war plants], and we felt we should follow suit. . . .
>
> In other words, the Double V was like a Roman candle. It flared up, it did its work and then it died down. It wasn't the sole reason things opened up [in the armed forces and industry], but it certainly woke people up.

Thus, both during the height of the Double V campaign and then in its decline, the paper played up the improving climate for black workers, which demonstrated "good faith intentions," with positive articles as well as photographic layouts frequently covering an entire page. This coverage included stories about defense plant workers, shipyard employees, servicemen and servicewomen, and black merchant marine seamen. Its new, highly patriotic tone was especially evident in picture cutlines. One of them said: "The 93rd Division is part of Uncle Sam's method of building up unexcelled fighting strength for a battle against enemy

forces. Okay, Uncle Sam, we're ready!" And another exclaimed:
"These black men [in the defense plants] realize they have as
much, or more, at stake than any other group of people. They
know that democracy must survive. They know that democracy
is their only hope. And, because they are conscious of these things,
they have rolled up their sleeves and are enthusiastically helping in
the development of America's might. 'America first, last and
always!' is their song as they work in the arsenals of democracy."

Jesse Vann, who took over the *Courier* from her husband,
Robert Vann, after he died in 1940, also may have played a major
role in cutting back on the Double V campaign. The paper provided her income, and she may have been concerned that the
campaign could endanger this support. In addition, she may have
worried that the campaign could harm morale and engender government enmity at the very moment that blacks were making
huge gains with government help. In any case, she apparently con
cluded that playing up the black gains while downplaying the
Double V was a way to satisfy everyone. She had to be pleased
with the increased money that the paper was making from national
advertising, and she may have felt that continuing an unabated
campaign to end black injustices might cause some of the advertisers to cut back on what they were spending. This reasoning
would have been in line with what several researchers in the 1940s
concluded: Increased profits affected the editorial content of black
papers. "Negro publishers are apt to be primarily business men
whose interest in race welfare is secondary to their interest in
selling newspapers," wrote Thomas Sancton in 1943. Five years
later, Vishnu V. Oak agreed: "Many [black] newspapers seem
quite willing to sell their pages to anyone who is willing to pay the
proper price." Finally, looking to the future, Vann may have realized it would be unwise to not tone down. The country's war

fortunes subtly changed as the United States went on the offensive, with victories over the Japanese in the Pacific starting in May 1942, and the Allies invaded North Africa in November.

But toned down or not, black newspapers were investigated heavily in World War II by seven government agencies—the Justice Department, the FBI, the Post Office Department, the Office of Facts and Figures, the Office of War Information, the Office of Censorship, and the Army. In fact, so many agencies were involved in looking at blacks and the black press that one official in 1942 described it as a "muddle."

One of the busiest agencies was the Post Office, which inspected 15,930 issues of newspapers and magazines during the war for Espionage Act violations. The Post Office occasionally barred specific issues from the mail, and it took away six second-class mailing permits. The black press was among those examined closely, and the Post Office asked the Justice Department on a number of occasions if certain issues of black newspapers contained seditious writing. The pivotal moment came in the fall of 1942, when the Justice Department, which had been struggling with trying to determine what constituted sedition, was asked about two issues of the *Pittsburgh Courier* and concluded:

> In the opinion of the analyst, the paper has been reporting honest and legitimate complaints. The *Pittsburgh Courier* and other large Negro newspapers express the existing unrest of 10% of the total population of the U.S., rather than create it. The question of sedition and mailability of Negro newspapers cannot be considered apart from the Negro problem. In other words, it is the grievances themselves that discourage recruiting and enlistment [in the armed services] rather than the reporting of them by the Negro press.

A policy of declaring Negro newspapers unmailable or of considering prosecution on charges of sedition—particularly a paper as prominent and as respected by the Negro population as the *Pittsburgh Courier*—could only result in aggravating further unrest and possibly arouse a spirit of defeatism among the Negro population.

Using that opinion as a guideline for the rest of the war, the Justice Department never agreed that any black publication was unmailable. That ended the threat to black newspapers from the Post Office. Because of the Justice Department's conclusions, Post Office officials refused to declare any of the black newspapers seditious or to strip them of their second-class mailing permits. It could not afford to go to court, if it was challenged legally, without the backing of the government's legal branch.

But the Post Office did not give up easily. For example, it asked the Justice Department to review the October 14, 1943, issue of Los Angeles's black *California Eagle* because of what it wrote about the imminent possibility of race riots. This included:

> Tonight the city is tense. A riot may happen in the next breath.
> . . .
>
> And somewhere tonight there is a man clearing his throat for the speech he will make after the next riot.
>
> "These niggers have got to be shown their place. Los Angeles is a Southern Town now, and we've got to let the darkies know it!"
>
> There are presses in our city tonight which will print the stories to start the next riot. . . . "Tonight Mrs. Lula Blotz, attractive housewife, was brutally assaulted by a hulking Negro rapist."
> . . .

And somewhere tonight there is the tongue which will send up the first lynch cry . . . "Get that Nigger!"

And the hate is here.

Like devilish sparks it bristles out of eyes that remember Mississippi and from the Dixie-accented voice of the street car conductor just in from Oklahoma.

In sending the paper to the Justice Department, a Post Office inspector stated that he felt those comments would create "fear and hatred of the white race, and racial tension which might easily explode into riots at little or no provocation, resulting in 'murder, arson and assassination.'" The Justice Department did not agree, declaring the paper mailable, and the Post Office never again inquired about the mailability of a black publication during the war, feeling that such requests were a waste of time.

The Post Office was not the only government agency to be rebuffed by the Justice Department during the war when it came to the question of taking action against black newspapers. There also was the FBI. Hoover had already believed during the Red Scare period of 1919–1921 that the black press was dangerous, and then he had had it investigated heavily between the two world wars. Thus, it could not have surprised anyone at the Justice Department that he suspected it was seditious immediately after the bombing of Pearl Harbor. Hoover pointed to five papers in the *Afro-American* chain that ran comments by five Richmond blacks on December 30, 1941, about Japan's possible attitude toward blacks if it won the war. "The colored races as a whole would benefit," said one man. "This would be the first step in the darker races coming back into their own." The Justice Department brushed off Hoover's complaint, however, noting that the comments were "mere expressions of individual opinion as to the possible course of future events" and not "false statements." In addition, evidence was lacking to prove that the statements were designed to harm the armed forces, either in recruiting or enlistment.

Hoover was undismayed by this setback, and the FBI continued its massive investigation of the black press. It also initiated unofficial censorship by subscribing to the papers and having them sent each week to the bureau's headquarters in Washington, as well as having agents visit the papers to complain that their articles on discrimination were hurting the war effort. P. B. Young Sr., publisher of the *Norfolk Journal,* said it was "a rare day" when the FBI did not visit a black paper early in the war. Bolden recalled a visit to the *Pittsburgh Courier* during that period:

> The investigation was a farce. They [the agents] never harassed anybody or threatened anybody. They just expressed their dissatisfaction at what we were doing. . . . They suggested that we protest in another way or wait until after the war. But to my knowledge, they never threatened to arrest anyone or told anyone they had to do something. . . .
>
> [Executive Editor Percival Prattis] just called them scared white people, Hoover's flunkies. We all said that. We just considered them Nazi strong men. We just ignored them. I guess you could call it contempt. I understood why they came around. I thought it was a stupid waste of time and taxpayers' money, but I could put myself in the white man's shoes—he was saying, "We'd better investigate them niggers. They might be forming a Communist cell." But none of us feared them. When you're not guilty, you have no fear.

As the war continued, the FBI tried unsuccessfully time after time to get the approval of the Justice Department to move legally against the black press, which clearly was not going to happen after

Biddle and Sengstacke met in June 1942. Then, in September 1943, the FBI mounted a major wartime attack on black publications in a 714-page report, "Survey of Racial Conditions in the United States." It claimed the black press was hurting the war effort because it was "a strong provocator [*sic*] of discontent among Negroes." The report continued: "It is claimed that its general tone is not at all, in many instances, informative or helpful to its own race. It is said that more space is devoted to alleged instances of discrimination or mistreatment of Negroes than there is to matters which are educational or helpful. The claim is that the sensational is foremost while true reportorial material is sidetracked." Forty-three publications were cited for causing problems through articles and headlines, thirteen of them were listed as having Communist connections or running articles that followed the Communist Party line, and five allegedly had used pro-Japanese material. In addition, the FBI claimed that six black papers in particular were causing enormous discontent among blacks and had Communist connections—the *Baltimore Afro-American,* the *Chicago Defender,* the *Michigan Chronicle* (Detroit), the *Oklahoma City Black Dispatch,* the *People's Voice* (New York City), and the *Pittsburgh Courier*—while a seventh paper, the *Amsterdam Star-News* in New York City, was lauded as a responsible black publication because it was "comparatively conservative" and had criticized communism several times. If Hoover hoped the survey would lead to some black press indictments, he was disappointed. It was sent to the White House, but there is no evidence that Roosevelt read the survey or urged any action based on it.

Undeterred by his lack of success with the report, Hoover went to the Justice Department again in October 1943 about an outspoken *Chicago Defender* column that complained about the treatment of blacks in Army camps. It said: "Mainly, their [the black soldiers'] bitterness adds up to—'I [would] just as soon die fightin' for democracy right here in Georgia, as go all the way to Africa or Australia. Kill a cracker in Mississippi or in Germany, what's the difference!'" Once again the Justice Department stopped Hoover by declaring the column legal. It would continue to do the same thing until February 1945, when Hoover finally gave up after attempting to get the *Pittsburgh Courier* for a critical article about the federal War Manpower Commission. In 1947, Young recalled the heavy FBI wartime investigation of the black press and boasted of the result: "The fact that years of watching and distilling of every line, every word printed in the Negro press that could by any process of reasoning have been classified as treasonable brought not one single arrest, not one single act of suppression, constituted irrefutable proof of the undiminished patriotism of the American Negro at a time when efforts to sabotage our war effort were quite general in other circles."

While it was true that the FBI was not involved in any suppressions, that was not the case with the Office of Censorship and the Army, neither of which was controlled or heavily influenced by the Justice Department. The Office of Censorship could censor or rule unmailable anything sent outside of the forty-eight states, and it first exercised this power with the February 1942 issue of the *New Negro World*. The problem was an article headlined "Let's Tell the Truth" that talked about whites killing blacks in the United States: "If my nation cannot outlaw lynching, if the uniform [of the Army] will not bring me the respect of the people that I serve, if the freedom of America will not protect me as a human being when I cry in the wilderness of ingratitude; then I declare before both GOD and man . . . TO HELL WITH PEARL HARBOR." The district postal censor complained that this was "distinctly subversive," the chief postal censor in Washington agreed, and it was not mailed outside of the country. The *Chicago Defender* had the same thing happen in the spring and summer of that year; in addition, one issue arrived in Havana, Cuba, with everything cut out by a censor except the border. The censors continued to carry out such practices until the spring of 1944.

The Army was particularly ruthless. Biddle recalled in 1962: "The military found it easier to clamp down on everything than to exercise the difficult practice of judgment [during World War II]." In 1941, even before the United States entered the war, all reading material in Army libraries was being examined, and anything considered subversive or damaging to morale was removed. Then, a year later, the Army expanded its order when it said that any printed material in the camps that commanding officers considered "unsuitable for soldier use from the standpoint of being subversive, obscene, or otherwise improper" should be destroyed. It also started a secret blacklist of publications that it felt were "undesirable."

Although there were numerous complaints from Army personnel that black newspapers were hurting the morale of black soldiers by writing about injustices to blacks, suppressions surprisingly did not begin until July 1943. At that point, the *Chicago Defender* said that its newsboys were stopped at Camp Rucker in Alabama, that their papers were seized, and that they were "chased" away. In addition, distribution of the *Defender* and the *Pittsburgh Courier* was stopped at several Mississippi Army camps. Then, following racial disturbances at the antiaircraft training center at Fort Bliss, Texas, the commanding general banned black papers from the post because they were of "such an agitational nature as to be prejudicial to military discipline." As a result, the camp's postal officer began to confiscate "objectionable newspapers" before the mail was delivered to black servicemen. When the War Department in Washington learned of the suppression in August, it ordered it halted and told camp commanders that an occasional issue of a paper could be suppressed, but banning them permanently "would only serve to supply ammunition for agitation to colored papers."

But that was not the end of Army suppression of black papers. It continued at camps in Alabama, Arizona, Georgia, Louisiana, Tennessee, and Washington, with papers affected including the *Amsterdam Star-News,* the *Baltimore Afro-American,* the *Chicago Defender,* the *Pittsburgh Courier,* and the *Washington Afro-American.* An order issued in late 1943 stating that no further publications could be banned without War Department approval was designed to finally end this, but in some cases the order was ignored until August 1944. After the *Pittsburgh Courier* was banned from Fort Benning in Georgia, Schuyler lashed out at the government in his column on April 8, 1944: "It becomes clearer and clearer that our white folks simply can't take it. . . . When Negro newspapers print the facts and criticize the criminal collusion between officialdom and crackerdom leading to treasonable discrimination against the mistreatment of Negro soldiers and sailors simply because they are colored . . . a cry goes up, not for a change of policy toward the Negroes, but for . . . suppression of the Negro newspapers."

In sharp contrast to the Army was the Navy, where there was not a large number of suppressions of black newspapers. The Navy thoughtfully addressed the problem and the dangers involved in military censorship of black papers in its "Guide to the Command of Negro Naval Personnel" in February 1945:

> Some concern has been expressed because a good proportion of Negro enlisted men read Negro newspapers which are severely critical of the Navy or because they belong to organizations working for the improvement of racial conditions. It is appar-

ently thought that such contacts may be a source of low morale. This is a doubtful assumption. Commanding officers who have been most successful with colored personnel commonly subscribe to Negro newspapers. . . .

It is true that Negro publications are vigorous and sometimes unfair in their protests against discrimination, but it is also true that they eagerly print all they can get about the successful participation of the Negro in the war. Negroes have to buy them if they want to read Negro news. Censorship and repression of such interests is not in the American tradition. It cannot be made effective, and has the reverse effect of increasing tension and lowering morale.

In February 1944, in the midst of the suppressions, the black press made two important gains at the White House. One involved Roosevelt's continual refusal to meet with black groups. A. Philip Randolph, one of the country's leading blacks, complained about this in the *Pittsburgh Courier* on April 11, 1942: "Practically every other minority group in America have systematic contact with the President. They can call upon the President to meet with their representatives and receive a cordial hearing. The President feels obligated to give consideration to the recommendations of organized labor, the Jews and Catholics and other minority groups but he has no such attitude toward the Negro."

That finally changed on February 5, 1944, when Roosevelt met for thirty-five minutes with the Negro Newspaper Publishers Association (NNPA), which had been founded by Sengstacke in 1940. Thirteen editors and publishers from ten black newspapers presented a twenty-one-point statement on the war aims and postwar aspirations of blacks, and the publisher of the *Norfolk Journal and Guide* said the president showed "heightened interest, or even agreement," as it was read. "It was obvious that this was no routine audience he was giving the Negro group; he was concentrating his attention on the subject at hand," he wrote, noting that the meeting "hit one tremendous climax after the other." Roosevelt pleased the editors by inviting them to make such a visit annually, and one month after his death in April 1945, his successor, Harry S Truman, met with fifteen NNPA publishers, editors, and reporters at the White House, confirming that it was no longer a liability for a U.S. president to meet with a group of American blacks.

Three days after the NNPA meeting with Roosevelt, a black reporter attended a presidential press conference for the first time in American history. Black journalists had been requesting permission to attend the press conferences since Roosevelt had become president in 1933, but they were always turned down because of a rule by the White House Correspondents Association stating that only those representing a daily newspaper could be admitted. Under this rule, none of the blacks who applied were eligible. The rule ostensibly was designed to keep the number of reporters small enough to fit into the Oval Office, where the press conferences took place. But it also clearly was designed to keep blacks out. Historian Graham J. White claimed that Stephen Early, the president's southern press secretary, was only able to enforce it because he had the "tacit approval" of Roosevelt. Disregarding any biases he had, Early felt that allowing blacks into the press conferences would be politically unwise because they would ask about civil rights, and whatever the president said was sure to offend someone. "By avoiding specifics," wrote historian Donald A. Ritchie, "Franklin Roosevelt could create the impression of commitment to equal rights without aggravating southern Democrats in Congress, and without losing a single southern state in any of his four presidential campaigns."

Nevertheless, in the summer of 1943, Biddle, a dependable friend of blacks, suggested to Roosevelt that a black should be admitted to the White House press corps, and the president told him to look into it. While it is unknown what information Biddle gathered and whether he prepared a report for Roosevelt, Harry S. McAlpin finally became the first black White House reporter six and a half months later as a joint representative of the *Atlanta Daily World,* the country's only black daily paper, and the NNPA. McAlpin had formerly worked for the *Defender* as a Washington correspondent and then deliberately left for a job at the *World* so he would be eligible to go to the White House, and Sengstacke secretly paid most, if not all, of his salary. But despite writing for a daily paper, McAlpin said more than forty years later that he felt he was allowed to become a White House correspondent only because the president now thought this would be a good move politically. "Roosevelt was the shrewdest politician ever in the White House," he said. "He had the knack to not offend too much or favor too much the deep South, the business interests, the blacks, etc."

On the day before the first press conference that McAlpin would attend, Paul Wooten, a White House correspondent for the *New Orleans Times-Picayune* and president of the White House Correspondents Association, asked him to come by his office. In his unpublished memoir, McAlpin recalled their remarkable conversation:

> "Harry, you have been accredited as a White House correspondent by President Roosevelt and there is nothing we can do about that. But I asked you to come in because I believed we could arrive at some agreement in connection with your attend-

ing the President's press conferences. We are anxious to cooperate with you in every way possible.

"Now, I suggest that when you come down tomorrow, you sit out in the reception hall. One of us regular correspondents will be glad to tell you what went on in the conference as soon as it is over. And, of course, if you have any question you would like to have asked, if you would let one of us know about it, we'd ask it for you and as soon as the conference is over, we'd let you know what answer the President gave.

"Now the reason I made these suggestions is because there is always a large crowd at the conferences. They gang up to the corridor leading to the President's office, and when the signal is given to enter, there is a grand rush. It's possible that you might step on someone's foot in the rush . . . and there would be a riot right in the White House."

While I was seething inside, I listened with an outward calmness to this suggestion. Then I said:

"I'm somewhat surprised at what you have said, Paul (it was probably the first time he had ever been addressed by a Negro using his first name). I have always had the impression that the men who reached the pinnacle of the reporting profession by becoming White House correspondents were the cream of the crop of journalism. I'd be surprised if any of them should start a riot in the White House because someone inadvertently stepped on his foot, but if they did it would be one of the biggest stories of the year and I'll be damned if I'd want to miss it. Thanks for the suggestion, but I'll take my chances. I'll be going in to get my own stories and to ask my questions myself." . . .

As I left his office, I said to myself, "Well, they're still at it. White folks won't let me forget [that I'm black]!"

So, he went to his first press conference in the Oval Office, and he deliberately walked past the president's desk when it was over. Roosevelt, who was sitting, as he frequently did, because he had polio, smiled warmly, stuck out his hand, and said, "I'm glad to see you McAlpin, and very happy to have you here."

Roosevelt's handshake and comment signaled to the white reporters that blacks were there to stay as White House correspondents, and McAlpin remained in that position until late 1945, filing a story each day with the *World* and the other papers that were members of the NNPA. During his twenty-one months at the White House, the white reporters gradually became friendly toward him, although they never socialized together; in fact, the correspondents' association blackballed him from the organization because he refused to promise that he would not come to its annual dinner. When he finally left the White House to become an information specialist with the government's Office of Price Administration, the NNPA replaced him with another black.

While McAlpin's admission to presidential press conferences, as well as the NNPA meeting with Roosevelt, were small gains, they were still significant. These were highly visible, tangible signs of the increasing equality of blacks, which was particularly evident in figures that showed that blacks experienced more occupational improvements between 1940 and 1944 than in the previous seventy-five years combined. They were in every branch of the armed services in increasing numbers, and the exploits of black servicemen around the world were played up dramatically in the black press by twenty-seven black war correspondents (compared to only one in World War I). Black women on the home front prospered, too. They worked alongside white women as "Rosie the Riveter" in the shipyards and aircraft plants, and they poured into government agencies, which expanded enormously to meet the wartime demand for labor.

Black newspapers trumpeted all of these gains as well as the injustices, frequently linking them to the constant drumbeat of a need for a double victory, and readers liked what they saw and avidly read the papers. From 1940 to 1945, the circulation of the country's more than 200 black newspapers rose from 1,276,000 to 1,808,060, an increase of 42 percent. But even those figures understated readership. As before the war, the papers were continually passed around, and it was estimated that 3.5 million to 6 million people read them every week during World War II, when one-third of the urban black families subscribed to a black paper. In 1944, two weeks after the black publishers and editors met with Roosevelt, the *Michigan Chronicle* proudly noted the rising prestige of the black newspapers:

> The minority presses have a tremendous responsibility especially in a time of crisis such as the present. The rising recognition of the Negro Press, we believe, bears witness to the fact that the Negro newspapers have shown themselves worthy of the public trust and have lived up to those responsibilities. The most significant achievement of the Negro Press during this crisis, in our estimation, lies in the fact that the Negro newspapers have brought home to the Negro people of America that this is their war and not merely a "white man's war." . . . We are determined to make this a people's war and we mean all the people, regardless of race, creed or color. It may well be that the tremendous struggle of the Negro Press in this democratic effort is responsible for the recognition which it is receiving today.

That recognition would not last long, however. In the twenty years following the war, black newspapers would suddenly go from leading their readers and telling them what to think, or at least printing what they wanted to read, to largely falling out of favor with them. The civil rights era, which quickened the pace of black demands for total equality, along with other unstoppable forces, would inexorably and rudely cause black papers to plummet into a subordinate and largely noninfluential role forevermore.

SEVEN

FROM AN INCREDIBLE HIGH TO AN INCREDIBLE LOW

Educated Negroes are reading the Negro press decreasingly.
—Allan Morrison, *Ebony*

Black newspapers were understandably optimistic about the future following World War II.

Not only had President Truman met at the White House with the Negro Newspaper Publishers Association in May 1945, thus continuing what Roosevelt had started the year before, but black reporters continued to make important inroads in the capital beyond being in the White House press corps. In another milestone in 1947, the NNPA's Louis Lautier and the Associated Negro Press's Alice Dunnigan became the first black reporters to be accredited to the congressional press galleries. Lautier was rapidly accepted by the white male reporters, but Dunnigan, who also had press passes to the White House and the State Department, encountered blatant and severe discrimination. Looking back almost thirty years later, she recalled: "Race and sex were twin strikes against me from the beginning. I don't know which of these barriers were [*sic*] the hardest to break down. I think sex was more difficult, because I not only had to convince members of the other race of my capacity, but [I] had to fight against discrimination of Negro men, as well as against envy and jealousy of female members of my own race." Then, in 1955, Lautier became the first black member of the prestigious, all-male National Press Club in Washington, while Dunnigan became the first black in the Women's National Press Club. While she appreciated that this "opened avenues for many exclusive stories and personal interviews with prominent dignitaries," she resented not being invited to join until the club's "professional liberals" finally decided, after waiting seven years, that "they could, in good faith, accept just one minority into their sacred society."

The financial picture also appeared brighter for black newspapers. Circulations had increased dramatically during the war, with the *Pittsburgh Courier* leading the way in 1945 at 350,000, which made it the largest mainstream black paper in U.S. history up to that time. Equally significant, according to an academic study, was that some white-owned national corporations had become convinced that the black press was a viable advertising market. During the war years, national advertising had increased more than two and a half times in the black papers, largely because of the government's excess profits tax, and with the end of the war in sight, black publishers wondered if these advertisers would go back to largely ignoring their papers when the tax incentives disappeared. However, in 1947, the *Courier* still had thirty-seven national advertisers, which was down from the high point of fifty-one in 1944 but still higher than in any other previous year, and far above the figure for 1941, when only nineteen national advertisers had appeared in the pages of the *Courier.* The number of national ads in 1947 was 15 percent higher than in 1941, and the average advertisement was larger than before the war. Thus, researchers concluded that for the first time, many advertisers were "gingerly using black newspapers."

Also encouraging were strong indications that black readers liked the newspapers. Two polls, for example, showed that more than 90 percent of the black respondents agreed with the papers' militant attitudes. Additionally, the *Chicago Defender* found that 81 percent of the blacks it polled in 1945 did not make decisions on local and national matters until they saw what the black press wrote about the issues, and 97 percent felt that the main reason that blacks were obtaining equal rights and becoming first-class citizens was that the black newspapers had sounded a continual drumbeat against inequalities.

Thus, the future looked promising, which several researchers pointed out. Gunnar Myrdal had been commissioned by the Carnegie Corporation to study American blacks, and one chapter of his classic 1944 book, *An American Dilemma: The Negro Problem and Modern Democracy,* dealt with the outlook for the black press. He wrote:

> The importance of the Negro press for the formation of Negro opinion, for the functioning of all other Negro institutions, for Negro leadership and concerted action generally, is enormous. The Negro press is an educational agency and a power agency. Together with the church and the school—and in the field of interracial and civic opinions, more than those two institutions—it determines the special direction of the process through which the Negroes are becoming acculturated. The Negro press causes, on the one hand, an intense realization on the part of the Negroes of American ideals. On the other hand, it makes them realize to how small a degree white Americans live up to them.

As the educational level of the Negro masses rises, as those masses become less dissimilar in culture from other Americans, as the isolation between the two groups increases under voluntary withdrawal on the part of the Negroes, as race consciousness and race solidarity are intensified, as the Negro protest is strengthened, and disseminated even among the lower classes—as all of these closely interrelated processes are proceeding, partly under the influence of the Negro press itself, the Negro press will continue to grow. With larger circulation, there will be increased possibilities of getting advertising. With a fortified economic basis the Negro press will be able not only to buy better equipment but also to engage better-trained journalists and to organize a better national news service. When the Negro press can produce a better product than now, it will sell even better. The Negro newspaper will probably remain a weekly, though perhaps in some regions it will become possible to launch Negro dailies. This is the prospect we see for the Negro press. It will flourish and become more conspicuous when the foreign-language papers die out. . . .

Whether or not this forecast of an increasing circulation for Negro papers comes true, the Negro press is of tremendous importance. It has rightly been characterized as "the greatest single power in the Negro race."

Three years later, John Burma of Grinnell College analyzed the black press and predicted there would be fewer but larger black papers, they would improve journalistically and have better printing facilities, and their overall circulation would rise because of declining illiteracy and the increase of the black population. He also speculated that local and national advertising would increase, which would make them more financially sound. "As the tide of

Negro protest continues to rise and becomes even more vocal and well organized and as race consciousness and race solidarity increase," he wrote in *Social Forces,* "the protest function of the Negro press will remain unimpaired or even will expand. . . . [G]reater growth is to be expected." Then, a year later, Charles H. Loeb, president of the Editorial Society of the Negro Newspaper Publishers Association, claimed there were "glorious years ahead" for the black press as it continued to flourish. Noting that white newspapers generally ignored blacks, he said black newspapers would be "indispensable" if blacks were going to continue to make progress toward equality, and to further that goal he foresaw the papers becoming better printed, better written, and more objective. He concluded, "[T]he Negro publisher hardly has reason to visualize impending doom."

He could not have been more incorrect, which would quickly become evident as black newspapers entered a deep downward spiral. But even in World War II, when the future looked promising, several largely praiseworthy articles about the papers in national magazines had noted troublesome points in passing. Thomas Sancton in the *New Republic* on April 26, 1943, strongly commended black papers for their fierce fight against injustices, noting that "[w]hen a white man first reads a Negro newspaper, it is like getting a bucket of cold water in the face." As an example, he pointed out what black readers expected to find when they read the papers: "When a squat little redneck, with none of the graces he says are inherent in his race, gets up in the Senate and proposes that 13,000,000 people—who for three centuries spilled their sweat into the American earth—be torn away from it and sent to the fever coast of Africa, Negroes want their press to call him a liar, a thug and a cheat. They don't want him handled with calm disdain, as *The New York Times* might handle him. They know what he is. They want to see it in print, or as near to it as possible under the libel laws."

But toward the end of the four-page article, Sancton turned to what he saw as the "fundamental weakness" of the black papers: overcompensation. If the white press, for example, criticized blacks for their crime rate, the black press would treat it apologetically; if the white papers downplayed black achievements, the black papers would praise them effusively. Furthermore, he condemned the "eye-for-an-eye philosophy," whereby the black papers lashed out at whites who criticized blacks. He said it was important for the black press to rise above such attacks and to be more factual if blacks were to achieve the goals they were seeking. "Racism is a bad game no matter who plays it," he wrote, adding that while much of the black newspapers' criticism of whites was deserved, it could create a feeling of bitterness in blacks and turn them into racists. "[T]he Negro press must learn objectivity," he warned, "before anything approaching a solution of the race problem can be achieved."

A year later, *Fortune* touched on the same subject in the conclusion of an otherwise laudatory article about black newspapers. It noted that a few papers, instead of trying to cultivate white respect for blacks, continually wrote about white criminals "to show that whites are no better than Negroes." The magazine said this worried black leaders more than the hostility of white northerners or the way many southern blacks still had a "yassah, massa" attitude, which was labeled "good niggerism." Then, it added ominously, black leaders saw in this racism "a danger to their whole program for achieving equality, for they know better than any white man where the slumbering hatreds among their own kind might lead if encouraged. That is one reason why they put such emphasis on Negro rights and Negro self-respect, hoping that thus they can build a structure in the shadow of which hatred will wither."

By 1950, the downward turn for black newspapers unquestionably had begun, although it was still too early to realize how dramatic it would be. One tipoff was that the acknowledged leader among the black papers, the *Pittsburgh Courier,* had dropped 22 percent of its circulation, from an all-time high of 357,212 when it had twenty-three editions to 280,000, in just three years (and it would continue to decline to 186,000 in 1954 and then to 100,000 by 1960). Writing in *Commonweal* about some of the papers' problems, Roland Wolseley, who taught journalism at Syracuse University, did not address the circulation decline but did express concern over the low amount of advertising in the black papers, which left them financially strapped. He noted that Vishnu V. Oak, who taught at Wilberforce University, had attributed the advertising problem in a 1948 book to two causes: Most black businesses could not afford to advertise very often, and national advertisers were either unaware of the black papers or ignored them. However, he pointed out that Roi Ottley, Abbott's biographer, considered this a plus because it left the black papers free to speak out on matters involving blacks without having to worry about alienating advertisers.

Wolseley was not the first to notice advertising problems in the black press following the war. In 1947, Burma had written: "Most businesses are run by whites and for whites, with Negro trade as incidental. The clientele these businesses primarily wish to reach is white, so there is an obvious lack of return from advertising in the Negro press. Moreover, the Negro press is an additional paper; most Negroes who read Negro papers also read white papers. Many firms, the makers of nationally advertised goods, for example, are deterred from using the media of the Negro press because they feel such advertising would be mere duplication." In the same year, P. L. Prattis, executive editor of the *Pittsburgh Courier,* was more blunt in *Phylon,* blaming the low amount of national advertising in black newspapers on the insidious evils of racial segregation. "The white advertisers, living in another world, see no need of advertising in media published for the benefit of a set-off, segregated, poor and 'inferior' segment of the population," he wrote angrily. Looking back in 1986, Roderick Doss of the *New Pittsburgh Courier* took a different tack in explaining the decline in advertising: He said it was the result of the flood of white veterans returning from the war and starting new households. When advertisers saw this, they quickly became interested in upgrading white living standards and took their advertising in that direction and away from blacks and the black newspapers. "The returning black veteran was never recognized," he said. "The double standard was reinforced and this condition persisted until the 1960s."

But while the decline in advertising hurt financially, this was not a major reason for the huge drop in circulation and influence from the late 1940s until the mid-1960s. Nor is there evidence that the stunning success of a new breed of black magazines at this time drew readers away from black newspapers, although it is tempting to draw that conclusion because circulation on one was rocketing upward just as it was plummeting on the other. John H. Johnson started *Ebony,* a picture magazine for blacks, in 1945 without any advertising and sold less than 25,000 copies. However, by the magazine's tenth anniversary issue, when he also was publishing three other money-making magazines for blacks (*Jet, Tan,* and *Hue*), it had $186,000 of advertising in 180 pages and a circulation of 506,000, and it continued to prosper in the years ahead, reaching a circulation of 6 million by 1980. Johnson attributed his success over the first decade to not only a drive for home subscriptions but also a shift in editorial focus. He dropped his early use of cheese-cake photographs of women and sensational articles loaded with gossip and instead began reporting seriously about blacks. "The Negro press has depended too much on emotion and racial pride," he told *Time* in 1955. "Negroes have grown out of that."

Johnson was correct about readers starting to become dissatisfied with black newspapers by the mid-1950s, but time would show that blaming this solely on the papers' overuse of "emotion and racial pride" was a gross oversimplification. In reality, the swift decline of the black papers in the 1950s and the 1960s was attributable to a number of highly interconnected factors that produced a complicated, unstoppable, and in some ways unpredictable drama.

With a long tradition of militant, protest journalism, black newspapers came out of the war proud of their accomplishments and comfortable in continuing their outspoken fight against black injustices that had increasingly attracted readers. Propelling them forward was a striking esprit de corps among their reporters and editors, who approached their work with almost the fervor of a religious calling. Phyl Garland, a reporter for the *Pittsburgh Courier* from 1958 to 1965, recalled in the *Columbia Journalism Review* in 1982 the deep sense of commitment that she and the other top new black reporters had at the time; they felt they were "warriors" who were privileged to be able to "strike out at the forces that denied us opportunity and respect." Harold L. Keith, who worked at the paper for eighteen years and was the editor when he left in 1963, shared that feeling. "The galvanizing force that made it [the *Courier*] go was the institution of racism—we were Negroes then," he said. "All of us felt involved and it gave us the impetus to work for little money to do the best job we could to fight that institution. We had outstanding reporters in the South, some of them white, who risked their lives to do things like infiltrate the Ku Klux Klan to bring us the news."

But striking out at injustices in the late 1940s and the first half of the 1950s could be particularly dangerous because of the climate of the times. The Cold War had begun, and too much militancy by a black newspaper could easily be construed as Communist inspired. That is what happened to Los Angeles's *California Eagle.* In World War II, it had been monitored closely by both the Post Office and the Federal Bureau of Investigation, and in 1943 officials of the latter felt that some articles in the *Eagle* followed the Communist Party line. Then, in July 1945, the paper praised Russia for being the only country with no racial discrimination. When the paper's outspokenness about government policies continued unabated after the war, rumors spread that it was too radical, making trouble, and Red-inspired, even though publisher Charlotta Bass was not a Communist, and circulation declined. Discouraged over the lack of community support as well as by heavy competition from the rival *Los Angeles Sentinel,* she sold the paper in 1951 after running it for forty years, and it lasted another thirteen years before going out of business. That ended an eighty-six-year run, which made the *Eagle* the country's oldest black newspaper. Edward "Abie" Robinson, who wrote for the paper, recalled in the late 1990s what the paper had meant to him and other blacks: "When the *Eagle* finally closed its doors for good, [what] can you say when you attend your own funeral? How can you do that? There would never be a group [of journalists] like this that would be able to do the things that we thought we were capable of doing. We were buried, we were dead, and it was . . . a tragedy, it was a loss. And Los Angeles has never recovered from that."

It is unknown how many other black papers, if any, were victims of the vicious Red-smearing tactics of this period, but a much more common reason for the decline in prestige and circulation of a number of papers was simply poor management decisions. During the 1950s, Keith became disillusioned as he watched what occurred at the *Courier.* White advertisers started pulling out of the paper at an increasing rate when it began covering the civil rights movement. With less advertising revenue, the management decided to trim the paper's staff, so there were fewer stories to print. There also was a heavy investment in a magazine section and color comics with black characters, neither of which was a success, and the paper downsized to become a tabloid, which left the public feeling cheated because the *Courier* was smaller. Then, after Martin Luther King Jr. led a widely heralded bus boycott in Montgomery, Alabama, in 1955–1956, the paper inexplicably ran a series entitled "What's Good about the South." This enraged readers and caused circulation to drop further. Radical Elijah Muhammad then became a columnist in the paper and began criticizing various religions while building up his Black Muslim organization. This not only outraged ministers, whose congregations read the paper, causing further subscription losses, but when the column, "Mr. Muhammad Speaks," was discontinued, another 25,000 drop in circulation occurred because his followers stopped pedaling the paper on the streets. Also not helping was the publisher's decision to keep endorsing Republicans when blacks solidly backed the Democratic Party.

Garland recalled that the situation deteriorated further in 1959 when S. B. Fuller, a conservative Chicago cosmetics manufacturer, took over the paper and disastrously changed its long-running, fundamental editorial direction: "He decided that the *Courier* would no longer be a black paper but an integrated news organ emphasizing 'positive' matters and avoiding all controversy, this at a time when blacks were becoming increasingly militant.

For those of us who experienced these sieges of mismanagement, the sense of helplessness and frustration—it seemed ridiculous that, due to a lack of correspondents, we should be covering the civil rights movement largely by telephone—was all but unendurable."

As the *Courier* slumped, so did other black papers, until *Newsweek* noted in 1963 that the country's 2 remaining dailies and its 131 weeklies, semiweeklies, and biweeklies had only 1.5 million circulation, even though the number of blacks had grown by about 50 percent over the past twenty years to 20 million. It labeled this a "sad plight." Allan Morrison, the New York editor of *Ebony,* said the problem was that the black papers were written for those in the ghettoes. "When the middle class escapes the ghetto, it rejects everything to do with the ghetto," he explained, "and it passes this rejection on to its children. Educated Negroes are reading the Negro press decreasingly."

That did not mean they were not reading newspapers or paying attention to the news. Now, however, the news came increasingly from white-owned papers and television stations. That was not true in the years immediately following World War II, when the only news about blacks in the white press was still virtually limited to those who were sports heroes, entertainment stars, or criminals. So, if blacks wanted news about themselves, from births to deaths to marriages to club news, they had to read the black newspapers. But then the civil rights movement, a natural follow-up to, and a beneficiary of, almost fifty years of militancy in the black press, started, and slowly, over more than a decade, it grew into the country's top domestic news story.

When that occurred, it attracted the attention of the white press to news about blacks for the first time. As Nicholas Blatchford, managing editor of the *Washington Daily News,* told *Newsweek* in 1968 in reference to articles about black areas in large cities, "Reporters and editors are discovering this other country." But that did not mean the white press knew what black readers wanted to see in the papers or even why any of them bought a white paper. Nat Goldstein, circulation director of the *New York Times*, bluntly admitted, "I have walked around black neighborhoods, and I have seen people carrying the *Times,* but we really have no formal research on who reads us in the ghetto." The *Atlanta Journal* also was in a quandary when it described local ghetto life in 1968 in a fourteen-part series, "Two Atlantas," which was written mainly for middle-class white readers with no ghetto experience. "We just don't know how to reach ghetto readers," said managing editor Durwood McAllister. "But we're open to suggestions."

The white press also had another problem, particularly as the civil rights movement escalated and violence became more and more common. Frequently, the only way that white reporters could enter black areas was by accompanying police cars going to quell a riot, and even then they sometimes were chased away. To overcome this, the white press finally began hiring black reporters. Some of them did not have the journalistic skills or experience of the white reporters, but they could go more easily into black areas, especially the ghettoes, and interview blacks.

These hirings had enormous implications for black newspapers and contributed to their decline. What made them ironic were recent complaints from blacks that the white press was all but closed to blacks who wanted to work in white newsrooms. In 1947, the *Courier*'s Prattis complained bitterly in *Phylon* about the opportunities for a black college graduate who wanted to become a journalist:

> Eventually, the Negro student is graduated with good marks. . . . Where can he turn to get a starting job on a good newspaper? His best chance so far has been with Negro newspapers. They are all

right, but they are in a restricted area of the field of journalism. They . . . are victims of segregation. Most of what practical Negro journalists know, they have learned by themselves and have taught themselves in terms of their special needs. They have been largely out of competition with the leaders in the great big world of [white] journalism, the ones who determine what par is and change it at their whim or wish. If our student of journalism elects to take his chance on a Negro newspaper, he has the opportunity for restricted growth in a restricted, segregated field. He can rise, just like the white boy, but instead of rising to the top of the accumulated world experience of the last three centuries, he rises merely to the top of the accumulated experience in Negro journalism during the last one hundred years. This is a kind of journalism, protest journalism, made necessary by the depressive and enervating effects of segregation.

Obviously, although he may become a star performer in the restricted field, he cannot be expected to show similar proficiency in the larger field because he has been denied an opportunity for growth in it. He and the white boy made the same marks in school. But in the intervening years, the white boy has risen to the top of the world heap and the Negro boy has been stopped short atop the Negro heap. White folk like to say that the brains of Negroes cease growing after a certain age is reached. What is truer is that segregation deprives Negroes of a developing life experience. The journalist, and Negroes in most professions requiring the skill and knowledge that come from experience and association, suffers from this segregation. The Negro would-be journalist starts off with the odds weighted against him. He can go so far and no farther when segregation cuts him off from normal assimilation of the dominant culture. In his own field, he reaches a state of experiential paralysis.

When the white press started hiring blacks, thus addressing Prattis's concerns to some degree, this created a different problem—it quickly became what Garland called "a brain drain [on the black papers] that was devastating." Suddenly the best young black journalistic talent was not staying very long on the black press, if, in fact, they even took a job there in the first place. Some of the black editors desperately tried to counter this trend by doing such things as identifying high school students who looked promising and then paying part of their way through college, hoping they then would join their papers and remain there. But this strategy was not very successful, and the defections continued, prompting *Chicago Defender* publisher John Sengstacke to complain that he was constantly "running a training school" for the white press. Some of the black reporters who left, even though they received higher salaries on the white press, were just as frustrated—and also sad. George Barbour, who resigned from a black newspaper to become the first black broadcaster at KDKA in Pittsburgh in forty-three years, recalled that he "loved" the black press. But he had a family to support, and when Westinghouse broadcasting offered him a higher salary, he felt that he had no choice but to accept it. Vernon Jarrett, who also started on black newspapers, had a similar love-hate relationship with the white press. "I enjoyed the audience of the white-owned publication, the fact that my messages were going out all over the country and everywhere, but there was something different about working for a black newspaper where no longer shall others speak for us," he said, echoing what was written in the first issue of *Freedom's Journal* in 1827.

But while being paid more was important, and writing for a larger audience enhanced their sense of self-importance, the black reporters frequently found their new jobs had downsides. For example, nobody really trusted them. The black community was leery that they were spies for the white establishment, and white editors were not entirely confident that they would report accurately about blacks. Furthermore, they sometimes had to work harder than their white colleagues because of artificial barriers that they were forced to hurdle. In the winter of 1969–1970, the *Columbia Journalism Review* provided an example:

> One of the few over-forty blacks in the Washington press corps recalls how, in his early days, just to stay even with white competitors in covering one racial trial in the Deep South, he had to go to the courthouse a day early, scout a place where he could eat, park his car, and phone his office in an Eastern city. "The next morning," he says, "I got up early again, went to the phone booth, and put an out-of-order sign on it. Then after the morning session, I ran out and called in my story. It worked the first day, but on the second, when I went to the same booth and asked the operator to get me Baltimore, she said, 'Ain't you the nigger boy who called yesterday? You just put that phone down.' I protested, but I had to go find another phone." Such stories, of which there are many, help explain why few young [black] boys looked to journalism [rather than other professions].

As the drain on black talent continued, and the white press increased its coverage of blacks because of the volatile civil rights movement, black newspapers changed in significant ways. For the first time in their history, they not only did not have news about blacks virtually all to themselves, but they also did not have the resources to compete with the far more well-financed white press. Consequently, they were beaten badly on many of the stories, particularly because they were essentially a weekly press, while the white press was daily, and, in the case of television, sometimes live. As the *Columbia Journalism Review* said tersely in 1967, "[N]ow that the big race stories are everybody's story, the Negro papers are usually out last with the least."

Furthermore, the black papers' writing subtly changed as the militant writers of the 1940s, who arguably were leading their readers and influencing what they thought, became the older conservatives of the 1960s. *Holiday* magazine noted in 1967: "Because the most gifted [black] writers so often work elsewhere, the editorials and columns in the Negro papers . . . rarely match the front-page news in intensity. Voices are modulated back there—chiding, questioning and criticizing, but rarely raging, exhorting or threatening. The journalists on even the most outspoken papers usually sound middle-aged; tired, exasperated and cautious." An Atlanta journalist was even more brutal and colorful in *Time* in 1976: "Once a sword for freedom, the black press is now a flaccid instrument." Suddenly readers had passed them by and were not very interested in what they had to say.

But there was more behind the newly conservative tone than just the aging of the journalists. In fact, it was largely intentional because black publishers faced a dilemma unlike any they had ever faced before. The *Columbia Journalism Review* stated it succinctly in 1970: "It [the black press] finds itself trying not to be too conservative for the black revolutionaries, and not too revolutionary for white conservatives upon whom it depends for advertising." Thus, ironically, the black papers had done what was inconceivable as late as World War II: In one important way, they had become just like their white counterparts. They were businesses run by businessmen, and whatever it took to make money—in this case, not being too critical in order to retain white advertisers—took precedence over everything else. So the black papers purposely softened their editorial tone. Publisher John Murphy of the *Baltimore Afro-American* put it simply when he admitted that instead of the papers being "spearheads of protest," they now were "much more informational." C. B. Powell, the publisher of the *Amsterdam News,* echoed that theme, noting that when his paper considered issues to be "too revolutionary," it now spoke out against them. You've got to realize," he said, "that we don't see our role as leaders."

Researcher Henry G. La Brie III, writing in the *Negro History Bulletin* in 1973, predicted that paying more attention to what advertisers liked would make the black newspapers more like the white press and less "black." "There is nothing necessarily wrong with this," he continued. "In fact it is encouraging to see the black newspaper becoming a viable business since for many years it was viewed by many as something of a 'charity.' Subscribers bought the papers to help a brother."

In many ways, that comment indicated the strange, new world that black newspapers found themselves in by the 1960s and 1970s, and they would never be the same again. Nor would they ever have the influence that they once enjoyed.

EIGHT

THE CIVIL RIGHTS ERA AND
THE BLACK PRESS

The black press was the advocate of all of our dreams, wishes, and desires.
—Frank Bolden, *The Black Press: Soldiers without Swords*
(PBS documentary)

On May 17, 1954, a racial thunderbolt hit the United States when the Supreme Court announced its decision in *Brown v. Board of Education.* The case was the result of the National Association for the Advancement of Colored People deciding nine years before to challenge segregation. After careful planning, it filed a suit in 1950 in Charleston, South Carolina, asking that sixty-seven black children be allowed to attend the public schools of Clarendon County. That case, along with four similar ones, proceeded up through the federal court system for four years. The Supreme Court did not disappoint the NAACP. In a unanimous decision, which was even more stunning because three of the judges were from the South, it ruled that it was unconstitutional to segregate children in elementary and secondary public schools solely because of their race. This reversed the famous 1896 decision, *Plessy v. Ferguson,* which had established a separate but equal society.

Historian Benjamin Quarles noted that the *Brown* decision was "a revolutionary step in American race relations" and that it had a much wider impact than a narrow reading would suggest:

> The decision itself applied only to schools below the college level, but it had unmistakable implications for public institutions of higher education. And it had similar implications for any publicly operated facility—library, museum, beach, park, zoo, or golf course. Indeed, the Brown decision could be extended to any field in which segregation was imposed by state law. It did not apply to private groups and organizations, but it would undoubtedly cause many of them to re-examine their racial policies.
>
> In fine, the Brown decision meant that America would have to look anew at its colored citizens. "The abiding subconsciousness of the Negro turned overnight into an acute and immediate awareness of the Negro," wrote James Jackson Kilpatrick, editor of the *Richmond News Leader.* And as the nation came to grips with this historic decision, it would come face to face with a Negro who seemed to have grown taller.

Black newspapers understandably praised the outcome in a torrent of news stories, features, columns, and editorials. In a front-page editorial headlined "Let's Give Thanks," the *Pittsburgh Courier,* for example, called the decision "the most powerful affirmation of the ideals of our country" since the Emancipation Proclamation of 1863, which freed the slaves in the Confederacy during the Civil War. It claimed the decision showed that God was on the side of the blacks, adding, "It was no wonder that church bells rang [when the decision was announced] and many people shouted, 'Hallelujah! I'm free at last.'" On the same day, the *Cleveland Call and Post* labeled the decision "one of the most important milestones in their [blacks'] slow and tortuous journey upward from slavery to freedom" and said it applied to all rights, not just those in public schools, guaranteed to U.S. citizens of any color. Warning, however, that there was a difference between the Supreme Court interpreting a right and blacks actually getting it, the paper accurately predicted what lay ahead:

> Negro Americans may be sure that the Southland will exhaust every device at its command, and some not yet evolved, to stall, delay—and perhaps sabotage this new interpretation of American freedom. There will be wild denunciations from some states, hypocritical double-talk from others; in some violence and threats, and in others an outbreak of legislative trickery, all aimed at preventing Negro and white children from attending the same schools.
>
> In the opposing camp there will be hot-heads of immediacy, the "pink" intellectuals and psuedo [*sic*]-liberals—and our erstwhile friends, the Communists—who will engage in gyrations and oratory calculated to arouse the Negro people to anger and revolt. . . .
>
> The stakes are the highest this generation has ever played for. Let us not lose the prize through errors of hasty action.

A paradox of the *Brown v. Board of Education* decision was that the black papers became a victim of the shining prize for which they had sought so hard and so long: integration. As the civil rights movement revved up and then roared onward over the years with an increasing, throbbing intensity, sometimes resulting in destruction, violence, and even death, integration gradually spread out to encompass far more than public schools, and one of those integrating out of necessity was the white press. It began hiring away some of the best young black journalistic talent in order to cover the black communities, particularly when there were riots, and suddenly black papers did not have a virtual monopoly on black news. This, in turn, led to blacks starting to buy white papers rather than the black ones, and as circulation dropped, it became apparent that the black papers might be in a death spiral that few of them would survive. The connection between integration and the decline of the black papers—even the possibility that they might cease to exist—was noted widely by the press, which found this an easy explanation for what was occurring. But as has been shown, the downturn was far more complicated than that.

Nevertheless, while there were numerous reasons for what was happening to black papers, everyone agreed on one thing: There was definitely a crisis. Black papers reacted in different ways to it. The *Chicago Daily Defender* continued to show anger at what was happening to blacks and defiantly pushed for more rights. "I'm a nigger, but I'm a proud nigger," editor-in-chief C. Sumner ("Chuck") Stone Jr. told *Newsweek* in 1963. "If I don't push, nobody will." The approach at the country's only other daily black paper, the *Atlanta Daily World,* was just the opposite. Editor C. A. Scott, whose attitude was "don't rock the boat," felt that getting angry accomplished nothing and instead urged his readers to get smart. "We have everything to lose [by being mad] and nothing to gain," he said. "What we want is goodwill. The less friction we create today, the less we will have to undo tomorrow." Roy Wilkins, executive secretary of the NAACP and a former managing editor at the black *Kansas City Call,* noted it was important for each black paper to reexamine what it was doing and possibly set new goals in order to survive. However, he felt it would be a mistake for black papers to merely mirror the white press. "Negro papers came into being as crusaders," he said. "And the minute they stop being crusaders and become chroniclers, they're done."

But apparently not many black journalists were listening or agreed. By 1967, *Holiday* magazine noted that the black press, both newspapers and magazines, were doing what Wilkins had warned against:

> Ironically, the Negro press has a very low rate of visibility. Its publications don't catch the eye with foreign words or an exotic type face. The front-page pictures are the same ones you see everywhere else. Weekly and semiweekly Negro papers often look overfamiliar because they depend heavily on the wire services and news bureaus for their national coverage. The Negro magazines are also comfortably integrated among their neighbors on the magazine rack. *Time, Life* and *Esquire* are just as likely to have the Supremes or [black baseball player] Juan Marichal on the cover. Hurrying commuters usually get their first look at *Ebony* by accident, buying it under the impression this it is *Life,* which it resembles in size and design. . . . With the notable exception of the *Afro-American,* few Negro newspapers have giveaway names—the *World,* the *Independent,* the *Courier,* the *Journal and Guide,* the *Defender,* the *Blade*—nothing there to make the white public sit up and take notice. The extremist sheets, such as *Muhammad Speaks* and *Black Power,* rarely appear outside the ghettoes. This may partly explain why the Negro press has attracted so little attention. It's easy to forget that it's there.

The degree to which the black papers looked more and more like their white counterparts continued to be a topic of discussion as the years passed. In 1974, Milton Coleman, who had worked on two black papers before founding the All-African News Service, told the *Columbia Journalism Review* that writing like white newspapers or looking like them was a losing proposition for black papers. Instead, they needed to be distinctively black. Then, two years later, John Henrik Clarke, a black educator, pointed out in *Time* that the black press was "doing more copying of the white press than creating. Since the civil rights movement, it has collapsed."

Certainly it had not "collapsed" in one way. From 1971 to 1974, the number of black papers increased by thirty to more than 200 in thirty-four states and the District of Columbia, and the overall circulation went up 600,000 to about 4.1 million. But there was still concern about the future. During this period, Henry G. La Brie III received a Ford Foundation grant to study the black press and interviewed seventy-three prominent black journalists, many of whom were between the ages of sixty and ninety-one and had spent most of their careers on the black press in forty-two cities. Overall, the journalists did not believe that black newspapers, even with the problems they had, would die out; instead, they believed that they would become "community" oriented and cover the news about blacks that did not appear in the white press. "The daily [white] press will play up the newer class blacks, the successful doctors and lawyers, the NAACP and the Urban Leagues," said Simeon Booker, Washington bureau chief for John H. Johnson's magazine empire. "But they won't have the bulk of support in the black community. . . . We will continue to cover the home parties, receptions and so on; not the first black vice-president but the guy who got a promotion maybe from a janitor to a supervisor. If we cater to this group, we will always have a base." Others believed that black papers would last as long as discrimination existed, and some pointed out that only the black press was capable of covering black America in depth and really telling it like it was. "You'd be surprised at the difference there can be between a story in the Negro paper and the same story which appears in the downtown [white] paper," said Thomas L. Dabney, a reporter for the *Norfolk Journal and Guide:* " . . . It goes like I was saying awhile ago, can't no one speak for a people like they can speak for themselves. . . . His language may not be as good, but he can tell it better."

But not everyone agreed. The most noticeable dissent was by Percival Prattis, who had been executive editor of the *Pittsburgh Courier* when it was at its height of influence and power in World War II:

> I don't think the Negro press will continue much longer because community attitudes—and I refer here to attitudes of both blacks and whites—are going to continue to change. News that you would formerly only find in the Negro newspaper is going to be in the white papers before Negro reporters can get to it. And, the Negroes who are most qualified to be journalists are going to find their jobs with the white papers, radio and TV. The opportunities for them are going to be much greater and there won't be the same role for them to play and as a consequence, the [black] publishers will not have the opportunity to make the money they used to make and they will go into something else.

In 1982, Phyl Garland, who started out as a reporter on the *Pittsburgh Courier* in 1958 and then left for *Ebony* in 1965, where she became its New York editor before joining the faculty at Columbia University's journalism school, addressed the state of black newspapers in the *Columbia Journalism Review.* She noted its many problems, which included low revenues, the loss of black college-educated reporters to white publications, low prestige, and continued drops in circulation. But she particularly emphasized that black newspapers needed to make basic changes in what they covered and how they wrote those stories if they were going to survive.

Lou Ransom, managing editor of the *New Pittsburgh Courier,* noted that black papers could no longer be "everything for everybody" as they were in the past. Most of the readers were old and bought the papers simply because they always had read them. Meanwhile, black college graduates found little in the papers of interest to them and did not buy them, instead turning to white daily papers and magazines such as *Time* and *Newsweek.* Ransom concluded that these "young professionals" were "starving" for in-depth articles about black subjects and that the papers should offer them exactly that.

Raymond H. Boone, who worked for sixteen years in the *Afro-American* chain of newspapers and then became a visiting professor of journalism at Howard University, felt that black papers needed to concentrate on both internal and external enemies of the blacks. Solving the internal problems—those that could only be addressed by blacks themselves—involved such things as getting blacks to vote, making sure black children stayed in school so they would eventually get good jobs, teaching blacks how to best use their money, and combating black-on-black crime. "Black papers need to offer leadership to the community and to encourage greater self-reliance," he said. As for external enemies, he noted the black press was necessary because there was a racial "war of ideas" going on, and blacks were not well equipped to deal with it. "Most owners of white papers are conservative and are concerned about maintaining white power in this country," he said. "Their papers are political weapons and *not* simply objective disseminators of the news."

Garland concluded by praising the vision of William H. Lee, publisher of the black *Sacramento Observer.* He had told her: "I honestly see us assuming a new role, becoming the urban newspapers of the future. Our cities have become increasingly black, and white papers have been unable or unwilling to reach this audience. Some have brought blacks in and tried to incorporate them into the operation, but this still can't give them the kind of credibility we can have. Our papers can fulfill the function of providing urban news and showing people how to cope with the urban environment, a role that white newspapers ultimately may give up. That can be our future."

As the twentieth century ended, black newspapers were still largely struggling. They had never regained the influence and power that they had during and immediately after World War II, but they had not died either, as Prattis had predicted would occur. And there was still a nostalgia—and a regret—among the dwindling number of black newspaper veterans who remembered the old days of glory. "I felt bad, even when I went to work somewhere else, because they [the black papers] taught me how to write, how to make up a newspaper, the value of news, and the value of being truthful," said Frank Bolden, who worked on the *Pittsburgh Courier* during and after World War II, on a 1999 PBS television documentary on the history of black newspapers. "The black press was the advocate of all of our dreams, wishes, and desires. I still think it was the greatest advocate for equal and civil rights that black people ever had in America. It had an effect on everybody."

If they had still been alive, such a comment would have brought a smile to the giants of black newspaper history, such as Frederick Douglass, Ida B. Wells, Robert Abbott, Robert Vann, and John Sengstacke. What they accomplished, what they did for blacks, is not forgotten. No matter what the black papers became in the last half of the twentieth century, their distant roar can still be heard. And it is magnificent.

NOTES

CHAPTER ONE

2 *'Winter of discontent':* See Major Robinson, "Carmichael Hit by Adam Powell," *Pittsburgh Courier,* October 22, 1966, 3; and Toki Schalk Johnson, "Danger May Lie Ahead in 'The Pill' for Youth," *Pittsburgh Courier,* October 22, 1966, 11.

'Kicking around in your stable': "Lady Fortune," *Pittsburgh Courier,* October 22, 1966, 4.

Pages of the Courier *today:* "Sengstacke Purchases *Courier,*" *New Pittsburgh Courier,* October 29–November 4, 1966, 1.

3 *Discussing the sale:* See "Daily *Defender* Buys Courier Group Papers," *Chicago Tribune,* October 22, 1966, sec. 2, 7; "Chicago Editor Buys *Courier,*" *Pittsburgh Press,* October 22, 1966, 13; and "Sengstacke Buys Courier Papers," *Chicago Defender,* October 25, 1966, 4.

4 *Nothing but praise:* Roland E. Wolseley, *The Black Press, U.S.A.: A Detailed and Understanding Report on What the Black Press Is and How It Came to Be* (Ames: Iowa State University Press, 1971), 78.

Portals of heaven for us: Joseph D. Bibb, "We Gain by War," *Pittsburgh Courier,* October 10, 1942, 13.

6 *Reader to reader:* Charles H. Loeb, president of the editorial society of the Negro Newspaper Publishers Association, spoke about the influence and the power of the black newspaper in comparison to black preachers in the introduction to Vishnu V. Oak, *The Negro Newspaper* (Yellow Springs, Ohio: Antioch Press, 1948), 26.

Sharp as a steel trap: I. Garland Penn, *The Afro-American Press and Its Editors* (1891; New York: Arno Press, 1969), 408.

7 *Leading journalists and papers:* See, for example, Andrew Buni,

Robert L. Vann of the Pittsburgh Courier: Politics and Black Journalism (Pittsburgh: University of Pittsburgh Press, 1974); Lee Finkle, *Forum for Protest: The Black Press during World War II* (Cranbury, N.J.: Associated University Presses, 1975); Lawrence D. Hogan, *A Black National News Service: The Associated Negro Press and Claude Barnett, 1919–1945* (Cranbury, N.J.: Associated University Presses, 1984); Patrick S. Washburn, *A Question of Sedition: The Federal Government's Investigation of the Black Press during World War II* (New York: Oxford University Press, 1986); Henry Lewis Suggs, *P. B. Young, Newspaperman: Race, Politics, and Journalism in the New South, 1910–1962* (Charlottesville: University Press of Virginia, 1988); Clint C. Wilson II, *Black Journalists in Paradox: Historical Perspectives and Current Dilemmas* (Westport, Conn.: Greenwood Press, 1991); Frankie Hutton, *The Early Black Press in America, 1827 to 1860* (Westport, Conn.: Greenwood Press, 1993); Hayward Farrar, *The Baltimore Afro-American, 1892–1950* (Westport, Conn.: Greenwood Press, 1998); William G. Jordan, *Black Newspapers & America's War for Democracy, 1914–1920* (Chapel Hill: University of North Carolina Press, 2001); and Theodore Kornweibel, Jr., *"Investigate Everything": Federal Efforts to Compel Black Loyalty during World War I* (Bloomington: Indiana University Press, 2002).

8 *DuPont/Columbia Award:* See Armistead S. Pride and Clint C. Wilson II, *A History of the Black Press* (Washington, D.C.: Howard University Press, 1997); and *The Black Press: Soldiers without Swords,* produced and directed by Stanley Nelson, Half Nelson Productions, 1999, television documentary.

9 *A fight well fought:* P. L. Prattis, "The Role of the Negro Press in Race Relations," *Phylon* 7, 3 (Third Quarter 1946): 274.

CHAPTER TWO

11 *Black newspaper had finally arrived:* Carter R. Bryan, "Negro Journalism in America before Emancipation," *Journalism Monographs* 12 (September 1969): 8. "Righteousness Exalteth a Nation" was taken from the Book of Proverbs. After a year, the newspaper's motto was changed to "Devoted to the Improvement of the Colored Population." See Pride and Wilson, 14.

12 *900 papers in the country:* Michael Emery and Edwin Emery, with Nancy L. Roberts, *The Press and America: An Interpretive History of the Mass Media,* 8th ed. (Boston: Allyn and Bacon, 1996), 17, 19, 21–24, 88.

13 *A place to live:* Benjamin Quarles, *The Negro in the Making of America* (New York: Macmillan, 1964; rev. ed., New York: Collier Books, 1979), 33–34.

 Ads offering blacks for sale: See Jean Folkerts and Dwight L. Teeter, Jr., *Voices of a Nation: A History of Media in the United States* (New York: Macmillan, 1989), 18; and Frank Luther Mott, *American Journalism: A History of Newspapers in the United States through 250 Years, 1690 to 1940* (1941; reprint, New York: Macmillan, 1947), 56, 58.

 Forty-eight in 1775: Wm. David Sloan, *The Media in America: A History,* 5th ed. (Northport, Ala.: Vision Press, 2002), 49.

 Equal treatment for blacks: David A. Copeland, *Debating the Issues in Colonial Newspapers: Primary Documents on Events of the Period* (Westport, Conn.: Greenwood Press, 2000), 82–83.

14 *Executed to morrow:* Ibid., 84.
 'Till he be dead: Ibid., 88.

15 *Charged with murder and put in jail:* Ibid., 89.
 To be severely punished: Ibid., 91. For a brief discussion of the abolitionist movement, see Folkerts and Teeter, 187–95; and Sloan, 143–49.
 First literary expressions: Bryan, 3.

16 *O Mary, don't you weep:* Quarles, *The Negro in the Making of America,* 76–77.

17 *They only did so occasionally:* Bryan, 3–7.
 Perpetrator of evil: Wilson, 6–7.

18 *College graduate in the country:* Ibid., 25–29.

19 *Lay the case before the publick:* Ibid., 25, 27.

19   *Support to continue publishing:* See ibid., 29; Bryan, 9–10; Martin E. Dann, *The Black Press, 1827–1890: The Quest for National Identity* (New York: G. P. Putnam's Sons, 1971), 39; and Hutton, 7. There is disagreement about when *Rights of All* stopped publishing. Penn said it was in 1830, but other historians believe it was the year before. See Penn, 30.

   A most tenacious grip: Penn, 27.

20   *Await their trial:* Bryan, 8.

   Such an effort: Ibid., 8–9.

   Might be attacked and killed and his press destroyed: Hutton, 39. Hazel Dicken-Garcia noted that newspapers taking items from other publications became less common in the eighteenth century as journalists shifted from being news gatherers to reporters. See Hazel Dicken-Garcia, *Journalistic Standards in Nineteenth-Century America* (Madison: University of Wisconsin Press, 1989), 19–20.

   Useful members of society: Hutton, 55.

21   *Advance in their jobs:* Ibid., 88.

   Others' convenience and rights: Ibid., 108.

22   *Since she was black:* Ibid., 66–67, 70.

   Speeches, and ship sailings: Bryan, 8.

   To accomplish your end: Hutton, 112.

23   *Help free the black man:* Wolseley, 18.

   Sought to mold white attitudes: Jane H. Pease and William H. Pease, *They Who Would Be Free: Blacks' Search for Freedom, 1830–1861* (New York: Atheneum, 1974), 98.

   Exposure to his viewpoints: Benjamin Quarles, *Black Abolitionists* (New York: Oxford University Press, 1969), 89.

   Put money into the paper: Wilson, 29–30.

   Were becoming upwardly mobile: Dann, 16.

24   *Lasted for two months in 1837:* Bryan, 30–33.

   Then above the law: Ibid., 25, 27, 30–33.

25   *Fewer had the necessary money:* Ibid., 1–2.

   Till their brethren are free: Penn, 40.

26 *Athens, Co., Ohio:* Hutton, xiv, 94.
  Character and sobriety: Ibid.

27 *Funeral parlors or homes:* Ibid., 95–97.
  Shared them with others eagerly: Ibid., xiv–xv.
  Never were able to get enough money: Quarles, *Black Abolitionists,* 87–88.
  Had no connection to it: Ibid., 88.

28 *Waiting on tables:* See Bryan, 20; and Benjamin Quarles, *Frederick Douglass* (Washington, D.C.: Associated Publishers, 1948), 10.

29 *Second only to the Bible:* Frank E. Fee, Jr., "'Intelligent Union of Black with White': Frederick Douglass and the Rochester Press, 1847–48," *Journalism History* 31, 1 (Spring 2005): 35.
  Platform or pulpit: Quarles, *Black Abolitionists,* 63–64.
  Accustomed to buying slaves: See ibid., 136; Fee, 35; and Quarles, *Frederick Douglass,* 51–52.
  United States in 1847: Fee, 35.

30 *Enslaved Fellow Countrymen:* Bryan, 19–20.
  And thought of liberty: Quarles, *Frederick Douglass,* 81.
  Lasting until 1860: See ibid., 83; and Bryan, 21–22.
  Burgeoning intellectual independence: Quoted in Fee, 35.
  Awakening interest in them: Ibid.

31 *Awkward grammatical phrases:* Quarles, *Frederick Douglass,* 86.
  Because they were black: Fee, 36, 38–41.

32 *Oh! The wretch!:* Ibid., 36.
  Killing in self-defense: Bryan, 21.
  Rob them of this liberty: Philip S. Foner, *The Life and Writings of Frederick Douglass,* vol. 2 (New York: International Publishers, 1950), 44.

33 *As well as by Douglass:* Bryan, 20–21.
  Will be vain and unavailing: Ibid., 21.
  To go to work: Quarles, *Frederick Douglass,* 97.

34 *Mortgage on his house:* See Bryan, 22; Quarles, *Frederick Douglass,* 82; and Quarles, *Black Abolitionists,* 87.

35 *It closed in 1875:* See William S. McFeely, *Frederick Douglass* (New York: W. W. Norton, 1991), 197–208; Bryan, 22–23; Quarles, *Black Abolitionists,* 87–88; and Emery and Emery, 130.

36 *Prison-house of slavery:* Quarles, *Frederick Douglass,* 96–98.
Lowly stations in life: Hutton, 157.
Acceptance by whites: Ibid., 157–59, 161.

37 *Remainder of the 1800s:* Ibid., 160.

CHAPTER THREE

40 *Bail bondsman came for him:* Harvey Fireside, *Separate and Unequal: Homer Plessy and the Supreme Court Decision that Legalized Racism* (New York: Carroll & Graf, 2004), 1–3, 25.
Basic rights to all citizens?: Ibid., 25.

41 *Upon the same plane:* Gerald Gunther, *Cases and Materials on Constitutional Law,* 10th ed. (Mineola, N.Y.: Foundation Press, 1980), 755–56.

42 *Wrong this day done:* Ibid., 756.
Two most "shameful" decisions: Fireside, 7. The only case that he felt was more "shameful" was *Dred Scott v. Sanford* in 1857, in which the Supreme Court, in a 7–2 decision, denied that blacks had constitutional rights.
Dare to challenge it?: Ibid., 273.

43 *Blacks were on trains:* Ibid., 221–25.
Demand for itself protection: Quoted in David Domke, "The Black Press in the 'Nadir' of African Americans," *Journalism History* 20, 3–4 (Autumn-Winter 1994): 134–35.

44 A *He never can become free:* Ibid., 135.
Stands like a stone wall: Ibid.

45 *1866, 1870, 1871, and 1875:* Ibid., 131.
Lose their new rights: For a brief discussion of reconstruction, see *Funk & Wagnalls New Encyclopedia,* 1975 ed., s.v. "Reconstruction."

46 *Referred to as "ghouls":* Stanley F. Horn, *Invisible Empire: The Story of* the *Ku Klux Klan, 1866–1871* (1939; Montclair, N.J.: Patterson Smith, 1969), 9–13.

46   *Fearsome nature:* Ibid., 13.

47   *Fried nigger meat:* Ibid., 17–18, 67.
          Good will follow from it: Ibid., 67–70.

48   *Until after World War II: Funk & Wagnalls New Encyclopedia,* 1975 ed., s.v. "Reconstruction."
          Number of possible subscriptions: See Pride and Wilson, 97–98; and Henk La Brie III, "Black Newspapers: The Roots Are 150 Years Deep," *Journalism History* 4, 4 (Winter 1977–1978): 111.

49   *55 percent by 1900:* Michael Schudson, *Discovering the News: A Social History of American Newspapers* (New York: Basic Books, 1978), 93.
          Foot soldiers storming a fortress: See Penn, 112, 114; Frederick G. Detweiler, *The Negro Press in the United States* (Chicago: University of Chicago Press, 1922), 60; La Brie, 111; and Pride and Wilson, 88–89.

50   *An entire neighborhood:* See Dann, 111.
          Freedom's Journal in 1827: Hutton, 161–62.

51   *Undermine the black community:* Dann, 22–23.
          Artificial barriers erected by whites: For a discussion of what black newspapers meant to blacks, see ibid., 11–30.

52   *Used to hold them back:* Ibid., 21–22.

53   *Previous condition of servitude:* Quoted in Rayford W. Logan, *The Betrayal of the Negro from Rutherford B. Hayes to Woodrow Wilson,* 5th ed. (1954; New York: Collier Books, 1970), 115. This book was originally titled *The Negro in American Life and Thought: The Nadir, 1877–1901.*
          Cohabitation with white women: Ibid., 115–16.
          Aliens in our native land: Quoted in Domke, 133.
          Will of the people: Ibid.

54   *Formerly been slaves:* Ibid.
          Offensively demand any social rights: Ibid.

55   *Stronger than ever:* Ibid., 134.
      Beefed up existing laws: Logan, 117–18.
      Pressing aggressively for further rights: Domke, 134.
      Innate inferiority of blacks: Pride and Wilson, 118. For a thorough dis-
      cussion of Social Darwinism, see Richard Hofstadter, *Social Dar-
      winism in American Thought,* rev. ed. (1944; New York: George
      Braziller, 1969).

56   *Not talking about negroes:* Logan, 173.
      Legislation or judicial decree: Pride and Wilson, 118.

57   *He died in 1915:* See *Funk & Wagnalls New Encyclopedia,* 1975 ed., s.v.
      "Washington, Booker Talisferro"; Logan, 276–77; and Pride and
      Wilson, 54.
      Penitentiary in the United States: Quarles, *The Negro in the Making of
      America,* 166–67.

58   *One of the opening speeches:* Pride and Wilson, 119.
      History of the United States: Logan, 276–78.

59   *A new heaven and a new earth:* Ibid., 278–80.

60   *Supremacy once more:* Ibid., 278, 281, 310.

61   *Compromise the national policy:* See Pride and Wilson, 119; Herbert
      Aptheker, ed., *A Documentary History of the Negro People in the
      United States* (New York: Citadel Press, 1951), 876; and Logan,
      276.
      Equal but separate accommodations: Wilson, 117–18.

62   *They do not understand:* Domke, 135–36.
      Shape and reflect their values: Ibid., 136.

63   *Lynchings (1,217) took place:* Aptheker, 792.
      Murdered in this fashion in 1892: Funk & Wagnalls New Encyclopedia,
      1975 ed., s.v. "Lynching."
      Oklahoma Territory: Logan, 348.

64   *The place of the crime:* "Swung from a Limb," *Atlanta Constitution,*
      May 20, 1896, 2.

65   *Those outrageous transactions:* Aptheker, 86.
      Even as publishers: Emery and Emery, 58–59.

65 *Till then shall we strive:* Dann, 61–67.

66 *Tennessee Supreme Court reversed the decision:* See Rodger Streitmatter, *Voices of Revolution: The Dissident Press in America* (New York: Columbia University Press, 2001), 81; and Linda O. McMurry, *To Keep the Waters Troubled: The Life of Ida B. Wells* (New York: Oxford University Press, 1998), 27–30.
    Princess of the Black Press: See Streitmatter, 82–83; and Penn, 408.

67 *A halt be called in wholesale lynchings:* Streitmatter, 83–84.

68 *Smiles of white women:* Ibid., 84.
    Pair of tailor's shears: Jacqueline Jones Royster, ed., *Southern Horrors and Other Writings: The Anti-Lynching Campaign of Ida B. Wells, 1892–1900* (Boston: Bedford/St. Martin's, 1997), 52.

69 *The paper and its press were destroyed:* Ibid., 52–53.
    Outraged and lynched: Streitmatter, 85–87.

70 *Conscience of the nation:* Ibid., 87–96.
    It became a weekly: Pride and Wilson, 228.

71 *Enterprising in business matters:* Aptheker, 643.
    The first black illustrated paper: Dann, 23, 26.

CHAPTER FOUR

74 *Upcoming presidential election:* Logan, 312.
    Unbeknownst to the public: Pride and Wilson, 122. Washington purchased the *New York Age* in 1907. See Wolseley, 22.
    A separate agrarian economic role: Wilson, 54.

75 *Leading the way backward:* See Quarles, *The Negro in the Making of America,* 172; and *Funk & Wagnalls New Encyclopedia,* 1975 ed., s.v. "Du Bois, William E(dward) B(urghardt)."

76 *Deserting Washington and his program:* Quarles, *The Negro in the Making of America,* 172–73.
    Moral clergymen and skilled engineers: Pride and Wilson, 152.
    Jail for a short time: See ibid., 123–24; and Wolseley, 34.

77   *The leadership of Booker T. Washington:* Logan, 342.

Shameful deeds toward us: Wilson, 56; and Quarles, *The Negro in the Making of America,* 173. What the Niagara Movement called for in its initial meeting was essentially no different from what was sought by the Afro-American National League, a movement that had been started in 1890 by Fortune. It died after three years because of money problems. See Quarles, *The Negro in the Making of America,* 173–74.

Du Bois was arrogant: See Quarles, *The Negro in the Making of America,* 174; and Logan, 342.

78   *Final year of World War I:* See Quarles, *The Negro in the Making of America,* 174–75; and Logan, 343.

79   *White Church Sunday:* Roi Ottley, *The Lonely Warrior: The Life and Times of Robert S. Abbott* (Chicago: Henry Regnery, 1955), 6, 13.

Washington's conciliatory approach: Martin Jackson Terrell, "A Study of the *Chicago Defender*'s 'Great Northern Drive'" (master's thesis, Ohio University, 1991), 22–23.

80   *Now earn $20 a week:* Ottley, 61–80.

Days of struggle in Chicago: Ibid., 83.

81   *Soliciting advertising:* Ibid., 81–88.

A saving of 4 cents: See ibid., 87–88, 93; and James R. Grossman, "Blowing the Trumpet: The *Chicago Defender* and Black Migration during World War I," *Illinois Historical Journal* 78, 2 (Summer 1985): 83.

82   *To Play Piano:* Ottley, 93–99.

83   *Passed from hand to hand:* See ibid., 104–5, 109; Grossman, 88; Pride and Wilson, 137; Terrell, 30; and Streitmatter, 142–43.

Now was on the wane: Hogan, 28. For a brief account of the Yellow Journalism period, see Margaret A. Blanchard, ed., *History of the Mass Media in the United States: An Encyclopedia* (Chicago: Fitzroy Dearborn, 1998), 709–10.

84   *Advertising revenue soared:* Streitmatter, 143–44.

Organ of racial propaganda: See Ottley, 104–5, 120; and Dicken-Garcia, 98. Dicken-Garcia noted that journalists strove for "impartiality" before "objectivity" became the standard in white newspapers.

84 *Constant state of intimidation:* Streitmatter, 141.

Great Northern Drive: Pride and Wilson, 136.

85 *They did in the South:* See Logan, 132; and Quarles, *The Negro in the Making of America,* 156–58.

From the South to the North: There is disagreement about the number of blacks who left the South in the decade. Rodger Streitmatter said that between 1916 and 1919, the migration numbered 500,000, which is the figure cited by many historians; Roi Ottley claimed it was a half million in 1917 and 1918 alone; and Martin Terrell noted that a government publication in 1919 put the number at almost 750,000 from 1915 to 1918. See Streitmatter, 141; Terrell, 13; and Ottley, 161.

86 *Wearing overalls and housedresses:* See Streitmatter, 142; Terrell, 1, 17; and Ottley, 170.

87 *If he want to work:* See Terrell, 7–11; and Richard B. Sherman, ed., *The Negro and the City* (Englewood Cliffs, N.J.: Prentice-Hall, 1970), 12.

A racial magnet: Streitmatter, 142.

Alabama, Texas, and Arkansas: Terrell, 16.

88 *Race relations in the United States:* See Ottley, 160; and Streitmatter, 142, 152.

Marched north: See Terrell, 33–34; and Streitmatter, 147.

Negative aspects of the South: Alan D. DeSantis, "A Forgotten Leader: Robert S. Abbott and the *Chicago Defender* from 1910–1920," *Journalism History* 23, 2 (Summer 1997): 66.

Never envisioned by Abbott: Ottley, 161.

89 *$2,000 back home in two months:* See Terrell, 35, 40; Grossman, 92; and Streitmatter, 142.

90 *Glory in its accomplishment:* See Grossman, 86; and Terrell, 37.

Becomes an outlaw: Terrell, 39.

91 *The great Lincoln intended:* Ibid., 41.

92 *Beulah Land:* Ibid., 10, 43, 46–48.
        Adjust to the North: Ibid., 50, 60.

94 *Keeping the peace:* Ibid., 60–61.

95 *Complied with their wishes:* See ibid., 39, 54–55, 57–58; Streitmatter, 154; and Ottley, 165.
        This is a sad condition: Ottley, 164–65.

96 *Influenced by the white community:* See Streitmatter, 143, 154; Sherman, 7; Terrell, 19, 28; Grossman, 86, 88–90; and Ottley, 145.

97 *By the First Amendment:* See Streitmatter, 146; Sherman, 7; Terrell, 19, 24; *The Black Press: Soldiers without Swords;* and Ottley, 145–46. Ottley said that more than a dozen agents and correspondents for the *Defender* were forced to leave their home towns.
        Would never experience: Terrell, 25.

98 *Made southerners even angrier:* See ibid., 25–26, 36–37; Grossman, 86; Streitmatter, 145–46; and *The Black Press: Soldiers without Swords.*

99 *Nothing was done:* Kornweibel, *"Investigate Everything,"* 119.
        Bounds of propriety: See Leo Spitz, "Department Intelligence Office Report," April 25, 1918, Record Group 165, MID 10218-133, Box 3191, National Archives, College Park, Maryland; and Washburn, 17.
        South and its resources: See Durand Whipple to A. M. Briggs, July 3, 1917, Record Group 65, Entry 12E, Box 64A, File O. G. 5911, National Archives; and Washburn, 16.

100 *Negroes of the South:* DeSantis, 69.
        In the midst of a war: See Woodrow Wilson to Rep. E. Y. Webb, May 22, 1917, as quoted in Donald Johnson, *The Challenge to American Freedoms* (Lexington: University of Kentucky Press, 1963), 55; and Washburn, 11–12.
        Mail bulk items profitably: See Zechariah Chafee Jr., *Free Speech in the United States* (1941; reprint ed., New York: Atheneum, 1969), 36–38; and George Juergens, *News from the White House: The Presidential-Press Relationship in the Progressive Era* (Chicago: University of Chicago Press, 1981), 195–96.
        Armed forces' uniforms: Chafee, 39–41, 100–102.

101 *1,055 were convicted:* Washburn, 13–14.
       Forty-one others to life imprisonment: Ibid., 20.

102 *Overturn the conviction:* Jordan, 92–95, 112. Also see Kornweibel,
       170–75.
       In their own defense: Theodore Kornweibel Jr., "The Messenger
       Magazine: 1917–1928" (Ph.D. dissertation, Yale University,
       1971), 9–10.
       Focused upon Germany: "Pro-Germanism among Negroes," *The Mes-
       senger,* July 1918, 13.
       Restored in 1921: See Detweiler, 171; Washburn, 22; and Jordan,
       112–13.

103 *Than the Chicago Defender:* Washburn, 212–27.
       To sixty a year later: Ibid., 15.

104 *Charred ashes and bones:* See Grossman, 85; and Streitmatter, 148.
       Encouraged readers to do the same: Finkle, 46.
       Evidence of German influence: Kornweibel, "Investigate Everything,"
       122–23.

105 *Caution should be his guide:* Ibid., 124.
       To see that he does: Robert S. Abbott to Maj. W. H. Loving, May 11,
       1918, Record Group 165, MID 10218-133, Box 3191, National
       Archives.

106 *In a patriotic fashion:* Kornweibel, "Investigate Everything," 126–28.
       Discontentment and unrest: Emmett J. Scott to George Creel, June 5,
       1918, Record Group 165, MID 10218-154, Box 3192, National
       Archives.

107 *Discrimination against blacks:* Jordan, 125.
       By the black editors: Ibid., 127–28.
       Numerous black newspapers: Alfred Lawrence Lorenz, "Ralph W.
       Tyler: The Unknown Correspondent of World War I," *Journal-
       ism History* 31, 1 (Spring 2005): 2–4.

108 *Public profession of loyalty:* Kornweibel, "Investigate Everything," 126.
       President of the United States: "Thirteen," *The Crisis,* January 1918,
       114.
       Our eyes lifted to the hills: See Lt. Col. M. Churchill to Charles H.

Studin, June 3, 1918, Record Group 165, MID 10218-139, Box 3191, National Archives; Elliott M. Rudwick, "W. E. B. Du Bois in the Role of Crisis Editor," *Journal of Negro History* 43, 3 (1958): 226; and "Close Ranks," *The Crisis,* July 1918, 111.

109 *Win in the fifth:* See Finkle, 48–49; Rudwick, 226; "Our Special Grievances" and "The Reward," *The Crisis,* September 1918, 216–17; and Jordan, 115.

110 *The prosecution of the war:* Kornweibel, *"Investigate Everything,"* 129. *White neighbors and fellow-citizens:* Streitmatter, 156–57; DeSantis, 69; and Ottley, 185–86.

111 *Most prolific of advocacy presses:* Streitmatter, 157–58. Even though the *Defender* ended its campaign, almost 1 million blacks continued to stream out of the South in the 1920s. See Grossman, 82.

112 *Up to that time:* See Grossman, 88; and Ottley, 138–39, 188.

CHAPTER FIVE

114 *The Anarchist Fighters:* See Don Whitehead, *The FBI Story: A Report to the People* (New York: Random House, 1956), 39–40; Fred J. Cook, *The FBI Nobody Knows* (New York: Macmillan, 1964), 87–88; Stanley Coben, *A. Mitchell Palmer: Politician* (New York: Columbia University Press, 1963), 206; and http://www.intellectualconservative.com/article459 (accessed May 13, 2006). *Up to a block away:* Whitehead, 39–40.

115 *Division of the Justice Department:* See Jay Robert Nash, *Citizen Hoover: A Critical Study of the Life and Times of J. Edgar Hoover and His FBI* (Chicago: Nelson-Hall, 1972), 19; Cook, 89; and Coben, 207.
Dedication to duty: See Nash, 16–18; and Whitehead, 37.
High-charged electric wire: Nash, 23.

116 *Considered ultraradical:* See ibid.; Whitehead, 41; Cook, 94–95; Hank Messick, *John Edgar Hoover* (New York: David McKay, 1972), 14;

Max Lowenthal, *The Federal Bureau of Investigation* (New York: William Sloane Associates, 1950), 91; and Coben, 207.

116 *Outrages of all sorts:* Memorandum, J. E. Hoover to Mr. Fisher, September 10, 1919, Record Group 60, File 9-12-725, National Archives.

Does more harm than good: R. P. Stewart to James F. Byrnes, September 12, 1919, Record Group 60, File 9-12-725, National Archives.

117 *Nothing unlawful in its publication:* Francis G. Caffey to Attorney General, December 10, 1919, Record Group 60, File 9-12-725, National Archives. In the same file, also see Francis G. Caffey to Attorney General, September 17, 1919, and November 3, 1919.

House in June 1920: Lowenthal, 120.

Relatively negligible: Messick, 14.

Every issue of the more radical publications: Theodore Kornweibel, Jr., *"Seeing Red": Federal Campaigns against Black Militancy, 1919–1925* (Bloomington: Indiana University Press, 1998), 9.

118 *Considered it a compliment:* See Lowenthal, 121; and Detweiler, 171.

No action was taken: See Buni, 108; and Robert K. Murray, *Red Scare: A Study in National Hysteria, 1919–1920* (Minneapolis: University of Minnesota Press, 1955), 178, 230–31, 244–46.

119 *Taking legal action against it:* Kornweibel, *"Seeing Red,"* 7, 36–53.

Radical advocacy: Ibid., 52–53.

120 *Subscription and advertising lists:* Detweiler, 152–56.

121 *Plow the fields:* Ibid., 1.

Even though it takes Death: Ibid., 152–53.

More than 1 million: Ibid., 1–3, 6–7, 10, 12, 24.

122 *People of the United States:* Ibid., 2–3.

Followed by group discussion: Ibid., 4–6.

Bad side: Ibid., 9.

123 *They showed our Ph.D.s: The Black Press: Soldiers without Swords.*

124 *This was heady stuff:* See Robert T. Kerlin, *The Voice of the Negro, 1919* (New York: E. P. Dutton, 1920), ix–x; and *The Black Press: Soldiers without Swords.*

124   *Support to the Negro press:* Detweiler, 30.

125   *Ours for the asking:* Ottley, 207–8, 211–12, 219. For a content analysis of how the *Chicago Defender* slowly changed editorially through six time periods, see T. Ella Strother, "The Black Image in the *Chicago 'Defender,'* 1905–1975," *Journalism History* 4, 4 (Winter 1977–1978): 137.

126   *Absences from the office:* Ottley, 294–96, 298–300. Also see Felecia G. Jones Ross and Joseph P. McKerns, "Depression in 'The Promised Land': The *Chicago Defender* Discourages Migration, 1929–1940," *American Journalism* 21, 1 (Winter 2004): 55–73.
      His mother's high standards: Buni, 3–6.

127   *The top student:* Ibid., 6–12.
      Oblivion and despair: Ibid., 12.

129   *An attorney that December:* Ibid., 13–19, 31–40.
      Three or four people: Ibid., 42–44.
      Not *reading Negro newspapers:* Ibid., 44.

130   *Circulation to survive:* Ibid., 45–52.
      Arouse readers' interest: Ibid., 52–53.

131   *Will lead toward advancement:* Ibid., 53–54.
      OPINIONS OF AMERICANS: Ibid., 102.

132   *Should be printed each week:* Ibid., 107–8, 119–20, 132.

133   *Paper's main editorial writer:* Ibid., 137–38, 171.
      British West Indies: Ibid., 146, 173, 223.

134   *250,000 by 1937:* Ibid., 243–44, 251–57.

135   *A huge hit with readers:* Ibid., 243–48. The *Courier,* as well as other large black papers, played up a number of sports stories in the 1930s beside Louis, including major league baseball's refusal to take black players. For more on this, see Chris Lamb, *Blackout: The Untold Story of Jackie Robinson's First Spring Training* (Lincoln: University of Nebraska Press, 2004), chapter 2; and Brian Carroll, "'A Perfect Day': The Black Press Begins Making the Case for Professional Baseball's Integration" (paper presented at the annual

meeting of the American Journalism Historians Association, San Antonio, Texas, October 2005).

135 *Quality of its writing:* Buni, 243–44.

136 *Every fron page:* See ibid., 257; and Finkle, 131–33, 143–44. The struggle to get proportional representation of blacks in the military also is discussed in Buni on 299–318.

137 *Nature of black publications:* Washburn, 29.

Will go down with her: "Japanese Propaganda among the Negro People," *Report on Japanese Propaganda in the United States,* 1939, OF 10B, Box 11, Justice Department, FBI Reports, 1939-40 Folder, No. 12, Roosevelt Library, Hyde Park, New York.

138 *Communist sympathizers, or radicals:* Sherman Miles to J. Edgar Hoover, July 11, 1941, Record Group 165, MID 10110-2452-1174, Box 3085, National Archives.

Holding America up to ridicule: Frank Bolden, interview by author, January 14, 1983, Pittsburgh, Pennsylvania, handwritten notes.

Articles were not unlawful: See J. E. Clegg to Director, Federal Bureau of Investigation, September 30, 1940; Memorandum, John Edgar Hoover to Lawrence M. C. Smith, October 10, 1940; and Memorandum, Hugh A. Fisher to J. Edgar Hoover, November 7, 1940. All are in File 100-122319, Federal Bureau of Investigation, Washington, D.C.

FBI investigate Prattis: See Finkle, 164; and Washburn, 35–36.

139 *Country's foreign policy:* See Special Agent Report, Federal Bureau of Investigation, October 21, 1941; and John Edgar Hoover to Assistant Chief of Staff, G-2, November 29, 1941. Both are in File 100-31159, Federal Bureau of Investigation.

140 *Aggression felt by Negroes:* See Finkle, 11, 116; George S. Schuyler, *Fifty Years of Progress in Negro Journalism* (1950; reprint ed., Ann Arbor, Mich.: University Microfilms, 1971), 6; "The Third Annual Institute of Race Relations—A Summary," *Events and Trends in Race Relations—A Monthly Summary* 4, 1 (August 1946): 26; and Charles S. Johnson, *Patterns of Negro Segregation* (New York: Harper, 1943), 314.

140 *Read the papers every week:* See Finkle, 51–54; Pride and Wilson, 138;
         Gunnar Myrdal, *An American Dilemma: The Negro Problem and
         Modern Democracy* (1944; New York: Harper and Row, 1962),
         1423; *Editor and Publisher, the Fourth Estate: 1942 International
         Year Book Number* (New York: Editor & Publisher, 1942), 182;
         Arnold M. Rose, *The Negro's Morale: Group Identification and Protest*
         (Minneapolis: University of Minnesota Press, 1949), 104–5; and
         U.S. Department of Commerce, *Negro Newspapers and Periodicals
         in the United States, 1940,* Negro Statistical Bulletin, no. 1, May
         1942, 1. *Courier* President Ira Lewis claimed in May 1941 that the
         paper's circulation was fluctuating between 150,000 and 180,000,
         but no other source makes the claim that it was that high at that
         time. See Buni, 383.

141 *A deliberate slant: The Black Press: Soldiers without Swords.*

CHAPTER SIX

144 *Surely as the Axis forces:* James G. Thompson, "Should I Sacrifice to
         Live 'Half American'?" *Pittsburgh Courier,* January 31, 1942, 3.

145 *Portals of heaven for us:* Bibb, 13.
         Push to win the war: For the patriotic feeling of Americans in World
         War II, see Studs Terkel, *"The Good War": An Oral History of World
         War Two* (New York: Pantheon Books, 1984).

146 *Stars and Stripes?:* See "A Hero from the Galley," *Pittsburgh Courier,*
         January 3, 1942, 6; and Washburn, 53, 99.
         That service's highest honor: "Navy Cross for Dorie Miller," *Pittsburgh
         Courier,* May 16, 1942, 1.
         Defending America Our Way: "Defending America Our Way," *Balti-
         more Afro-American,* January 31, 1942, 4.

147 *Under the Hitler heel:* "Now Is the Time Not to Be Silent," *The Cri-
         sis,* January 1942, 7.
         Influence with black readers: Ulysses Lee, *United States Army in World War
         II: Special Studies; The Employment of Negro Troops,* vol. 8, no. 8

(Washington, D.C.: Office of the Chief of Military History, U.S. Army, 1966), 77.

148 *At home— abroad:* Patrick S. Washburn, "The *Pittsburgh Courier*'s Double V Campaign in 1942," *American Journalism* 3, 2 (1986): 75.

WE ARE AMERICANS, TOO!: "The Courier's Double 'V' for a Double Victory Campaign Gets Country-Wide Support," *Pittsburgh Courier,* February 14, 1942, 1.

149 *Gary Cooper:* Washburn, "The *Pittsburgh Courier*'s Double V Campaign in 1942," 75–76.

150 *Avoid the above situation:* "Means More Race Interest," *Pittsburgh Courier,* March 7, 1942, 12.

Hypocritical North: See "An Important Campaign," *Pittsburgh Courier,* April 4, 1942, 12; and "Means New Day for the Race," *Pittsburgh Courier,* March 7, 1942, 12.

COURAGE AND SACRIFICE—COLORED AMERICANS!: Frank E. Bolden, "'We Want Full Participating Rights in War to Save Democracy,'" *Pittsburgh Courier,* March 7, 1942, 12.

151 *We pledge our all!:* See "All Americans Can Rally around the 'Double V' Slogan," *Pittsburgh Courier,* March 21, 1942, 12; and "'Double V' Creed," *Pittsburgh Courier,* April 11, 1942, 1.

30 cents a copy: Washburn, "The *Pittsburgh Courier*'s Double V Campaign in 1942," 77–78, 80.

152 *Victory at Home and Abroad:* Ibid., 79.

Wichita's 6,000 Negro citizens: George S. Schuyler, "'Make Democracy Real,' Says Double V Originator," *Pittsburgh Courier,* April 18, 1942, 5.

153 *The service in February 1943:* "Ky. Pastor Speaks on 'Double V,'" *Pittsburgh Courier,* July 25, 1942, 19; and photograph, *Pittsburgh Courier,* February 27, 1943, 1.

Training camps in Dixie: See Washburn, *A Question of Sedition,* 57–58; and John Morton Blum, *V Was for Victory: Politics and American Culture during World War II* (New York: Harcourt, Brace, Jovanovich, 1976), 189.

154 *Outright subversive publications:* Memorandum, Maj. Gen. George V. Strong to Assistant Chief of Staff, G-3, June 17, 1942, Record Group 165, 291.21, Box 43, Volume 1 through August 1943 Folder, National Archives.

155 *Preventing their subversive language:* See private handwritten notes, Francis Biddle, "May 22, 1942," Francis Biddle Papers, Cabinet Meetings, Jan.-June 1942 Folder, Roosevelt Library, Hyde Park; and Washburn, *A Question of Sedition,* 80–82.

Can't do anything about her: See Nathan Miller, *FDR:An Intimate History* (Garden City, N.Y.: Doubleday, 1983), 361; and Washburn, *A Question of Sedition,* 81. The Sedition Act, which had been passed in 1918, did not reappear in World War II because it had been repealed in 1921.

Something that controversial: Washburn, *A Question of Sedition,* 130.

156 *Any nation that indulges in it:* See Memoranda, Breen to O'Brien, June 8 and June 10, 1942. Both are in Record Group 28, File No. 103777-E, Case No. 134, National Archives. Also see Washburn, *A Question of Sedition,* 125–26.

Formulated anew: See Calvin W. Hassell to L. M. C. Smith, June 10, 1942; Memorandum, Ralph S. Boyd to Lawrence M. C. Smith, June 30, 1942; and L. M. C. Smith to Calvin Hassell, June 30, 1942. All are in Record Group 28, File No. 103777-E, Case No. 134, National Archives. Also see Washburn, *A Question of Sedition,* 126–28.

157 *Watched closely by the Justice Department:* See Washburn, *A Question of Sedition,* 87–90; John H. Sengstacke, interview by author, April 21, 1983, Chicago, tape recording; and John H. Sengstacke, telephone interview by author, September 15, 1983, handwritten notes. For a discussion of the differing views of Francis Biddle and Franklin D. Roosevelt about whether constitutional rights changed during wartime, see Patrick S. Washburn, "FDR versus His Own Attorney General: The Struggle over Sedition, 1941–42," *Journalism Quarterly* 62, 4 (Winter 1985).

158 *"Glad" to support the war effort:* Sengstacke, interviews by author.

159 *Too much pressure on the government to do that:* Sengstacke, interview, April 21, 1983; and Bolden, interview.

Could not be overlooked: Washburn, *A Question of Sedition,* 131. For information on the way that black newspapers covered black workers during World War II, see Patrick S. Washburn, "The *Pittsburgh Courier* and Black Workers in 1942," *Western Journal of Black Studies* 10, 3 (Fall 1986).

161 *Despite what Biddle had promised:* Mary Alice Sentman and Patrick S. Washburn, "How Excess Profits Tax Brought Ads to Black Newspaper in World War II," *Journalism Quarterly* 64, 4 (Winter 1987): 769–74.

Thirty-one weeks of the year: Washburn, "The *Pittsburgh Courier's* Double V Campaign in 1942," 80.

162 *'Remember Jim Crow' too:* See Finkle, 63–65, 77, 112; Earnest L. Perry Jr., "It's Time to Force a Change: The African-American Press' Campaign for a True Democracy during World War II," *Journalism History* 28, 2 (Summer 2002): 92; and *Funk & Wagnalls New Encyclopedia,* 1975 ed., s.v. "Four Freedoms."

Certainly woke people up: See Frank E. Bolden, telephone interview by author, October 31, 1980, handwritten notes; and Frank E. Bolden, telephone interview by author, November 21, 1980, handwritten notes.

163 *We're ready!:* Photograph caption, *Pittsburgh Courier,* June 21, 1942, 4.

Arsenals of democracy: Photograph caption, *Pittsburgh Courier,* May 23, 1942, 5.

Willing to pay the proper price: See Thomas Sancton, "The Negro Press," *New Republic,* April 26, 1943, 560; Oak, 47–48; and Washburn, "The *Pittsburgh Courier's* Double V Campaign in 1942," 83.

164 *North Africa in November:* Washburn, "The *Pittsburgh Courier's* Double V Campaign in 1942," 83–84.

A muddle: See George A. Barnes to Ulric Bell, June 5, 1942, Record Group 208, 002.11, E-5, Box 3, OFF 1941-43, June 1–10 Folder, National Archives; and Washburn, *A Question of Sedition,* 7–8.

164   *Second-class mailing permits:* Washburn, *A Question of Sedition,* 145.

165   *Defeatism among the Negro population:* See Memorandum, Coral
Sadler to D. W. Barco, October 29, 1942, File 146-7-64-354, Justice Department; and Washburn, *A Question of Sedition,* 140.
Backing of the government's legal branch: Washburn, *A Question of Sedition,* 140–46.

166   *Just in from Oklahoma:* Kieferle to O'Brien, November 5, 1943, File
146-28-1227, Justice Department, Washington, D.C.
A waste of time: See Calvin W. Hassell to Tom C. Clark, November
8, 1943; and Tom C. Clark to Calvin W. Hassell, November 15,
1943. Both are in File 146-28-1227, Justice Department. Also see
Washburn, *A Question of Sedition,* 194–95.
Bombing of Pearl Harbor: Patrick S. Washburn, "J. Edgar Hoover and
the Black Press in World War II," *Journalism History* 13, 1 (Spring
1986): 27.

167   *Either in recruiting or enlistment:* See "The Inquiring Reporter," *Balti-
more Afro-American,* December 20, 1941, 4; Memorandum, John
Edgar Hoover to Wendell Berge, January 30, 1942; and Memo-
randum, Wendell Berge to J. Edgar Hoover, February 5, 1942.
The two latter documents are in File 100-63963, Federal Bureau
of Investigation.
Visit a black paper early in the war: Robert Durr, *The Negro Press: Its
Character, Development and Function* (Jackson: Mississippi Division,
Southern Regional Council, 1947), 2–3.
You have no fear: Bolden, interview, January 14, 1983.

168   *Any action based on it:* Federal Bureau of Investigation, "Survey of
Racial Conditions in the United States," undated, 430–59, OF
10B, no. 2420, Justice Dept., FBI, Reports folder, Roosevelt Library. A letter, which was sent with the report to the White
House, indicated it was completed in September 1943.

169   *Declaring the column legal:* See Memorandum, John Edgar Hoover to
Tom C. Clark, October 11, 1943; Tom C. Clark to Director,
Federal Bureau of Investigation, November 9, 1943; J. Edgar
Hoover to Tom C. Clark, December 16, 1943; and Tom C.

Clark to Director, Federal Bureau of Investigation, January 1, 1944. All are in File 100-122319, Federal Bureau of Investigation.

169 *War Manpower Commission:* Washburn, "J. Edgar Hoover and the Black Press in World War II," 30–31.

Quite general in other circles: Durr, 2–3.

170 *Mailed outside of the country:* See Jas. R. Stewart, "Let's Face the Truth," *New Negro World,* February 1942, 1–2; Col. George C. Van Dusen to Lt. Col. W. Preston Corderman, March 9, 1942; and Maj. Chet W. Wadsworth to District Postal Censor, Miami, March 14, 1942. The latter two documents are in Record Group 216, File 007-B/2, National Archives. Also see Washburn, *A Question of Sedition,* 110.

Until the spring of 1944: Washburn, *A Question of Sedition,* 110–11, 157–58, 196–97.

Difficult practice of judgment [during World War II]: Francis Biddle, *In Brief Authority* (Garden City, N.Y.: Doubleday, 1962), 186.

Felt were "undesirable": See Adjutant General's Office, War Department, "Donations of Reading Material to Service Club Libraries," June 24, 1941, Record Group 407, AG 461; 1st Lt. Elias C. Townsend to Assistant Chief of Staff, G-2, Atlanta, July 1, 1941, Record Group 165, MID 10110-2452-1160, Box 3085; War Department, "Special Service Officer," May 12, 1942, Record Group 407, File 062.11, TM 21-205; and Adjutant General's Office, War Department, "Undesirable Literature in Camps," June 18, 1942, Record Group 407, AG 461. All are in the National Archives. Also see Washburn, *A Question of Sedition,* 111–12.

Several Mississippi Army camps: Washburn, *A Question of Sedition,* 154.

171 *Agitation to colored papers:* Lee, 384.

Ignored until August 1944: Washburn, *A Question of Sedition,* 191–92.

Suppression of the Negro newspapers: George Schuyler, "The World Today," *Pittsburgh Courier,* April 8, 1944, 1, 4.

172 *Increasing tension and lowering morale:* Morris J. MacGregor and Bernard C. Nalty, eds., *Blacks in the United States Armed Forces: Basic Documents,* vol. 6 (Wilmington, Del.: Scholarly Resources, 1977), 12.

172 *No such attitude toward the Negro:* See "'Need Frank Talk with President'—Randolph," *Pittsburgh Courier,* April 11, 1942, 3; and Washburn, *A Question of Sedition,* 197.

173 *One tremendous climax after the other:* See "Off the Record," *PEP: Negro Publisher, Editor and Printer,* May 1945, 10–11; and Washburn, *A Question of Sedition,* 198–200.

    Group of American blacks: Washburn, *A Question of Sedition,* 201–02. While Roosevelt avoided meeting with black groups until near the end of his presidency, he did meet before then with black individuals, such as Walter White, executive secretary of the NAACP. See *A Question of Sedition,* 93.

    His four presidential campaigns: See Graham J. White, *FDR and the Press* (Chicago: University of Chicago Press, 1979), 18–19; and Donald A. Ritchie, *Reporting from Washington: The History of the Washington Press Corps* (New York: Oxford University Press, 2005), 30–31.

174 *The blacks, etc.:* See Harry McAlpin, telephone interview by author, March 15, 1983, handwritten notes; and Washburn, *A Question of Sedition,* 198–200. According to a Secret Service report, the *Defender* paid most of McAlpin's salary, but Sengstacke said in 1983 that he paid all of it. See Ritchie, 33; and John Sengstacke, interview by author, April 21, 1983.

176 *Happy to have you here:* Harry S. McAlpin, typewritten autobiographical manuscript, 125–30, used with permission.

    Replaced him with another black: McAlpin, telephone interview; and Harry McAlpin, interview by author, March 17, 1983, Fairfax, Va., handwritten notes.

    Seventy-five years combined: Robert C. Weaver, *Negro Labor: A National Problem* (New York: Harcourt, Brace, 1946), 78.

    Only one in World War I: John D. Stevens, "From the Back of the Foxhole: Black Correspondents in World War II," *Journalism Monographs* 27 (February 1973): 10. Also see Jinx Coleman Broussard and John Maxwell Hamilton, "Covering a Two-Front War: Three African American Correspondents during World War II," *American Journalism* 22, 3 (Summer 2005): 33–54. For a sample of what was written by the black war correspondents, see Ross F. Collins and Patrick S. Washburn, eds., *The Greenwood Library of American War Reporting,* vol. 5, *World War I & World War II, The European Theater* (Westport, Conn.: Greenwood Press, 2005), 313–15, 318–19, 331, 344–46, 354, 357–58, 383–84, 398–401, 414–15.

177 *Subscribed to a black paper:* See Finkle, 52–54; and John H. Burma, "An Analysis of the Present Negro Press," *Social Forces* 26, 2 (December 1947): 172. Burma noted that an Office of Price Administration report in October 1944 said there were 205 black newspapers, which was in sharp contrast to the Bureau of the Census, which reported that only 155 black papers existed in 1945. He speculated that the census figure was substantially lower because it classified some of the papers as periodicals instead of counting them as newspapers.

Which it is receiving today: "Publishers at the White House," *Michigan Chronicle,* February 19, 1944, 1.

CHAPTER SEVEN

179 *Blatant and severe discrimination:* Ritchie, 36–37. The Associated Negro Press was a news agency for black newspapers that was founded by Claude Barnett in 1919. For information on the ANP, see Hogan.

180 *Female members of my own race:* Ritchie, 37.
Minority into their sacred society: Ibid., 42–43.

181 *Gingerly using black newspapers:* Sentman and Washburn, 771, 867.
A continual drumbeat against inequalities: Burma, 174; "Readers Back Crusading Policy of Negro Press," *Chicago Defender,* February 24, 1945, 9.

182 *Power in the Negro race:* Myrdal, 923–24. The reference to the black press being "the greatest single power in the Negro race" appeared in Edwin Mims, *The Advancing South: Stories of Progress and Reaction* (Garden City, N.Y.: Doubleday, Page, 1926), 268.

183 *Visualize impending doom:* See Burma, 180; and Oak, 27–28.

184 *Possible under the libel laws:* Sancton, 558.
   A solution of the race problem can be achieved: Ibid., 559–60.

185 *Hatred will wither:* "Fortune Press Analysis: Negroes," *Fortune,* May
   1945, 238.
   100,000 by 1960: Buni, 325–26.
   Alienating advertisers: Roland E. Wolseley, "The Vanishing Negro
   Press," *Commonweal,* September 22, 1950, 578. For Oak's discussion of advertising, see Oak, 112–21.

186 *Advertising would be mere duplication:* Burma, 178.
   Persisted until the 1960s: See P. L. Prattis, "Racial Segregation and
   Negro Journalism," *Phylon* 8, 4 (Fourth Quarter 1947): 310; and
   Sentman and Washburn, 773, 867.

187 *Negroes have grown out of that:* See "The Negro Press: 1955," *Time,*
   November 7, 1955, 64; and Blanchard, 28.

188 *Bring us the news:* Phyl Garland, "The Black Press: Down but Not
   Out," *Columbia Journalism Review,* September/October 1982,
   43–45.
   No racial discrimination: Washburn, *A Question of Sedition,* 175, 180.
   Never recovered from that: The Black Press: Soldiers without Swords.

189 *Backed the Democratic Party:* Garland, 45–46.

190 *Was all but unendurable:* Ibid., 46.
   Reading the Negro press decreasingly: "A Victim of Negro Progress,"
   Newsweek, August 26, 1963, 50.

191 *Open to suggestions:* "Good-by, Hambone," *Newsweek,* July 22, 1968,
   56.
   And interview blacks: Ibid.

192 *Experiential paralysis:* Prattis, "Racial Segregation and Negro Journalism," 308.

193 *Freedom's Journal in 1827:* See *The Black Press: Soldiers without Swords;*
   and "Newspapers: Playing It Cool," *Time,* July 28, 1967, 66.

194 *Rather than other professions:* See Nick Kotz, "The Minority Struggle
   for a Place in the Newsroom," *Columbia Journalism Review,*

March/April 1979, 28; and Jules Witcover, "Washington's White Press Corps," *Columbia Journalism Review,* Winter 1969–1970, 43.

195 *Last with the least:* See Allan Morrison, "The Crusading Press," *Ebony,* September 1963, 208, 210; and Bernard Roshco, "What the Black Press Said Last Summer," *Columbia Journalism Review,* Fall 1967, 6.

   Now a flaccid instrument: See Elaine Kendall, "The Negro Press," *Holiday,* May 1967, 84; and "Coping with the New Reality," *Time,* June 14, 1976, 70.

196 *Don't see our role as leaders:* L. F. Palmer, Jr., "The Black Press in Transition," *Columbia Journalism Review,* Spring 1970, 33–34. The same point was made by *Time,* which noted that Nathan Hare, who had published a militant intellectual magazine, *Black Scholar,* said it was "very difficult to make money and be a voice for black revolution." See "Coping with the New Reality," 70.

   To help a brother: Henry G. La Brie III, "The Future of the Black Press: A Silent Crusade," *Negro History Bulletin* 36, 8 (December 1973): 169.

CHAPTER EIGHT

197 *A separate but equal society:* Quarles, *The Negro in the Making of America,* 237–38.

198 *Seemed to have grown taller:* Ibid., 238.
   I'm free at last: "Let's Give Thanks," *Pittsburgh Courier,* May 29, 1954, 1.

199 *Errors of hasty action:* "An End to This—?" *Cleveland Call and Post,* May 29, 1954, C2.

200 *Few of them would survive:* "A Victim of Negro Progress," 50.
   They're done: Ibid., 51.

201 *Forget that it's there:* Kendall, 82.

202 *It has collapsed:* See Thomas DeBaggio and Julia Aldridge, "Black

News Services: Dying of Neglect?" *Columbia Journalism Review,* July-August 1974, 49; and "Coping with the New Reality," 70.

202 *About 4.1 million:* See DeBaggio and Aldridge, 48; and La Brie, "The Future of the Black Press," 166.

Always have a base: La Brie, "The Future of the Black Press," 166.

203 *He can tell it better:* Ibid., 168.

Go into something else: Ibid.

204 *Should offer them exactly that:* Garland, 43.

Disseminators of the news: Ibid., 47. Italics in original.

205 *That can be our future:* Ibid., 50.

It had an effect on everybody: The Black Press: Soldiers without Swords.

BIBLIOGRAPHY

BOOKS

Aptheker, Herbert, ed. *A Documentary History of the Negro People in the United States.* New York: Citadel Press, 1951.

Biddle, Francis. *In Brief Authority.* Garden City, N.Y.: Doubleday, 1962.

Blanchard, Margaret, ed. *History of the Mass Media in the United States: An Encyclopedia.* Chicago: Fitzroy Dearborn, 1998.

Blum, John Morton. *V Was for Victory: Politics and American Culture during World War II.* New York: Harcourt, Brace, Jovanovich, 1976.

Buni, Andrew. *Robert L. Vann of the Pittsburgh Courier: Politics and Black Journalism.* Pittsburgh: University of Pittsburgh Press, 1974.

Chafee, Zechariah, Jr. *Free Speech in the United States.* 1941; New York: Atheneum, 1969.

Coben, Stanley. *A. Mitchell Palmer: Politician.* New York: Columbia University Press, 1963.

Collins, Ross F., and Patrick S. Washburn, eds. *The Greenwood Library of American War Reporting.* Vol. 5, *World War I & World War II, The European Theater.* Westport, Conn.: Greenwood Press, 2005.

Cook, Fred J. *The FBI Nobody Knows.* New York: Macmillan, 1964.

Copeland, David A. *Debating the Issues in Colonial Newspapers: Primary Documents on Events of the Period.* Westport, Conn.: Greenwood Press, 2000.

Dann, Martin E. *The Black Press, 1827–1890: The Quest for National Identity.* New York: G. P. Putnam's Sons, 1971.

Detweiler, Frederick G. *The Negro Press in the United States.* Chicago: University of Chicago Press, 1922.

Dicken-Garcia, Hazel. *Journalistic Standards in Nineteenth-Century America.* Madison: University of Wisconsin Press, 1989.

Durr, Robert. *The Negro Press: Its Character, Development and Function.* Jackson: Mississippi Division, Southern Regional Council, 1947.

Editor and Publisher, The Fourth Estate: 1942 International Year Book Number. New York: Editor & Publisher, 1942.

Emery, Michael, and Edwin Emery, with Nancy L. Roberts. *The Press and America: An Interpretive History of the Mass Media.* 8th ed. Boston: Allyn and Bacon, 1996.

Farrar, Hayward. *The Baltimore Afro-American, 1892–1950.* Westport, Conn.: Greenwood Press, 1998.

Finkle, Lee. *Forum for Protest: The Black Press during World War II.* Cranbury, N.J.: Associated University Presses, 1975.

Fireside, Harvey. *Separate and Unequal: Homer Plessy and the Supreme Court Decision that Legalized Racism.* New York: Carroll & Graf, 2004.

Folkerts, Jean, and Dwight L. Teeter, Jr. *Voices of a Nation: A History of Media in the United States.* New York: Macmillan, 1989.

Foner, Philip S. *The Life and Writings of Frederick Douglass.* Vol. 2. New York: International Publishers, 1950.

Gunther, Gerald. *Cases and Materials on Constitutional Law.* 10th ed. Mineola, N.Y.: Foundation Press, 1980.

Hofstadter, Richard. *Social Darwinism in American Thought.* 1944; rev. ed., New York: George Braziller, 1969.

Hogan, Lawrence D. *A Black National News Service: The Associated Negro Press and Claude Barnett, 1919–1945.* Cranbury, N.J.: Associated University Presses, 1984.

Horn, Stanley F. *Invisible Empire: The Story of the Ku Klux Klan, 1866–1871.* 1939; Montclair, N.J.: Patterson Smith, 1969.

Hutton, Frankie. *The Early Black Press in America, 1827 to 1860.* Westport, Conn.: Greenwood Press, 1993.

Johnson, Charles S. *Patterns of Negro Segregation.* New York: Harper, 1943.

Johnson, Donald. *The Challenge to American Freedoms.* Lexington: University of Kentucky Press, 1963.

Jordan, William G. *Black Newspapers & America's War for Democracy, 1914–1920.* Chapel Hill: University of North Carolina Press, 2001.

Juergens, George. *News from the White House: The Presidential Press Relationship in the Progressive Era*. Chicago: University of Chicago Press, 1981.

Kerlin, Robert T. *The Voice of the Negro, 1919*. New York: E. P. Dutton, 1920.

Kornweibel, Theodore, Jr. *"Investigate Everything": Federal Efforts to Compel Black Loyalty during World War I*. Bloomington, Ind.: Indiana University Press, 2002.

———. *"Seeing Red": Federal Campaigns against Black Militancy, 1919–1925*. Bloomington: Indiana University Press, 1998.

Lamb, Chris. *Blackout: The Untold Story of Jackie Robinson's First Spring Training*. Lincoln: University of Nebraska Press, 2004.

Lee, Ulysses. *United States Army in World War II: Special Studies; The Employment of Negro Troops*. Vol. 8, no. 8. Washington, D.C.: Office of the Chief of Military History, U.S. Army, 1966.

Logan, Rayford W. *The Betrayal of the Negro from Rutherford B. Hayes to Woodrow Wilson*. 5th ed. 1954; New York: Collier Books, 1970.

Lowenthal, Max. *The Federal Bureau of Investigation*. New York: William Sloane Associates, 1950.

MacGregor, Morris J., and Bernard C. Nalty, eds. *Blacks in the United States Armed Forces: Basic Documents*. Vol. 6. Wilmington, Del.: Scholarly Resources, 1977.

McFeely, William S. *Frederick Douglass*. New York: W. W. Norton, 1991.

McMurry, Linda O. *To Keep the Waters Troubled: The Life of Ida B. Wells*. New York: Oxford University Press, 1998.

Messick, Hank. *John Edgar Hoover*. New York: David McKay, 1972.

Miller, Nathan. *FDR: An Intimate History*. Garden City, N.Y.: Doubleday, 1983.

Mims, Edwin. *The Advancing South: Stories of Progress and Reaction*. Garden City, N.Y.: Doubleday, Page, 1926.

Mott, Frank Luther. *American Journalism: A History of Newspapers in the United States through 250 Years, 1690 to 1940*. 1941; reprint, New York: Macmillan, 1947.

Murray, Robert K. *Red Scare: A Study in National Hysteria, 1919–1920*. Minneapolis: University of Minnesota Press, 1955.

Myrdal, Gunnar. *An American Dilemma: The Negro Problem and Modern Democracy.* 1944; New York: Harper & Row, 1962.

Nash, Jay Robert. *Citizen Hoover: A Critical Study of the Life and Times of J. Edgar Hoover and His FBI.* Chicago: Nelson-Hall, 1972.

Oak, Vishnu V. *The Negro Newspaper.* Yellow Springs, Ohio: Antioch Press, 1948.

Ottley, Roi. *The Lonely Warrior: The Life and Times of Robert S. Abbott.* Chicago: Henry Regnery, 1955.

Pease, Jane H., and William H. Pease. *They Who Would Be Free: Blacks' Search for Freedom, 1830–1861.* New York: Atheneum, 1974.

Penn, I. Garland. *The Afro-American Press and Its Editors.* 1891; New York: Arno Press, 1969.

Pride, Armistead S., and Clint C. Wilson II. *A History of the Black Press.* Washington, D.C.: Howard University Press, 1997.

Quarles, Benjamin. *Black Abolitionists.* New York: Oxford University Press, 1969.

———. *Frederick Douglass.* Washington, D.C.: Associated Publishers, 1948.

———. *The Negro in the Making of America.* 1964; rev. ed., New York: Collier Books, 1979.

Ritchie, Donald A. *Reporting from Washington: The History of the Washington Press Corps.* New York: Oxford University Press, 2005.

Rose, Arnold M. *The Negro's Morale: Group Identification and Protest.* Minneapolis: University of Minnesota Press, 1949.

Royster, Jacqueline Jones, ed. *Southern Horrors and Other Writings: The Anti-Lynching Campaign of Ida B. Wells, 1892–1900.* Boston: Bedford/St. Martin's, 1997.

Schudson, Michael. *Discovering the News: A Social History of American Newspapers.* New York: Basic Books, 1978.

Schuyler, George. *Fifty Years of Progress in Negro Journalism.* 1950; Ann Arbor, Mich.: University Microfilms, 1971.

Sherman, Richard B., ed. *The Negro and the City.* Englewood Cliffs, N.J.: Prentice-Hall, 1970.

Sloan, Wm. David *The Media in America: A History.* 5th ed. Northport, Ala.: Vision Press, 2002.

Streitmatter, Rodger. *Voices of Revolution: The Dissident Press in America.* New York: Columbia University Press, 2001.

Suggs, Henry Lewis. *P. B. Young, Newspaperman: Race, Politics, and Journalism in the New South, 1910–1962.* Charlottesville: University Press of Virginia, 1988.

Terkel, Studs. *"The Good War": An Oral History of World War Two.* New York: Pantheon Books, 1984.

Washburn, Patrick S. *A Question of Sedition: The Federal Government's Investigation of the Black Press during World War II.* New York: Oxford University Press, 1986.

Weaver, Robert C. *Negro Labor: A National Problem.* New York: Harcourt, Brace, 1946.

White, Graham J. *FDR and the Press.* Chicago: University of Chicago Press, 1979.

Whitehead, Don. *The FBI Story: A Report to the People.* New York: Random House, 1956.

Wilson, Clint C., II. *Black Journalists in Paradox: Historical Perspectives and Current Dilemmas.* Westport, Conn.: Greenwood Press, 1991.

Wolseley, Roland E. *The Black Press, U.S.A.: A Detailed and Understanding Report on What the Black Press Is and How It Came to Be.* Ames: Iowa State University Press, 1971.

MONOGRAPHS

Bryan, Carter R. "Negro Journalism in America before Emancipation." *Journalism Monographs* 12 (September 1969).

Stevens, John D. "From the Back of the Foxhole: Black Correspondents in World War II." *Journalism Monographs* 27 (February 1973).

GOVERNMENT DOCUMENTS

Federal Bureau of Investigation. "Survey of Racial Conditions in the United States," undated. OF 10B, no. 2420, Justice Dept., FBI, Reports Folder, Roosevelt Library, Hyde Park, New York.

U.S. Department of Commerce. *Negro Newspapers and Periodicals in the United States, 1940.* Negro Statistical Bulletin, no. 1, May 1942.

JOURNALS AND PERIODICALS

Broussard, Jinx Coleman, and John Maxwell Hamilton. "Covering a Two-Front War: Three African American Correspondents during World War II." *American Journalism* 22, 3 (Summer 2005): 33–54.

Burma, John H. "An Analysis of the Present Negro Press." *Social Forces* 26, 2 (December 1947): 172–80.

"Close Ranks." *The Crisis,* July 1918, 111.

"Coping with the New Reality." *Time,* June 14, 1976, 70–72.

DeBaggio, Thomas, and Julia Aldridge. "Black News Services: Dying of Neglect?" *Columbia Journalism Review,* July-August 1974, 48–49.

DeSantis, Alan D. "A Forgotten Leader: Robert S. Abbott and the *Chicago Defender* from 1910–1920." *Journalism History* 23, 2 (Summer 1997): 63–71.

Domke, David. "The Black Press in the 'Nadir' of African Americans." *Journalism History* 20, 3–4 (Autumn-Winter 1994): 131–38.

"Fortune Press Analysis." *Fortune,* May 1945, 233–38.

Frank, Fee, Jr. "'Intelligent Union of Black with White': Frederick Douglass and the Rochester Press, 1847–48." *Journalism History* 31, 1 (Spring 2005): 34–45.

Garland, Phyl. "The Black Press: Down but Not Out." *Columbia Journalism Review,* September/October 1982, 43–50.

"Good-by, Hambone." *Newsweek,* July 22, 1968, 56.

Grossman, James R. "Blowing the Trumpet: The *Chicago Defender* and Black Migration during World War I." *Illinois Historical Journal* 78, 2 (Summer 1985): 82–96.

Kendall, Elaine. "The Negro Press." *Holiday,* May 1967, 82–84.

Kotz, Nick. "The Minority Struggle for a Place in the Newsroom." *Columbia Journalism Review,* March/April 1979, 23–31.

La Brie, Henk, III. "Black Newspapers: The Roots Are 150 Years Deep." *Journalism History* 4, 4 (Winter 1977–1978): 111–13.

LaBrie, Henry G., III. "The Future of the Black Press: A Silent Crusade." *Negro History Bulletin* 36, 8 (December 1973): 166–69.

Lorenz, Alfred Lawrence. "Ralph W. Tyler: The Unknown Correspondent of World War I." *Journalism History* 31, 1 (Spring 2005): 2–12.

Morrison, Allan. "The Crusading Press." *Ebony,* September 1963, 204–10.

"The Negro Press: 1955." *Time,* November 7, 1955, 64–66.

"Newspapers: Playing It Cool." *Time,* July 28, 1967, 66.

"Now Is Not the Time to Be Silent." *The Crisis,* January 1942, 7.

"Off the Record." *PEP: Negro Publisher, Editor and Printer,* May 1945, 10–11.

"Our Special Grievances." *The Crisis,* September 1918, 216–17.

Palmer, L. F., Jr. "The Black Press in Transition." *Columbia Journalism Review,* Spring 1970, 31–36.

Perry, Earnest L., Jr. "It's Time to Force a Change: The African-American Press' Campaign for a True Democracy during World War II." *Journalism History* 28, 2 (Summer 2002): 85–95.

Prattis, P. L. "Racial Segregation and Negro Journalism." *Phylon* 8, 4 (Fourth Quarter 1947): 305–14.

———. "The Role of the Negro Press in Race Relations." *Phylon* 7, 3 (Third Quarter 1946): 273–83.

"Pro-Germanism among Negroes." *The Messenger,* July 1918, 13.

"The Reward." *The Crisis,* September 1918, 217.

Roshco, Bernard. "What the Black Press Said Last Summer." *Columbia Journalism Review,* Fall 1967, 6–9.

Ross, Felecia G. Jones, and Joseph P. McKerns. "Depression in 'The Promised Land': The *Chicago Defender* Discourages Migration, 1929–1940." *American Journalism* 21, 1 (Winter 2004): 55–73.

Rudwick, Elliott M. "W. E. B. Du Bois in the Role of Crisis Editor." *Journal of Negro History* 43, 3 (1958): 214–40.

Sancton, Thomas. "The Negro Press." *New Republic,* April 26, 1943, 557–60.

Sentman, Mary Alice, and Patrick S. Washburn. "How Excess Profits

Tax Brought Ads to Black Newspaper in World War II." *Journalism Quarterly* 64, 4 (Winter 1987): 769–74.

Stewart, Jas. R. "Let's Face the Truth." *New Negro World,* February 1942, 1–2.

Strother, T. Ella. "The Black Image in the *Chicago 'Defender,'* 1905–1975." *Journalism History* 4, 4 (Winter 1977–1978): 137–41.

"The Third Annual Institute of Race Relations—A Summary." *Events and Trends in Race Relations—A Monthly Summary* 4, 1 (August 1946): 21–28.

"Thirteen." *The Crisis,* January 1918, 114.

"A Victim of Negro Progress." *Newsweek,* August 26, 1963, 50–51.

Washburn, Patrick S. "FDR versus His Own Attorney General: The Struggle over Sedition, 1941–42." *Journalism Quarterly* 62, 4 (Winter 1985): 717–24.

———. "J. Edgar Hoover and the Black Press in World War II." *Journalism History* 13, 1 (Spring 1986): 26–33.

———. "The *Pittsburgh Courier* and Black Workers in 1942." *Western Journal of Black Studies* 10, 3 (Fall 1986): 109–18.

———. "The *Pittsburgh Courier*'s Double V Campaign in 1942." *American Journalism* 3, 2 (1986): 73–86.

Witcover, Jules. "Washington's White Press Corps." *Columbia Journalism Review,* Winter 1969–1970, 42–48.

Wolseley, Roland E. "The Vanishing Negro Press." *Commonweal,* September 22, 1950, 577–79.

NEWSPAPERS

"All Americans Can Rally around the 'Double V' Slogan." *Pittsburgh Courier,* March 21, 1942, 12.

Bibb, Joseph D. "We Gain by War." *Pittsburgh Courier,* October 10, 1942, 13.

Bolden, Frank E. "'We Want Full Participating Rights in War to Save Democracy." *Pittsburgh Courier,* March 7, 1942, 12.

"Chicago Editor Buys *Courier.*" *Pittsburgh Press,* October 22, 1966, 13.

"The Courier's Double 'V' for a Double Victory Campaign Gets Country Wide Support." *Pittsburgh Courier,* February 14, 1942, 1.

"Daily *Defender* Buys Courier Group Papers." *Chicago Tribune,* October 22, 1966, sec. 2, 7.

"Defending America Our Way." *Baltimore Afro-American,* January 31, 1942, 4.

"'Double V' Creed." *Pittsburgh Courier,* April 11, 1942, 1.

"An End to This—?" *Cleveland Call and Post,* May 29, 1954, C2.

"A Hero from the Galley." *Pittsburgh Courier,* January 3, 1942, 6.

"An Important Campaign." *Pittsburgh Courier,* April 4, 1942, 12.

"The Inquiring Reporter." *Baltimore Afro-American,* December 20, 1941, 4.

Johnson, Toki Schalk. "Danger May Lie Ahead in 'The Pill' for Youth." *Pittsburgh Courier,* October 22, 1966, 11.

"Ky. Pastor Speaks on 'Double V.'" *Pittsburgh Courier,* July 25, 1942, 19.

"Lady Fortune." *Pittsburgh Courier,* October 22, 1966, 4.

"Let's Give Thanks." *Pittsburgh Courier,* May 29, 1954, 1.

"Means More Race Interest." *Pittsburgh Courier,* March 7, 1942, 12.

"Means New Day for the Race." *Pittsburgh Courier,* March 7, 1942, 12.

"Navy Cross for Dorie Miller." *Pittsburgh Courier,* May 16, 1942, 1.

"'Need Frank Talk with President'—Randolph." *Pittsburgh Courier,* April 11, 1942, 3.

"Publishers at the White House." *Michigan Chronicle,* February 19, 1944, 1.

"Readers Back Crusading Policy of Negro Press." *Chicago Defender,* February 24, 1945, 9.

Robinson, Major. "Carmichael Hit by Adam Powell." *Pittsburgh Courier,* October 22, 1966, 3.

Schuyler, George. "'Make Democracy Real,' Says Double V Originator." *Pittsburgh Courier,* April 18, 1942, 5.

———. "The World Today." *Pittsburgh Courier,* April 8, 1944, 1, 4.

"Sengstacke Buys Courier Papers." *Chicago Defender,* October 25, 1966, 4.

"Sengstacke Purchases *Courier.*" *New Pittsburgh Courier,* October 29–November 4, 1966, 1.

"Swung from a Limb." *Atlanta Constitution,* May 20, 1896, 2.

Thompson, James G. "Should I Sacrifice to Live 'Half American'?" *Pittsburgh Courier,* January 31, 1942, 3.

DISSERTATIONS, THESES, AND PAPERS

Carroll, Brian. "'A Perfect Day': The Black Press Begins Making the Case for Professional Baseball's Integration." Paper presented at the Annual Meeting, American Journalism Historians Association, October 2005.

Kornweibel, Theodore, Jr. "The Messenger Magazine: 1917–1928." Ph.D. dissertation, Yale University, 1971.

Terrell, Martin Jackson. "A Study of the *Chicago Defender*'s 'Great Northern Drive.'" Master's thesis, Ohio University, 1991.

INTERVIEWS

Bolden, Frank E. Telephone interview by author, October 31, 1980. Handwritten notes.

———. Telephone interview by author, November 21, 1980. Handwritten notes.

———. Interview by author, January 14, 1983, Pittsburgh. Handwritten notes.

McAlpin, Harry S. Telephone interview by author, March 15, 1983. Handwritten notes.

———. Interview by author, March 17, 1983, Fairfax, Va. Handwritten notes.

Sengstacke, John H. Interview by author, April 21, 1983, Chicago. Tape recording.

————. Telephone interview by author, September 15, 1983. Handwritten notes.

VIDEORECORDINGS

The Black Press: Soldiers without Swords. Produced and directed by Stanley Nelson. Half Nelson Productions, 1999. Television documentary.

INDEX

Patrick S. Washburn is a professor of journalism at the E. W. Scripps School of Journalism at Ohio University, the author of *A Question of Sedition: The Federal Government's Investigation of the Black Press during World War II,* and a historical consultant for the PBS television documentary *The Black Press: Soldiers without Swords.* He has been an invited speaker about the black press at the Smithsonian Institution, the National D-Day Museum, and numerous universities.

Clarence Page is a nationally syndicated columnist, a member of the editorial board of the *Chicago Tribune,* winner of a Pulitzer Prize for commentary, and the author of *Showing My Color: Impolite Essays on Race and Identity.*